HANNES LEOPOLDSEDER

DER PRIX ARS ELECTRONICA

Die Deutsche Bibliothek – CIP-Einheitsaufnahme

Der **Prix Ars Electronica,** internationales Kompendium der Computerkünste (Veranstalter: Österr. Rundfunk (ORF), Landesstudio Oberösterreich). Hannes Leopoldseder. – Linz – VERITAS-Verlag, 1993.
ISBN 3-7058-0601-7
NE: Leopoldseder, Hannes (Hrsg.); Österreichischer Rundfunk (Wien)/Landesstudio Oberösterreich.

Der Prix Ars Electronica – Internationales Kompendium der Computerkünste – Computergraphik, Computeranimation, Interaktive Kunst, Computermusik – **Edition 94 – Herausgeber:** Dr. Hannes Leopoldseder – **Redaktion:** Dr. Christine Schöpf, Christian Schrenk, Paul Pritchard, ORF, Landesstudio Oberösterreich, Europaplatz 3, A-4010 Linz – **Übersetzungen:** Paul Pritchard, Christian Schrenk, Maurice Roux, Helmut P. Einfalt – **Cover-Design, Layout:** Arthouse, Hansi Schorn – **Titelbild:** Eric Coignoux: „No Sex" – **Lektorat:** Aileen Derieg, Linz, Mag. Ingrid Fischer-Schreiber, Linz – **Satz:** Typeshop Linz – **Offsetreproduktion, Montage:** RM, Linz – **Druck, Bindung:** LANDESVERLAG Druckservice Linz – **Verlag:** VERITAS-VERLAG, Hafenstraße 1–3, A-4020 Linz. **ISBN** 3-7058-0601-7 – **Copyright** 1994 by Österreichischer Rundfunk (ORF), Landesstudio Oberösterreich. Alle Bildrechte liegen bei den Künstlern. Die Verbreitung, auch durch Film, Funk und Fernsehen, fotomechanische Wiedergabe, ist nicht ohne vorherige Genehmigung durch den ORF gestattet. Die Nutzung durch Tonträger jeder Art, der auszugsweise Nachdruck, die Einspeicherung und Rückgewinnung in Datenverarbeitungsanlagen aller Art sind vorbehalten.
Prix Ars Electronica – Internationaler Wettbewerb für Computerkünste – **Veranstalter:** Österreichischer Rundfunk (ORF), Landesstudio Oberösterreich – **Idee:** Dr. Hannes Leopoldseder – **Konzept:** Dkfm. Heinz Augner, Dr. Christine Schöpf, Wolfgang Winkler – **Kontaktadresse:** Prix Ars Electronica, ORF, Europaplatz 3, A-4010 Linz, Telefon (0 73 2) 69 00-267, Telefax (0 73 2) 69 00-270, Telex (02) 1616.

Der Prix Ars Electronica – International Compendium of the Computer Arts – Computer Graphics, Animation, Interactive Art, Computer Music – **Edition 94 – Publisher:** Dr. Hannes Leopoldseder – **Editors:** Dr. Christine Schöpf, Christian Schrenk, Paul Pritchard, ORF, Landesstudio Oberösterreich, Europaplatz 3, A-4010 Linz – **Translations:** Paul Pritchard, Christian Schrenk, Maurice Roux, Helmut P. Einfalt – **Cover design, layout:** Arthouse, Hansi Schorn – **Frontispiece:** Eric Coignoux: "No Sex" – **Proof-Reader:** Aileen Derieg, Linz, Mag. Ingrid Fischer-Schreiber, Linz – **Setting:** Typeshop, Linz – **Offset reproductions, assembly:** RM, Linz – **Print, binding:** LANDESVERLAG Druckservice Linz – **Publishing house:** VERITAS-VERLAG, Hafenstrasse 1–3, A-4020 Linz. **ISBN** 3-7058-0601-7 – **Copyright** 1994 by Österreichischer Rundfunk (ORF), Landesstudio Oberösterreich. All artistic rights of the images remain with the artists. Distribution in any kind of media including film, radio and television as well as photomechanical reproduction requires prior consent by the ORF. The rights of use in sound carriers of all kinds, partial reprints, storage in and retrieval from data processing units of all kinds are reserved.
Prix Ars Electronica – International Competition for Computer Arts – **Organizer:** Österreichischer Rundfunk (ORF), Landesstudio Oberösterreich – **Idea:** Dr. Hannes Leopoldseder – **Conception:** Dkfm. Heinz Augner, Dr. Christine Schöpf, Wolfgang Winkler – **Liaison office:** Prix Ars Electronica, ORF, Europaplatz 3, A-4010 Linz, telephone (0 73 2) 69 00-267, telefax (0 73 2) 69 00-270, telex (02) 1616.

HANNES LEOPOLDSEDER

DER PRIX ARS
INTERNATIONALES KOMPENDIUM DER COMPUTERKÜNSTE
ELECTRONICA
INTERNATIONAL COMPENDIUM OF THE COMPUTER ARTS

EDITORIAL

- **6** ..... Hannes Leopoldseder – 15 Jahre Ars Electronica/15 Years of Ars Electronica
- **11** ..... Christine Schöpf – Prix Ars Electronica 94

PRIX ARS ELECTRONICA

- **13** ..... Michael Tolson – Sie sollten die Menschen beunruhigen/
  ..... They should make people nervous
- **19** ..... Michael Naimark – Interaktive Kunst und der Mythos der „Alles-Heit"/
  ..... Interactive Art and the Myth of Everything-Ness
- **21** ..... Charles Amirkhanian – Eine Art Menschlichkeit/Some Kind of Humanity
- **23** ..... Begründung der Jury für Computergraphik/Statement of the Computer Graphics Jury
- **25** ..... Begründung der Jury für Computeranimation/
  ..... Statement of the Computer Animation Jury
- **27** ..... Begründung der Jury für Interaktive Kunst/Statement of the Interactive Art Jury
- **29** ..... Begründung der Jury für Computermusik/Statement of the Computer Music Jury

COMPUTERGRAPHIK

- **32** ..... Michael Joaquin Grey – Goldene Nica
- **38** ..... Keith Cottingham
- **42** ..... John Kahrs
- **46** ..... Linda Dement
- **48** ..... Pascal Dombis
- **50** ..... Mogens Jacobsen
- **52** ..... Ronaldo Kiel
- **54** ..... Don MacKay
- **56** ..... Stewart McSherry
- **58** ..... Gavin Miller/Ned Greene
- **60** ..... Anna Gabriele Wagner/Adelhard Roidinger

COMPUTERANIMATION

- **64** ..... Dennis Muren/Mark Dippé/ILM – Goldene Nica
- **68** ..... Marc Caro – Goldene Nica
- **71** ..... Maurice Benayoun
- **75** ..... Eric Coignoux
- **78** ..... Bériou
- **80** ..... Peter Callas
- **82** ..... Cassidy J. Curtis
- **84** ..... Eric Darnell/Michael Collery
- **86** ..... Yoichiro Kawaguchi
- **88** ..... Sabine Mai/Frank Pröscholdt
- **90** ..... John Tonkin
- **92** ..... Hideo Yamashita/Eihachiro Nakamae
- **94** ..... Thomas Zancker
- **96** ..... Tamás Waliczky

INTERAKTIVE KUNST

Christa Sommerer/Laurent Mignonneau – Goldene Nica **100**
Loren Carpenter **105**
TRANSIT **108**
Max Almy/Teri Yarbrow **112**
Edward Elliott **114**
Friedrich Förster **116**
Michael Girard/Susan Amkraut **118**
Richard Kriesche **120**
Wolfgang Krüger **122**
Brenda Laurel/Rachel Strickland **124**
George Legrady **126**
Patti Maes **128**
Christian Möller **130**
Christian Möller/Rüdiger Kramm **132**
Catherine Richards **134**

COMPUTERMUSIK

Ludger Brümmer **138**
Åke Parmerud **140**
Jonathan Impett **142**
Patrick Ascione **144**
Jean-François Cavro **145**
Akemi Ishijima **146**
Paul Koonce **147**
Mesias Maiguashca **148**
Juliet Kiri Palmer **149**
Michel Redolfi **150**
Michael Vaughan **151**
Alejandro Viñao **152**
Frances White **153**

PRIX ARS ELECTRONICA – JURY

Gesamtjury **156**
Jury Graphik & Animation **157**
Jury Interaktive Kunst **159**
Jury Computermusik **161**

PRIX ARS ELECTRONICA – TEILNEHMER 94

Teilnehmer Computergraphik **166**
Teilnehmer Computeranimation **175**
Teilnehmer Interaktive Kunst **180**
Teilnehmer Computermusik **185**

EDITORIAL

HANNES LEOPOLDSEDER
15 JAHRE ARS ELECTRONICA
15 YEARS OF ARS ELECTRONICA

Ein Festival als Frühindikator des Medienbruchs

Wenn der Zukunftsforscher Daniel Burrus in seinen „Technotrends unserer Zeit" als erste Spielregel den Satz „Sobald es funktioniert, ist es überholt" aufstellt, spricht er damit einen der Angelpunkte künftiger Entwicklungen und der Auseinandersetzung mit ihnen an.

Aus diesem Grund versucht Ars Electronica als Festival für Kunst, Technologie und Gesellschaft seit 1979, also von Beginn an, Wandel und Veränderungen mitzuvollziehen: nicht nur im gesellschaftlichen, kulturellen und technischen Umfeld, sondern auch in der Konzeption der Veranstaltung an sich. Partner des Festivals sind seit 15 Jahren das Brucknerhaus Linz, die größte Kultureinrichtung der Stadt, und der Österreichische Rundfunk (ORF)/Landesstudio Oberösterreich).

Die Rundfunk- und Fernsehunternehmen, auch der ORF, stehen heute, angesichts der digitalen Medienrevolution, voraussichtlich vor der größten Herausforderung in ihrer Geschichte. Was heute für die elektronischen Medien einen radikalen Wandlungsprozeß in der Position, in den Aufgabenfeldern sowie in der Marktsituation mit sich bringt, hat der ORF Ende der siebziger Jahre gemeinsam mit dem Brucknerhaus Linz mit der Initiative zu einem elektronischen Festival wie in einem Labor zu beobachten und zu entwickeln versucht.

Als Ars Electronica am 18. September 1979 um 19.30 Uhr vom Roboter SPA 12 im Linzer Donaupark vor 100.000 Menschen eröffnet wurde, war die Computerwelt durch Mainframes und Terminals beherrscht, der Personal Computer hatte gerade die Geburtsstunde hinter sich – mit ihm begann aber eine neue Ära. Stand also am Beginn von Ars Electronica vor 15 Jahren die Entwicklung des PC und die damit verbundene Dezentralisierung im Vordergrund, erleben wir jetzt den sich radikal abzeichnenden Wandel von Wirtschaft und Gesellschaft durch die sich ausbreitenden Computernetze: Die neunziger Jahre werden

A Festival for Advance Indications of Media Disintegration

"As soon as it works, it's obsolete": by adopting this phrase as the first rule in the game ("Techno-trends of our Time"), futurologist Daniel Burrus puts his finger on one of the crucial issues concerning future developments and their evaluation.

This is why Ars Electronica – festival for art, technology and society – has endeavoured since its inception in 1979 to keep pace with evolution and change, not just in the societal, cultural and technical context, but also in the planning of the event itself. For 15 years now the festival has been a basis for partnership between the Brucknerhaus Linz, the city's biggest cultural institution, and the Upper Austrian Region of the Austrian Broadcasting Corporation (ORF).

In the digital media revolution, today's radio and television broadcasters, including the ORF, are facing what will probably be the biggest challenge in their history. The developments which are now confronting the electronic media with a radical transformation in their position, areas of activity and market conditions are the same developments that the ORF tried to address in the late 70s by attempting to observe and foster them as if in a laboratory environment – this is what the ORF's joint initiative with the Brucknerhaus Linz for an electronic festival was intended to bring about.

On 18th September 1979, at 7.30 p.m., when Ars Electronica was opened by the robot SPA 12 in front of 100,000 people in Linz's Danube park, the computer world was ruled by mainframes and terminals. The personal computer had just been born – but it marked the beginning of a new era.

So if the birth of Ars Electronica 15 years ago was dominated by the development of the PC and the decentralisation associated with it, what we are now witnessing is radical economic and social change coursing through the spreading computer networks: the nineties will be shaped by the global race for digital information highways.

EDITORIAL

HANNES LEOPOLDSEDER
15 JAHRE ARS ELECTRONICA
15 YEARS OF ARS ELECTRONICA

durch das globale Wettrennen um die digitalen Infobahnen beherrscht.

Diese 15 Jahre seit 1979 sind allerdings nur ein Augenaufschlag in der Geschichte der Computertechnik von der „Ars Magna" des Scholastikers Raimundus Lullus um 1300 (Werner Künzel und Peter Bexte nennen Lullus in ihrem „Ursprung des Computers" den „ersten Hacker in den himmlischen Datenbanken") über die „Ars Combinatoria" eines Gottfried Wilhelm Leibniz hin zur kommenden digitalen „Nationalen Informationsinfrastruktur" (NII) – einer „Infociety", in der der „METAMAN" (Gregory Stock) des dritten Jahrtausends sichtbar wird: ein Universum als einziger Computer.

Wir leben heute inmitten eines sich abzeichnenden Medienbruchs, der mit der Einführung der Buchstabenschrift und mit der Ausbreitung des Buchdrucks durch Gutenberg verglichen wird. Während der Buchdruck unsere Erfahrung in schriftlicher Form ausdrückt, geht das digitale Medium Computer weit darüber hinaus, indem Texte, Bilder und Töne integriert werden können. Wolfgang Coy (Universität Bremen) unterstreicht mit Recht die enorme kulturelle Bedeutung dieses Medienbruchs: „Der Medienbruch bedeutet, daß die Medien, die in den letzten 150 Jahren entstanden sind, also die elektronischen Medien von Telegraphie bis Fernsehen und die optischen Medien wie Photographie und Film, in Frage gestellt und über die Umformbarkeit in ein allgemeines, alles integrierendes Medium neu definiert werden. Mit dieser Umformbarkeit wird letztlich die Existenz der neueren elektronischen und optischen Medien in Frage gestellt." (Kunstforum 124/93).

Während heute Megaindustrien in dem Zusammenwachsen von Computer, Fernsehen und Telekommunikation eines der großen Wachstumspotentiale um die Jahrtausendwende sehen, denken andere Forscher, wie George Gilder vom Discovery Institute in Seattle, den Medienbruch um einen Quantensprung weiter: Gilder hält Fernsehen und Telefon bereits für überkommene Medien, die die digitale Revolu-

The fifteen years since 1979 are, however, only a blink in the history of computer technology which stretches from "Ars Magna", written around 1300 by the scholar Raimundus Lullus (in their "Ursprung des Computers" [Origin of the Computer], Werner Künzel and Peter Bexte call Lullus the "first hacker in the heavenly data banks"), by way of "Ars Combinatoria" by Gottfried Wilhelm Leibniz, to the imminent digital "National Information Infrastructure" (NII) of an "Infociety" in which the "METAMAN" (Gregory Stock) of the third millennium becomes apparent: a universe as one big computer.

Today we are living through an emerging media disintegration which is being compared to the introduction of alphabet script or the proliferation of Gutenberg's letterpress printing.

While letterpress printing expresses our experience in written form, the digital medium computer goes far beyond that through its ability to integrate text, pictures and sounds. Wolfgang Coy (University of Bremen) is right to emphasise the enormous cultural importance of this media disintegration: "Media disintegration means that those media that have taken shape over the last 150 years, in other words, electronic media all the way from telegraphy to television as well as optical media like photography and film, are called into question and by way of their capacity for transformation are re-defined into an overall, all-encompassing medium. In the end it is this capacity for transformation that calls into question the very existence of the recent electronic and optical media." (Kunstforum 124/93).

While today's multinationals view the convergence of computer, television and telecommunications around the turn of the century as one of the areas with the most growth potential, other researchers like George Gilder from the Discovery Institute in Seattle see media disintegration as being a quantum leap further ahead. As he tries to demonstrate in his book "Life after Television", television and

EDITORIAL

HANNES LEOPOLDSEDER
15 JAHRE ARS ELECTRONICA
15 YEARS OF ARS ELECTRONICA

tion nicht überleben, wie er in seinem Buch „Life after Television" darzulegen versucht. Wie die achtziger Jahre den Zusammenbruch der zentralen Systeme der Mainframes und der Terminals gebracht haben, erwartet Gilder in den neunziger Jahren den Zusammenbruch von Telefon und Fernsehen. Seine Zukunftsvision liegt in der selbständigen Nutzung der Computernetze durch den einzelnen, ermöglicht durch das enorme Anwachsen der Computerkapazität und der globalen Kommunikationsnetze. Wir stehen vor der Geburt eines neuen Kommunikationsmediums, eine gewaltige Herausforderung für die jetzigen elektronischen Medien.

Das Linzer Festival Ars Electronica von 1979 bis 1994 spiegelt 15 Jahre dieser Entwicklung zu einer digitalen Welt wider. Als einer der Mitbegründer von Ars Electronica (gemeinsam mit Prof. Herbert W. Francke, Hubert Bognermayer und Ulli A. Rützel) nannte ich 1979 als eine der Zielsetzungen des Festivals „Auseinandersetzung mit Manifestationen und Konsequenzen neuer Technologien für Kunst, Kultur und Gesellschaft", ein Postulat, das Linz über eineinhalb Jahrzehnte immer mehr zu einem Reflexions- und Ereignisort für neue Medien, Technologien und deren künstlerischen Einsatz werden ließ – von der Skyart über Virtual Reality bis zum Leben im Netz.

„Sobald es funktioniert, ist es überholt" – entsprechend dieses Grundsatzes, den ich vorangestellt habe, versucht Ars Electronica, Wandel und wechselnden Perspektiven konsequent Rechnung zu tragen – als Labor, das sich bewußt zum Unfertigen bekennt. Die 15 Jahre Ars Electronica lassen sich in drei Phasen gliedern:
– die Konzeptionsjahre 1979/80,
– die Phase der jährlichen Institutionalisierung, Thematisierung und Fokussierung durch das jährliche Generalthema auf der einen Seite sowie durch die Schaffung des Prix Ars Electronica als Fokus digitaler Entwicklungen (1986/87) und
– schließlich die dritte Phase der Überlegungen zur Verankerung, Vertiefung und Vernetzung

telephone should be considered obsolete media that will not survive the digital revolution. Just as the central systems of mainframes and terminals lost the upper hand in the eighties, Gilder expects telephone and television to fade away in the nineties. His vision of the future lies in the independent use of computer networks by the individual, made possible by the enormous increase in computing power and by the growth of global communications networks. We are about to witness the birth of a new communications medium, a major challenge to present-day electronic media.

Between 1979 and 1994, Linz's Ars Electronica Festival has reflected 15 years of this movement toward a digital world. As one of the co-founders of Ars Electronica in 1979 (together with Prof. Herbert W. Francke, Hubert Bognermayer and Ulli A. Rützel), I defined one of the goals of the festival as being "to examine the manifestations and consequences of new technologies for art, culture and society". In the course of the following decade and a half, this ideal was to increasingly make Linz a place for reflection and events addressing new media and technologies, and their artistic exploitation – from Skyart by way of virtual reality to life in the network.

"As soon as it works, it's obsolete" – in accordance with this principle that I have already quoted, Ars Electronica consistently tries to do justice to evolution and changing perspectives – a laboratory that consciously devotes itself to the unfinished. The 15 years of Ars Electronica can be divided into three phases:
– the planning years 1979/80,
– the phase of annual institutionalization, adopting a theme and focusing on it (1986/87); this was done on the one hand through the development of the annual, overall theme, as well as through the creation of the Prix Ars Electronica as a focus for digital developments; and
– the third and final phase: the commitment to definition, in-depth examination, and networking which is to be honoured through

EDITORIAL

HANNES LEOPOLDSEDER
15 JAHRE ARS ELECTRONICA
15 YEARS OF ARS ELECTRONICA

durch die Errichtung eines Ars Electronica Centers und Planung eines Ars Electronica Networks in den Jahren 1993/94, verbunden mit dem Ziel, 1996 das Ars Electronica Center als digitales Mediencenter eröffnen zu können.

Damit präsentiert sich Linz nach 15 Jahren mit dem Ars Electronica Triangle: Ars Electronica Festival – Prix Ars Electronica Wettbewerb – Ars Electronica Center als Museum der Zukunft.

Ausgangspunkt von Ars Electronica sind Kunst und Kultur. Künstler sind Indikatoren für künftige Entwicklungen. Auch im Technologie- und Medienbereich. Aus diesem Grund läßt sich Ars Electronica insgesamt als Frühindikator für technische, kulturelle und gesellschaftliche Entwicklungen sehen.

Die Idee des Prix Ars Electronica, 1987 durch den ORF initiiert, ist einfach: der Wettbewerb begreift den Computer als universales Medium, das allmählich alle Bereiche des kreativen Gestaltens umfassen wird.

Der Prix Ars Electronica betrifft derzeit vier Bereiche – Musik, Graphik, Animation, Interaktive Kunst. In der Zukunft werden die Bereiche anwachsen. Der Prix Ars Electronica ist für Linz ein Botschafter in der Welt geworden – der Prix Ars Electronica ist heute weltweit der umspannendste Wettbewerb von Nord nach Süd, von Ost nach West: Fast 6000 Künstler aus über 50 Ländern der Erde sind mit insgesamt 9000 digitalen Arbeiten bisher beim Prix Ars Electronica vertreten.

Die Teilnehmer am Prix Ars Electronica aus dem Kunst- und Musikbereich, aus den Universitäten, wissenschaftlichen Institutionen und Technologieunternehmen aus der ganzen Welt bilden rund um den Globus das „Grassroot-Network" der Ars Electronica.

Die Attraktivität des Prix Ars Electronica als Wettbewerb für digitale Medien für Künstler und Wissenschafter liegt unter anderem in der Konzentration der Preise, in der Auseinandersetzung und der Diskussion innerhalb der qualifizierten Fachjury, im Nichtaufteilen nach unterschiedlichen Sparten, sondern in dem Anspruch, jeweils Kreativität, Innovation,

the creation of an Ars Electronica Center, as well as through the planning of an Ars Electronica Network in the years 1993/94. On this basis, the Ars Electronica Center is to open as a digital media center in 1996.

Thus after 15 years, the Ars Electronica triangle takes shape: Ars Electronica Festival – Prix Ars Electronica competition – Ars Electronica Center, a museum of the future.

Ars Electronica's starting point is art and culture. Artists are harbingers of future developments, not least in the technology and media areas. For this reason Ars Electronica can, in general, be seen as an advance indicator for technical, cultural and societal developments.

The idea of the Prix Ars Electronica, initiated by the ORF in 1987, is a simple one: the competition views the computer as a universal medium which will gradually come to span all areas of creative work.

At present the Prix Ars Electronica covers four areas – Music, Graphics, Animation, Interactive Art. In the future more areas will be added. The Prix Ars Electronica has become an ambassador at large for Linz. It is now the world's most comprehensive competition north, south, east and west: So far, almost 6,000 artists from over 50 countries have entered a total of 9,000 digital works.

Prix Ars Electronica entrants from the art and music fields, from the universities, and from scientific institutions and technological businesses all over the world make up the 'grassroots network' of Ars Electronica.

As a digital media competition, the Prix Ars Electronica's attraction for artists and scientists lies in the concentration of the prizes, the debates and discussions within a jury of competent experts, the dedication to weighing up each individual work's creativity, innovation and computer-specificity rather than assigning it to a category.

For the region of Upper Austria, for Austria, and even globally for the "electronic community", Ars Electronica's 15 years represent an event with continuity, but at the same time a position for the future. From the

EDITORIAL

HANNES LEOPOLDSEDER
15 JAHRE ARS ELECTRONICA
15 YEARS OF ARS ELECTRONICA

Computerspezifität am Einzelprodukt abzuwägen.

Weltweit hat sich Ars Electronica innerhalb der großen Veranstaltungen SIGGRAPH und Imagina als drittes, eigenständiges Forum etabliert, das, im Gegensatz zu den anderen Institutionen, nicht kommerziell, sondern vom Anspruch her kulturell ausgerichtet ist.

Die nächsten 15 Jahre – bis zum Jahre 2009 – zählen gewiß zu den abenteuerlichsten Jahren des Wandels. Wenn Gregory Stock von der Princeton University Recht hat, überwindet „METAMAN" in unserem Jahrzehnt seine Geburtswehen: Wir stehen am Morgen einer neuen Phase unserer Evolution – die menschliche Gesellschaft ist unterwegs zu einem globalen Superorganismus, in dem die Menschen durch moderne Technologien und Kommunikation verbunden sind wie Zellen in einem großen Körper. Gleichzeitig aber stehen wir an einem Angelpunkt in der Geschichte: Wird die kommende „National Information Infrastructure" (NII), wie die amerikanische Regierung das Schaffen der landesweiten Breitbandkommunikationsstruktur nennt, geheime Hintertüren offen halten, die die Bürgerrechte der privaten Kommunikation und Freiheit beeinträchtigen, wie das Trendmagazin „Wired" in einem dramatischen Report über Freiheit und Privatsphäre in den Netzwerken 1994 darlegt? Was steht am Ende der Infobahnen? Die Entwicklung im nächsten Jahrzehnt erfordert mehr denn je die Auseinandersetzung über die Auswirkungen der neuen Technologien auf unsere Gesellschaft.

Ars Electronica ist dafür weiterhin ein Forum.

point of view of Linz, Ars Electronica has contributed to the moulding of a new profile and image for the city; for Austria, which is traditionally a land of culture, Ars Electronica represents one of the few festivals to credibly link art, media and forward-looking technology.

On the world stage, Ars Electronica has established itself among the large scale events such as SIGGRAPH and Imagina as a third, independent forum which differs from the other festivals in that it is by design culturally, not commercially, oriented.

The next 15 years – leading up to the year 2009 – will certainly be among the most adventurous years of change. If Gregory Stock of Princeton University is right, "METAMAN" will overcome the pains of birth in this decade: we are at the dawn of a new era in our evolution – human society is on its way to a global superorganism in which modern technology and communication connect people together like the cells in a great body. At the same time, however, we have reached a fulcrum in our history: Will the imminent "National Information Infrastructure" (NII), as the American government calls the creation of the nationwide, broad-band communications structure, hold open secret back doors that will restrict civil rights, confidential communication and freedom, as "Wired" magazine expounded this year in a dramatic report about freedom and privacy in the networks? What lies at the end of the data highways? The next decade's developments will require more investigation of the effects of new technology on our society than has ever occurred before.

Ars Electronica will continue to be a forum for such investigation.

EDITORIAL

CHRISTINE SCHÖPF
PRIX ARS ELECTRONICA 94

In seiner achten Ausgabe hat der diesjährige Prix Ars Electronica die Entwicklung der letzten Jahre weitergeführt und gefestigt: Das von Jahr zu Jahr steigende Interesse an diesem Wettbewerb, das sich in jährlich steigenden Teilnehmerzahlen manifestiert (1994 haben sich 844 Künstler aus 38 Nationen mit insgesamt 1.584 Arbeiten beteiligt) und die Verbreiterung des Prix Ars Electronica, der 1987 als Wettbewerb für Computerkünste ins Leben gerufen wurde und mittlerweile zum gemeinsamen Forum für Kunst, Wissenschaft, Forschung und Entertainment geworden ist.

Der Prix Ars Electronica will von seinem Grundanliegen her hervorragende Leistungen im Einsatz neuer Technologien auszeichnen. Nicht Computer- und Manpower stehen im Vordergrund, sondern Kreativität und Innovation, sei es die einer Gruppe oder die eines einzelnen.

Der Prix Ars Electronica wird vom Österreichischen Rundfunk/Landesstudio Oberösterreich innerhalb des seit 1979 gemeinsam mit dem Brucknerhaus Linz veranstalteten Festival Ars Electronica durchgeführt. Die Gesamtdotation des Preisgeldes beträgt 1,25 Millionen öS, gesponsert von Kapsch AG, Stadt Linz und Land Oberösterreich. Die Höhe des Preisgeldes sowie die Verbindung mit dem international reputierten Festival Ars Electronica machen den Prix Ars Electronica zum jährlichen Pflichttermin für Aktive aus Kunst, Wissenschaft, Forschung und Unterhaltung, was sich auch im Ergebnis des diesjährigen Prix Ars Electronica dokumentiert.

5 Goldene Nicas, 8 Auszeichnungen, also insgesamt 13 Geldpreise, und 40 Anerkennungen wurden im Prix Ars Electronica 94 vergeben: Die Goldenen Nicas, die Elektronik-Oscars, gehen nach Frankreich, Österreich, Deutschland und in die USA, und zwar an Dennis Muren/Mark Dippé (ILM), USA, für „Jurassic Park" und an Marc Caro (Midi Minuit), Frankreich, für „K.O. KID" in der Sparte Computeranimation (zweimal öS 150.000); in der Sparte Computergraphik (öS 100.000) an Michael Joaquin Grey, USA, für „Jellylife"; in der

This year's Prix Ars Electronica, the eighth, has continued and consolidated the direction it has taken over the past few years: interest in the competition grows year by year, manifesting itself in annually growing ranks of entrants (this year 844 artists from 38 countries entered a total of 1,584 works), also in the diversification of the Prix Ars Electronica which was started in 1987 as a competition for computer arts and has since become a common forum for art, science, research and entertainment.

The Prix Ars Electronica's prime concern is to honour outstanding achievements in the use of new technologies. This is less a question of computer power and manpower than of creativity and innovation, whether it is in the effort of a group or an individual.

The Prix Ars Electronica is organised by the Austrian Broadcasting Corporation's Upper Austrian Division as part of the Ars Electronica Festival, a joint effort with the Brucknerhaus Linz since 1979. The prize money adds up to 1.25 million Austrian schillings (US$ 100,500), sponsored by the Kapsch company, the City of Linz and the Province of Upper Austria.

The amount of prize money together with the association with the internationally renowned Ars Electronica Festival makes the Prix Ars Electronica an annual must for people from the worlds of art, science, research and entertainment, as demonstrated by the results of this year's Prix Ars Electronica.

5 Golden Nicas and 8 Distinctions, 13 cash prizes altogether, and 40 Honourable Mentions were awarded in the Prix Ars Electronica 94:

The Golden Nicas – electronic Oscars – went to artists in France, Austria, Germany and the USA, namely:

to Dennis Muren/Mark Dippé (ILM), USA, for "Jurassic Park" and to Marc Caro (Midi Minuit), France, for "K.O. KID" in the Computer Animation category (2 x ATS 150,000); in Computer Graphics (ATS 100,000) to Michael Joaquin Grey, USA, for "Jellylife"; for Interactive Art (ATS 150,000) to Christa Sommerer, Austria, and Laurent Mignonneau, France, for the interactive real-time computer

EDITORIAL

CHRISTINE SCHÖPF
PRIX ARS ELECTRONICA 94

Sparte Interaktive Kunst (öS 150.000) an Christa Sommerer, Österreich, und Laurent Mignonneau, Frankreich, für die interaktive Echtzeit-Computerinstallation „A-Volve"; und in der Sparte Computermusik (öS 150.000) an Ludger Brümmer, Deutschland, für seine Komposition „The Gates of H.".

Die Auszeichnungen in der Sparte Computeranimation (zweimal öS 100.000) erhalten Maurice Benayoun (Z. A. Productions), Frankreich, für „Ils sont tous là! (Les QUARXS)" und an Eric Coignoux (Mikros Image), Frankreich, für „No Sex".

Die mit je öS 50.000 dotierten Auszeichnungen gehen an Keith Cottingham, USA, für „Fictitious Portraits" und an John Kahrs, USA, für „Supercluster" (Computergraphik), an den österreichischen Kunstverein TRANSIT für das Radio-TV-Projekt „Realtime" und an Loren Carpenter (Cinematrix), USA, für „Kinoetic Evolution: Collective Collaborative Computer-Mediated Creation" (Interaktive Kunst) und an Åke Parmerud, Schweden, für „Strings & Shadows" und an Jonathan Impett, Großbritannien, für „Mirror-Rite" (Computermusik).

Die Preisverleihung des Prix Ars Electronica 94 wird auch heuer wieder live im Österreichischen Fernsehen und im Satellitenprogramm 3SAT übertragen und gibt dem Prix Ars Electronica damit eine europaweite TV-Präsenz.

Das vorliegende Buch „Der Prix Ars Electronica" und die zum Buch erscheinende Videokassette mit den besten Computeranimationen sowie die CD mit den ausgezeichneten Musikstücken dokumentiert die Ergebnisse des Prix Ars Electronica 94 über den aktuellen Anlaß hinaus und gibt einen Überblick über den Stand der Computerkultur in der Mitte der neunziger Jahre.

In der Zukunftsperspektive ist der Prix Ars Electronica Saatbeet für das Ars Electronica Center, das als permanenter Präsentationsort und Museum der Zukunft 1996 eröffnet wird und sowohl dem Besucher vor Ort als auch dem virtuellen Gast im Netz der Information offen steht.

installation "A-Volve"; and for Computer Music (ATS 150,000) to Ludger Brümmer, Germany, for his composition "The Gates of H."

The Distinctions for computer animation (2 x ATS 100,000) go to Maurice Benayoun (Z. A Productions), France, for "Ils sont tous là! (Les QUARXS)" and Eric Coignoux (Mikros Images), France, for "No Sex".

The Distinctions, worth ATS 50,000 each, go to Keith Cottingham, USA, for "Fictitious Portraits" and John Kahrs, USA, for "Supercluster" (Computer Graphics), to the Austrian art group TRANSIT for their radio/TV project "Realtime", to Loren Carpenter (Cinematrix), USA, for "Kinoetic Evolution: Collective Collaborative Computer-Mediated Creation" (Interactive Art), to Åke Parmerud, Sweden, for "Strings & Shadows", and to Jonathan Impett, Great Britain, for "Mirror-Rite" (Computer Music).

As usual, the Prix Ars Electronica 94 award ceremony will be broadcast live on Austrian television and on 3SAT satellite television, giving the Prix Ars Electronica a TV presence all over Europe.

This book, "The Prix Ars Electronica", the accompanying video cassette with the best computer animations and the CD with the best music works document the results of the Prix Ars Electronica 94 beyond the competition event itself and give an overview of the state of computer culture in the mid-nineties.

Looking to the future, the Prix Ars Electronica provides fertile ground for the Ars Electronica Center, which will open as a permanent presentation venue and museum of the future in 1996, and will be an information center open both to the visitor who arrives in person and to the virtual guest present in the network.

PRIX ARS ELECTRONICA

MICHAEL TOLSON
SIE SOLLTEN DIE MENSCHEN BEUNRUHIGEN
THEY SHOULD MAKE PEOPLE NERVOUS

Frage: Wir stehen einer wahren Flut von Computerbildern, bewegten wie unbewegten, gegenüber. Einige sind interessant, viele sind mittelmäßige Konsumware. Hängt das damit zusammen, daß sowohl Hardware wie Software für fast jeden erschwinglich sind, daß andererseits sich nur wenige echte Künstler für das neue Medium interessieren?
M. Tolson: Ich glaube schon. Hochqualitative Rendering-Software und 3D-Werkzeuge werden für immer mehr Leute leichter zugänglich, und so erleben wir eine Menge von „Frühwerken" neuer Künstler, die das Medium erst erforschen – und solche Arbeiten sind natürlich unreif. Was die Künstler betrifft, so glaube ich, daß wir sicher mehr davon brauchen, die mit diesem Medium arbeiten. Ich möchte die Kunst stärker hervortreten sehen.

Frage: Und was sollten wir tun, um ganz allgemein mehr Künstler und mehr Kunst in die Technologie zu bringen?
M. Tolson: Man sollte die Technologie weniger betonen. Der Prix Ars Electronica ist eine Gelegenheit, wo man Leute ermutigen kann, die künstlerischen Möglichkeiten des Mediums zu erforschen. Die Technologie kommt alleine zurecht, sie wird besser und besser werden, und ich hoffe nur, daß die Kunst da Schritt halten kann. Es ist wie bei jedem neuen Medium: Es dauert eine Weile, bis das Medium seine eigene Sprache und sein eigenes Vokabular entdeckt, und das ist in der Computergraphik noch nicht passiert. Und es wird auch lange dauern, weil dieses Medium so reichhaltig ist.

Frage: Welches waren die Hauptaspekte in der Jurydiskussion, was wurde zuerst diskutiert, der technologische Aspekt oder das Stück als Fragment oder als Summe von Fragmenten? Können Sie die Diskussion und die Standpunkte zusammenfassen?
M. Tolson: Für mich war der Hauptpunkt in der Jurydiskussion folgender: Ich habe mich um den Kunstaspekt gekümmert. Es ist gar zu einfach, mit dem Computer Bilder in Mengen zu produzieren, die irgendwie interessant und

Question: We are facing a real flood of computer graphics both as still images and animations. Some of it is interesting, much is merely mediocre products. Does this relate to the fact that both hardware and software are readily available to almost everyone, but on the other hand very few real artists are interested in the new media yet?
M. Tolson: I think so. 3-D software, high quality rendering is becoming more accessible to more people, and we're seeing now a proliferation of "early work", new artists who are just exploring the medium, and that work is going to be immature. As for more artists, I think we still need more artists to work in this medium. I want to see the art come out more.

Question: What do you suggest we could do generally to bring the artists and the art more into the technology?
M. Tolson: I think, less emphasis on the technology. The Prix Ars Electronica is one example where we can encourage people to explore the artistic possibilities of the medium. The technology is going to take care of itself. The technology is going to get better and better and better, and I hope that art can keep pace. With any new medium, it takes a long time for that medium to discover its vocabulary and its language, and that hasn't happened in computer graphics yet. It will take a long time, because it is such a rich medium.

Question: What were the main aspects of the jury discussions? What had to be judged first, the state of the technology, or the piece as a fragment or as a sum of fragments? How would you sum up the discussion and the viewpoints?
M. Tolson: These were the main topics of discussion for me in the context of the jury: I was preoccupied with the artistic content. It's too easy with the computer to mass produce images that look sort of interesting and different and fascinating, but I think the thought and the concept is so important in the piece, and I want to encourage that to happen more. That was my attitude throughout the judging: it is a problem

PRIX ARS ELECTRONICA

MICHAEL TOLSON
SIE SOLLTEN DIE MENSCHEN BEUNRUHIGEN
THEY SHOULD MAKE PEOPLE NERVOUS

„anders" und faszinierend aussehen, aber ich glaube, das Konzept dahinter ist bei einem Stück ganz wichtig, und ich möchte das auch forcieren. Das war meine Einstellung in der gesamten Jurysitzung, aber es ist natürlich schwierig, wenn man nur einen Teil eines größeren Werkes bewerten kann oder wenn man eine rein kommerzielle Arbeit betrachtet, die durch hervorragende technische Qualität brilliert.

Frage: Ein Wort noch zur Jurysitzung und zu den Einreichungen: Das Publikum blickt natürlich auf die populären Sachen in der Computergraphik – Commercials, „Terminator" oder „Jurassic Park". Wie wirkt sich das auf die Beurteilung aus?
M. Tolson: Das macht es natürlich sehr schwer. Es gibt da große Erwartungen. Das sind Werke, auf die das Publikum schaut, die es kennt, und das Publikum wird all die anderen Sachen niemals beachten, wenn sie nicht in den Vordergrund gestellt werden. Es gibt eine Menge großartiger individueller Arbeiten von Leuten, die seit Jahren in ihrem Kunstbereich tätig sind, aber keinen Zugang zum Publikum, zu den Massenmedien außerhalb von Ereignissen wie dem Prix Ars Electronica haben. Deshalb ist es auch so wichtig, solche Arbeiten zu fördern, denn ohne Anerkennung entstehen solche Werke nicht. Als ich in den siebziger Jahren anfing, mich mit Computergraphik zu beschäftigen, mußte ich bald wieder aufhören, weil ich kein Geld hatte, mir einen eigenen Computer zu kaufen. Acht Jahre lang habe ich pausiert, und dann mußte ich eine eigene Firma gründen, um an die nötige Ausrüstung heranzukommen, und ich bin nicht allein mit diesem Problem.

Frage: Könnten Sie die Entscheidung in der Computeranimation näher erläutern? In der Graphik gab es ja keine großen Kontroversen, da waren die Meinungen recht einhellig, aber die Teilung der Goldenen Nica in der Animation war doch eher kontroversiell.
M. Tolson: Die Nica wurde zwischen „Jurassic Park" und „K.O. KID" geteilt. Bei „Jurassic

when you are just looking at a small fragment of a larger piece, or if you are looking at a commercial work that has technological excellence.

Question: One point about the jury meeting and the entries: the public's eyes are on the very popular things that happen in computer graphics – commercials, "The Terminator", or "Jurassic Park", for example. How does that affect things?
M. Tolson: That makes it very difficult. Clearly there are great expectations. These are things that are in the public eye, it's what the public knows, and the public will never experience the other things, unless they are brought forth. There's a lot of great individual work that is being done – people who work for years on their art, and they have no access to the public, no access to the mass media, other than things like the Prix Ars Electronica. That is why it is so important to encourage that kind of work, otherwise it won't happen. I remember when I started doing things like computer graphics in the 70s – I stopped, because I didn't have the money to get a computer. I had to stop for eight years, and I needed to start a company to get the equipment, so I know I'm not alone in this problem.

Question: Could you comment a little bit on the animation decision – there was no great controversy about the computer graphics, that was more or less unanimous, but there was a lot of discussion about splitting the Nica.
M. Tolson: The Nica was split between "Jurassic Park" and "K.O. KID". On the part of "Jurassic Park", this reflected something uniquely state of the art. "Jurassic Park"'s use of stunning technology and compositing makes it really believable. This has to be recognized. On the other hand, it had a huge budget and a huge staff of the best animators in the world.
On the other side we have the "K.O. KID", which is clearly a labour of love: made by a small team, working very hard. I suspect they did not have much of a budget, and they

PRIX ARS ELECTRONICA

MICHAEL TOLSON
SIE SOLLTEN DIE MENSCHEN BEUNRUHIGEN
THEY SHOULD MAKE PEOPLE NERVOUS

Park" reflektiert diese Entscheidung die einzigartige Qualität auf dem allerhöchsten Stand der Technik. Die Verwendung von umwerfender Technologie und Bildtechniken macht das Ergebnis wirklich glaubhaft. So etwas muß anerkannt werden. Andererseits gab es dafür ein enormes Budget, und ein riesiges Team der weltbesten Animatoren hat daran gearbeitet. Sieht man hingegen „K.O. KID" an, dann erkennt man, daß es ein offensichtliches Stück Liebhaberei ist, von einem kleinen Team in harter Arbeit produziert, ich vermute mal, mit so gut wie keinem Budget, und trotzdem haben sie eine nahezu perfekte Animation geschaffen, mit einer Menge innovativer Techniken. Eine großartige Integration von Animation und Filmbildern, großartige Lichteffekte, und nebenbei erzählt es noch eine Geschichte, und es macht einfach Spaß, den Streifen zu sehen. Deshalb glaube ich, daß es eine wichtige Aussage seitens der Jury ist, wenn diese beiden Arbeiten gleich gewichtet werden. Es gibt keinen Imperialismus im Bereich der Computeranimation.

Frage: Sie haben sich ja auch für ein anderes Stück eingesetzt, für „No Sex".
M. Tolson: Dazu stehe ich. Das ist eine ganz kraftvolle Arbeit. Es muß nicht alles High-End-Graphik sein. Dieses Werk entstand auf einer Paintbox, und was mich besonders fasziniert hat, war die Schnittechnik, die zeitliche Struktur. Rhythmus und Tempo sind großartig, und so etwas sieht man in der Computeranimation viel zu selten. Computeranimationen sind allgemein zu simpel. Jedes Einzelbild in „No Sex" steht als eigenständiges Kunstwerk da. Es ist ein gewalttätiges Stück, ein starkes Stück, vielleicht ein aufwühlendes Stück, aber das gefällt mir. Ich glaube, Werke sollten so etwas machen. Sie sollten die Leute erschrecken, sie sollten die Menschen beunruhigen.

Frage: Es gab ganz allgemein eine Diskussion über die Ästhetik von Computerbildern. Welche Entwicklung können Sie feststellen: eine Regression oder einen Fortschritt?
M. Tolson: Ich fürchte, ich sehe eine Phase der

produced an almost perfect animation with a lot of technical innovation, with great integration of animation with live footage, and great lighting – and it tells a story and it's fun to watch. So I think we're making a strong statement that there's an equivalence here. There's no such thing as imperialism in the computer graphics domain.

Question: You made a strong statement on one piece: "No Sex".
M. Tolson: I stand by it. This is a very powerful piece. Things don't have to be high end graphics. This was done on a paintbox. And another thing that attracted me was the editing, the time structure; the rhythm and pacing are great, and I don't see enough of that in computer graphics. Computer graphics is generally too simple. Each frame in "No Sex" stands on its own as a work of art. It's a violent piece, a strong piece, maybe it's even a disturbing piece, but I like that. I think pieces should do that, they should scare people, they should make people nervous.

Question: In general there was some discussion about the aesthetics of computer images. What kind of development do you see – a regression or a way ahead?
M. Tolson: I fear I see a regression coming: I fear that because of the proliferation of low-cost systems. 3D is now relatively inexpensive to do with very high quality rendering. It works on PCs now, and what this means is that we are going to see a lot of bad 3-D animation. But the next step will be that more and more people and more and more artists will have access to this technology, so we will see an acceleration of the aesthetics, and hopefully that will develop a critical community, a critical dialog. I think this needs to happen.

Question: How have the aesthetics of computer graphics developed, how will they develop? What state are we in?
M. Tolson: It's my opinion that the aesthetics of computer graphics to date have been

PRIX ARS ELECTRONICA

MICHAEL TOLSON
SIE SOLLTEN DIE MENSCHEN BEUNRUHIGEN
THEY SHOULD MAKE PEOPLE NERVOUS

Regression kommen, und ich glaube, das hängt mit dem enormen Anwachsen von Billigsystemen zusammen. 3D mit hochqualitativem Rendering ist heute relativ billig zu machen, es läuft auch auf PCs, und das bedeutet, daß wir eine Menge schlechter 3D-Animationen sehen werden. Aber der nächste Schritt wird sein, daß immer mehr Leute und immer mehr Künstler Zugang zu dieser Technologie bekommen, und so werden wir in der Folge auch eine Beschleunigung in der Ästhetik miterleben. Daraus wird sich hoffentlich eine kritische Gemeinde entwickeln, ein kritischer Dialog. Ich glaube, das muß auch so ablaufen.

Frage: Wie hat sich die Ästhetik der Computergraphik entwickelt, wie wird sie sich weiter entwickeln? Wo stehen wir jetzt?
M. Tolson: Meiner Ansicht nach wird die Ästhetik der Computergraphik derzeit viel zu sehr von der Technologie und ihren Beschränkungen bestimmt, aber ich denke, daß sich das ändern wird und daß uns da aufregende Möglichkeiten geboten werden. Ich glaube wirklich, daß wir bisher nur an der Oberfläche dessen gekratzt haben, was im graphischen Bereich am Computer möglich ist. Und auch hier gilt wieder: In dem Maß, in dem die Ausrüstung und die Technologie für immer mehr Menschen zugänglich wird, werden wir immer mehr mittelmäßige Arbeiten sehen, solange die Leute das Medium erlernen. Dann aber wird sich die Kommunikation entwickeln, und dann wird es wirklich spannend.

Frage: Hängen diese Fragen wirklich so eng mit der Technologie zusammen?
M. Tolson: Ich behaupte, daß schon in der Technologie eine Menge Ästhetik steckt, und damit meine ich nicht die Computer oder die Chips. Ich meine das Potential der Software-Umgebung, und das finde ich sehr aufregend. Heute wird ein Großteil der Technologie zur Problemlösung verwendet – wie bekommt man eine photorealistische Wiedergabe, wie erzielt man natürliche Bewegungen –, und ich glaube, daß diese Aufgaben bald gelöst sein werden.

determined too much by the technology and the limitations of the technology, and I think that is going to start changing, so that is going to yield an exciting opportunity. I really think we have only scratched the surface of what is possible in computer graphics. Again, as this equipment, this technology becomes available to more and more people, we'll start to see a lot of mediocre work as people learn about the medium, but then that communication will develop, and it will be very exciting.

Question: Are the issues closely related to the technology?
M. Tolson: I think there is a great deal of aesthetics in the technology itself, by which I don't mean the computers or the chips. I mean the potential of the software environment. So for me, this is very exciting. To date, a lot of the technology has been devoted to solving problems (how do you get photo-realistic rendering, how do you get naturalistic motion), and I think these problems are beginning to be solved, and that is going to revolutionize the film and TV industry. On the other hand, I think that in some of the research pieces we see something else coming out. We see the exploration of abstract concepts, abstract spaces, and I think there is a really interesting 'something' in the computer domain that can come out in the graphics – I call it the Dionysian. You could say that to date, computer graphics has been too much on the appollonian side, too rational, and there is this kind of behaviour and passion that can come out of the technology. I'm looking forward to seeing more of that.
When I mentioned the "Dionysian" I was referring to that grand old axis: Appollonian/ Dionysian. I was suggesting that computer graphics, due to its naissance in the Cartesian tradition, along with projective vector geometry and Newtonian dynamics, has been heavily biased in its expressive powers towards the former with, at best, an uneasy nostalgia for the latter. Relatively recent developments in mathematics and the sciences, which have been enabled to a great extent by computers, will, I

MICHAEL TOLSON
SIE SOLLTEN DIE MENSCHEN BEUNRUHIGEN
THEY SHOULD MAKE PEOPLE NERVOUS

Das wird vor allem den Film- und Fernsehbereich revolutionieren. Andererseits glaube ich, daß man in einigen der Forschungsarbeiten etwas Neues auftauchen sieht: Wir erleben die Erforschung von abstrakten Konzepten, von abstrakten Räumen, und ich meine, es gibt ein wirklich interessantes „Etwas" im Computerbereich, das in den graphischen Anwendungen hervorkommen kann. Ich nenne es das Dionysische. Man könnte, philosophisch gesprochen, behaupten, die Computergraphik stehe viel zu sehr auf der apollonischen Seite – sie ist zu rational, und da gibt es einfach eine Art von Verhalten und Leidenschaft, die aus der Technologie selbst kommen kann. Ich freue mich darauf, mehr davon zu sehen.

Wenn ich „dionysisch" gesagt habe, so habe ich dabei an die große alte Achse „apollonisch – dionysisch" gedacht. Ich meine damit, daß die Computergraphik – die ja zusammen mit einer projektiven Vektorgraphik und einer Newtonschen Dynamik aus einer kartesianischen Tradition geboren wurde –, in ihrer Ausdruckskraft viel zu sehr zum Rationalen neigt und nur im Idealfall eine verschwommene Sehnsucht nach dem Emotionalen in sich trägt. Die relativ neuen Entwicklungen in der Mathematik und den Naturwissenschaften, die zu einem guten Teil erst durch den Computer ermöglicht wurden, werden – das spüre ich – sowohl die expressiven Fähigkeiten wie die Inhalte der Computergraphik verändern. Ich spreche hier von einer Anzahl eng verbundener Forschungsbereiche – nicht-lineare Dynamik und Komplexität, immersive Systeme, künstliches Leben, computer-neurologische Wissenschaft und dergleichen. Alle gemeinsam bedeuten sie nichts anders als eine echte Revolution in der Wissenschaft und letztlich auch im Bewußtsein. Man könnte sie als „dionysisch" bezeichnen, nicht so sehr im Sinn von „trunkenem Zustand" als vielmehr unter dem leidenschaftlichen Aspekt, meta-rational, somatisch.

Das ganze mag vielleicht für die Wissenschaft neu sein, die Religionen oder die Philosophie des Abendlandes kennen es schon lange. Ironischerweise war dieselbe Renaissance, die der

feel, transform graphics' expressive powers and content completely. I am speaking here of a number of deeply connected areas of research – nonlinear dynamics and complexity, immersion systems, artificial life, computational neuroscience, etc. This represents nothing less than a revolution in the sciences and, ultimately, in consciousness. It also might be characterized as Dionysian, not so much in its drunken but more its passionate, meta-rational and somatic aspects.

All of this might be new to the sciences, but it is hardly new to religion or even western philosophy, and is certainly not new to the arts. Ironically, the same Renaissance that gave birth to perspective and laid the way for the "triumph of reason" was heavily steeped in mystical neo-platonism. Maybe the problem was that then, as now, cubes were easier to draw…

The serious question here then becomes to what extent a medium constrains its artist. If the bulk of computer graphics to date represents the "dreams of reason" (or more commonly "the banalities of reason"), does the medium in fact place a horizon on what is possible? I think not. Not only must each medium develop its own language and critical vocabulary – what of a medium whose language is in constant flux or – Ursprache?

As to artist/scientists such as Karl Sims and Michael Grey: they just might represent an avant-garde tugging the medium towards not only the Dionysian, but towards a Dionysian return. The serpent swallows its tail and the computer scientists and artists discover what other artists have known – intuitively – all along. The deepest dreams of reason become Dionysian rages.

Of course, if we consider computer art as an evolutionary medium embedded in a cultural/economic medium, the selection pressures exerted by the mass media market are enormous and growing (with the advent of interactive media). These pressures are terribly conservative and banal. In this context I fear that the real dinosaurs will not be found in "Jurassic Park", but rather will be certain artist/

MICHAEL TOLSON
SIE SOLLTEN DIE MENSCHEN BEUNRUHIGEN
THEY SHOULD MAKE PEOPLE NERVOUS

Perspektive den Durchbruch verschafft und den Weg gepflastert hat für den „Triumph des Rationalen", tief in einen mystischen Neo-Platonismus verstrickt. Vielleicht war das Problem damals – nicht anders als heute –, daß Würfel einfach leichter zu zeichnen sind …

Hier taucht dann natürlich die ernste Frage auf, bis zu welchem Grad ein Medium seine Künstler einschränkt. Wenn der Großteil der Computergraphik heute den „Traum der Vernunft" darstellt (oder allgemeiner die „Banalitäten der Vernunft"), ist es das Medium, das den Horizont des Möglichen begrenzt? Ich glaube nicht. Nicht nur, daß jedes Medium seine eigene Sprache entwickeln muß und sein eigenes kritisches Vokabular – was passiert mit einem Medium, dessen Sprache in ständigem Fluß ist oder eine Ursprache?

Was die Künstler/Wissenschaftler betrifft, wie etwa Karl Sims oder Michael Joaquin Grey: Sie können eine Art Avantgarde darstellen, die das Medium nicht nur in Richtung des Dionysischen schiebt, sondern zu einer dionysischen Rückkehr bewegt. Die Schlange beißt sich in den Schwanz, und die Computerkünstler und -Wissenschaftler lernen kennen, was andere Künstler rein intuitiv schon immer gewußt haben. Die tiefsten Träume der Vernunft werden ein dionysisches Furioso.

Natürlich, wenn wir die Computerkunst als ein evolutionäres Medium begreifen, das in ein kulturell-ökonomisches Umfeld eingebettet ist, dann wird der Auswahldruck durch den Markt der Massenmedien enorm stark, und er wird durch das Auftreten der interaktiven Medien noch wachsen. Dieser Druck ist schrecklich konservativ und banal, und in diesem Zusammenhang fürchte ich, daß die echten Dinosaurier nicht in „Jurassic Park" zu finden sind, sondern unter gewissen Künstler-Wissenschaftler-Persönlichkeiten. Die Veränderung des Bewußtseins, von der ich vorhin gesprochen habe, ist – glaube ich – unaufhaltsam. Aber da sie eben den trivialisierenden Kräften der kommerziellen Massenmedien unterworfen werden muß, wird sie nur ganz langsam stattfinden.

scientists. The transformation of consciousness I spoke of before is, I believe, inevitable. Because it must be subjected to the trivializing forces of commercial mass media, it will also be very slow.

Das Interview wurde von Regina Patsch geführt.
This interview was conducted by Regina Patsch.

PRIX ARS ELECTRONICA

MICHAEL NAIMARK
INTERAKTIVE KUNST UND DER MYTHOS DER „ALLES-HEIT"
INTERACTIVE ART AND THE MYTH OF EVERYTHING-NESS

Interaktive Technologien sind also jetzt (endlich) in Mode gekommen. Die Wirtschaft und die Medien haben sie zur nächsten „großen Sache" erkoren. Aber irgendetwas vermiest mir diesen Enthusiasmus einigermaßen.

Gehen Sie doch einmal auf einen der vielen Interaktiv-, Multimedia- oder VR-Kongresse oder auf ein Festival und hören Sie einmal zu, wie dort die Worte „alles", „allumfassend" und „vollständig" verwendet werden:

„Man kann alles, was der Verbraucher haben will, auf einer einzigen CD-ROM unterbringen."

„Ganze Bibliotheken werden auf Knopfdruck abrufbar."

„Jeder kann sich die ganze Kunst der Welt zu Hause ansehen."

Einen Kollegen habe ich auf die letzte Aussage hin angesprochen. Wir waren gerade dabei, so eine „allumfassende" Disc für den Schulgebrauch herzustellen, und er hatte vor, die „ganze" Kunst in einem Bereich unterzubringen. Ich fragte ihn, wie viele Bilder er denn für den Bereich „Kunst der Welt" vorgesehen hätte. Er murmelte ein paar Zahlen und meinte dann: „1.200". Ich meinte darauf ihm gegenüber, daß in einigen der Kunstgeschichte-Texte an Colleges von 1.200, wenn nicht von mehr Künstlern die Rede sei und daß er ja dann nur je ein Bild zur Verfügung hätte, um das ganze Lebenswerk eines Künstlers darzustellen (abgesehen davon, daß er nicht einmal ein Bild des Künstlers selbst unterbringen könne).

Naivität stört mich keineswegs. Was mich aber stört, das ist die Auffassung der Produzenten interaktiver Medien, gar keine Entscheidungen treffen zu müssen, da sie dem Konsumenten ja ohnehin „ALLES" gäben. Das ist schlimmer als Unaufrichtigkeit dem Publikum gegenüber: Das ist nämlich Unaufrichtigkeit sich selbst gegenüber.

Wie dem auch sei, ich war einer der ersten schwärmerischen Lanzenbrecher für die Interaktivität in der Kunst. (1980 verdiente ich mehr mit Vorträgen über Interaktivität als mit Produktionen selbst.) Die Kunstwelt, die Mainstream-Kunstwelt, war ursprünglich skeptisch.

Interactive technologies have become in vogue (finally!). The business and press communities have proclaimed them the next Big Thing. But there's something that's been bugging me about all this enthusiasm.

Go to one of the many interactive/multimedia/virtual reality conferences or festivals and listen to how words like "everything" and "all" and "entire" are used.

"You can put everything the user will want on a single CD-ROM."

"Entire libraries can now be instantly accessed."

"All the world's art can now be seen by everyone in their homes."

I asked a colleague once about this last statement. We were involved in a large educational "everything disc", and he intended to put all of art on one section. I asked him how many laserdisc stillframes he planned to allocate for the world art section. He mumbled a few numbers and declared "1,200". I pointed out to him that some college art history texts make mention of 1,200 artists or more, so at most he could exhibit only one image representing the entire life of each artist (and couldn't even use a picture of the artist as well).

I don't mind the naiveté, but I do mind the implication that producers of interactive material don't need to make decisions, because they're giving the user ... EVERYTHING. This is worse than being dishonest with your audience: it's being dishonest with yourself.

For better or worse, I was one of the early rant-and-ravers of interactive technologies in the arts. (In 1980 I earned more income giving presentations about interactivity than producing!) The artworld, the mainstream artworld, was initially skeptical. Much of this is natural and healthy, a critical eye toward the new. Good art ultimately is judged by surviving the test of time. The hype around interactivity was often overwhelming. And most mainstream artworlders didn't have enough frame of reference to stick their necks out.

But there's a deeper reason, I think, for a resistance to interactivity, and it stems from Michelangelo's famous statement, 'I see the

MICHAEL NAIMARK
INTERAKTIVE KUNST UND DER MYTHOS DER „ALLES-HEIT"
INTERACTIVE ART AND THE MYTH OF EVERYTHING-NESS

In einem gewissen Rahmen ist das ja natürlich und gesund, dem Neuen mit einem kritischen Blick zu begegnen. Und wirklich gute Kunst ist letztendlich doch nur dadurch zu bewerten, ob sie den Zeit-Test besteht und überlebt. Der Medienrummel rund um die Interaktivität war oft überwältigend, und viele Vertreter der Kunstwelt hatten einen zu geringen Bezugsrahmen, um sich zu trauen, da hineinzuschnuppern.

Aber da gibt es noch einen tieferen Grund für den Widerstand gegen die Interaktivität, und der leitet sich von Michelangelos berühmtem Ausspruch ab: „Ich sehe die Figur im Marmorblock und werde sie daraus befreien." Diese Feststellung des „Ich rede, und Du hörst zu!" hat (zumindest im Westen) die Grundlage für die Auffassung vom Künstler als Schöpfer und vom Kunstliebhaber als passiv Lernendem geschaffen. Die Kunstwelt jedenfalls hat die Interaktivität als etwas „verrückt" eingestuft. Sie wurde ja nur von jenen Künstlern verwendet, die entweder keine Visionen hatten, die stark genug waren oder die sich nicht dazu entscheiden konnten, wie sie ihre Arbeit fertigstellen sollten.

Wir haben jetzt gut und gerne 15 Jahre hinter uns, in denen Künstler die Interaktivität erforscht haben, und, wie wir in der Jury zum Prix Ars Electronica gesehen haben, tauchen langsam einige poetische und provokative Arbeiten auf. Aber wir müssen lernen, sowohl kritisch als auch begeistert zu sein, wenn wir uns erwarten, daß interaktive Kunst aufhört, widersprüchlich zu bleiben.

figure in the marble and I will free it'. This declaration of 'I talk, you listen' set the stage (in the West, at least) for artist-as-creator and art-lover as passive learner. The artworld saw interactivity as, well, flakey. It was used by artists who didn't have a strong vision or couldn't decide how to finish.

We've now had a good fifteen years of artists exploring interactivity, and as we've seen in the Ars Electronica jury, there's some poetic and provocative work emerging. But we must learn to be both critical and enthusiastic, if we expect interactive art to stop being an oxymoron.

PRIX ARS ELECTRONICA

CHARLES AMIRKHANIAN
EINE ART MENSCHLICHKEIT
SOME KIND OF HUMANITY

Frage: Zwei Fakten waren bei den Musikeinreichungen in diesem Jahr auffallend: viele neue Namen junger Komponisten und die starke Beteiligung von Frauen. Welche Gründe sehen Sie dafür?
C. Amirkhanian: Es ist offensichtlich, daß es innerhalb der elektronischen Musik eine starke Demokratisierung gibt, das heißt, es gibt jetzt eine Art Basisbewegung, weil die Leute die technologische Ausrüstung recht billig kaufen und sie zu Hause einsetzen können – ohne formelles Studium. Aber die allerneueste Tendenz ist, daß nun auch immer mehr Frauen elektronische Musik machen, während es früher fast ausschließlich Männer waren. Wir sehen auch, daß sehr viele davon auf recht fortgeschrittene Weise mit den Computerprogrammen umgehen, daß sie auf eine neue Weise an Klang interessiert sind, etwa durch die Manipulation von Samples. Ich glaube, die Idee und die Möglichkeit, mit akustischen Klängen oder Samples zu arbeiten, haben die elektronische Musik viel zugänglicher gemacht, romantischer – sie klingt menschlicher, nicht mehr so kalt wie in früheren Jahren. Sehen Sie, wenn man elektronische Klänge synthetisch erzeugt, so erhält man irgendwie „eisige", gläserne Klänge, wenn man aber mit realem Klangmaterial arbeitet, dann entsteht eine freundlichere Art von Klang, die meiner Ansicht nach auch „wirklicher" klingt.

Frage: Sie erwähnten vor allem im Zusammenhang mit dem diesjährigen Gewinner der Goldenen Nica, Ludger Brümmer, eine neue Romantik in der Computermusik. Was konkret meinen Sie damit?
C. Amirkhanian: Ludger Brümmer hat sich schon in der Vergangenheit beispielsweise für Ravel interessiert. In vielen seiner Arbeiten hat er Klaviermusik von Ravel verwendet und transformiert. In seinem prämierten Stück benützt er eine Aufnahme eines bulgarischen Frauenchors, und bis zum Ende des Werks merkt man nicht, daß er Chormusik verarbeitet, erst ganz zum Schluß enthüllt er seine Quelle. So ergibt sich eine Verwandlung von Frauenstimmen durch das ganze Stück hin-

Question: When looking at this year's Prix Ars Electronica Music entries one immediately notices two things: many new names of young composers and a strong female participation. Which do you think are the reasons for this development?
C. Amirkhanian: It is apparent that there is a great deal of democracy going on in the electronic music movement. That is to say, there's a kind of grass-roots approach now, because people can buy the technology very cheaply and can use it in their own homes without studying formally. But the newer trend is that a lot of women are now making electronic music where formerly it was only men who were making it. This shows that there are a lot of women who are now working in a very advanced way with computer programs and have become interested in sound in a new way, working with manipulated samples, for example. I think the idea of working with acoustic sounds or samples has made electronic music almost more accessible, more romantic, more ... it sounds more human, it doesn't sound as cold as it did in former days. That is, when you synthesize electronic sounds, you get a kind of very icy, glassy sound, and when you make them from real sounds, the way you can now with samples, you get a more friendly kind of sound, which sounds more real, I think.

Question: You used the term "New Romanticism" in connection with this year's Golden Nica winner Ludger Brümmer. What exactly do you mean by that?
C. Amirkhanian: Ludger Brümmer has, in the past, been interested in the music of Ravel, for example. And in many of his pieces he took the piano music of Ravel and transformed it. In this piece he uses a recording of a Bulgarian women's choir, and you never know till the end of the piece that he is using the choir sound – not until at the very end, when he reveals the source. So you have the transformation of female voices through the whole piece in a way which only slightly refers to the original, but in the end it gives you a feeling for the real, beautiful choral

CHARLES AMIRKHANIAN
EINE ART MENSCHLICHKEIT
SOME KIND OF HUMANITY

durch, und zwar auf eine Weise, die nur entfernt an das Original erinnert. Am Schluß aber läßt er den wirklich wunderschönen Chorgesang durchklingen, aus dem er die Musik zusammengesetzt hat, und in diesem Sinn vermittelt er das Gegenteil eines „kalten" Gefühls, eben ein recht romantisches.

Frage: Und würden Sie das als einen neuen Trend bezeichnen?
C. Amirkhanian: Ich glaube, daß es besonders in Deutschland und Mitteleuropa schon in den frühen achtziger Jahren eine Suche nach dem Romantizismus gegeben hat, und jetzt entwickelt sich – durch die Verwendung von gesampelten Klängen – vielleicht nicht gerade eine „romantische" Bewegung, aber doch eine Art von Musik, die nicht mehr einfach aus der Manipulation von Sinusschwingungen und einfachen Wellenformen entsteht, sondern aus der Manipulation realer Klänge. Ich würde sagen, die alles überrollende Tendenz in der Computermusik scheint die Vermeidung einer Nüchternheit zu sein, die Akzeptanz einer Art Menschlichkeit in der Musik, und dies entsteht eben aus der Verwendung von akustischem Klangmaterial.

singing from which he composed the music. So it has the opposite of a cold feeling, a very romantic feeling.

Question: And you would say this is a new tendency?
C. Amirkhanian: I think there was a search for romanticism in the early eighties, especially in Germany and central Europe, and now again, maybe because of the use of samples, you have not so much a romanticism, but a kind of music that is no longer just a manipulation of sine waves and pure wave forms, but a manipulation of real, acoustic sounds. So I would say that the overriding force now in computer music seems to be the avoidance of austerity and the acceptance of a kind of humanity in the music which derives from the acoustic sounds.

Das Interview wurde von Regina Patsch geführt.
This interview was conducted by Regina Patsch.

PRIX ARS ELECTRONICA

BEGRÜNDUNG DER JURY FÜR COMPUTERGRAPHIK
STATEMENT OF THE COMPUTER GRAPHICS JURY

Goldene Nica:
- Michael Joaquin Grey, USA, für „Jellylife"

Auszeichnungen:
- Keith Cottingham, USA, für „Fictitious Portraits" und
- John Kahrs, USA, für „Supercluster"

Diese drei Arbeiten sind Beispiele für drei Zugänge zur Computergraphik, drei Möglichkeiten, unbewegte computergenerierte Bilder herzustellen, die einen guten Querschnitt darstellen. Die Jury ist der Meinung, daß diese drei unterschiedlichen Ansätze mit Preisen ausgezeichnet und in diesem Zusammenhang erläutert werden sollten.

„Jellylife" von Michael Joaquin Grey ist eine sehr gute Arbeit. Sie ist sowohl graphisch sehr kraftvoll als auch im technologischen Sinn sehr tiefgründig. Künstlerische und technologische Aussage halten sich in „Jellylife" die Waage und ergänzen einander. Hier liegt tatsächlich eine Verquickung von 3D-Zugang einerseits und wissenschaftlichen Konzepten andererseits vor, die in diesem Fall zur Herstellung von Computerbildern eingesetzt werden.

Außerdem wird in „Jellylife" auch ein Prozeß untersucht, d. h. eine Evolution innerhalb des digitalen Materials, die Grundzüge des Artificial Life in die Algorithmen einbezieht, also in jenen Prozeß, der das Werk beherrscht. Das Ergebnis ist eine zeitliche Lösung, die von einem hybriden Ansatz ausgeht.

Das Bild – speziell das Gesicht – in Keith Cottinghams „Fictitious Portraits" wirkt äußerst beunruhigend und deshalb sehr aussagekräftig. Kunst sollte diese Fähigkeit, den Betrachter zu beunruhigen, besitzen. Die Details, wie das Bild zustandegekommen ist, sind in diesem Zusammenhang eher zweitrangig, wichtiger ist seine Fähigkeit, Menschen zu bewegen. Darin liegt das eigentlich Interessante.

Anders als die meisten Photographien, wirkt das Portrait auf eigenartige Weise eher wie ein Gemälde und besteht in Wirklichkeit doch aus manipulierten Pixeldaten und wurde mittels eines zweidimensionalen Prozesses zusam-

Golden Nica:
- Michael Joaquin Grey, USA, for "Jellylife"

Distinctions:
- Keith Cottingham, USA, for "Fictitious Portraits" and
- John Kahrs, USA, for "Supercluster"

These three pieces are examples of three approaches to computer graphics, three ways of producing computer-generated still images which represent a good range. It is the opinion of the jury that all these approaches should be rewarded or mentioned in connection with the prizes awarded.

Michael Joaquin Grey's "Jellylife" is a very good piece. It is graphically very powerful, but also very deep in a technological sense. It demonstrates a balance between the artistic statement and the technological statement, the two complementing each other. It is really a mixture of the 3-D approach and of deep concepts coming from the world of science and being used – in this case – for the generation of computer images.

It is also an investigation of a process, an evolution within the digital material, using the terms of artifical life in the algorithm, the process that governs this work. The result is a temporal solution using a hybrid approach.

The image from Keith Cottingham's "Fictitious Portraits" – the face – is a very disturbing one, and therefore very powerful. Art should have the capacity to disturb. The details of how it was produced are less important for these purposes than its capacity to move people, which is what makes it so very interesting.

Although in a very bizarre way it looks more like a painting than most other photographic images, the portrait is in fact a manipulation of pixel data and was composed using a two-dimensional process.

As a still image, this portrait really addresses a classical tradition of portraiture which goes back a long way. The way it is integrated into this classic form is, of course, an element within this context, as is the way in which the computer is

PRIX ARS ELECTRONICA

BEGRÜNDUNG DER JURY FÜR COMPUTERGRAPHIK
STATEMENT OF THE COMPUTER GRAPHICS JURY

mengestellt. Als unbewegtes Bild bezieht sich dieses Portrait auf eine klassische Tradition der Portraitmalerei, die sich weit zurückverfolgen läßt. Die Art und Weise, wie es in diese klassische Form eingebettet ist, ist natürlich ein Element in diesem Zusammenhang, genauso wie die Art, in der der Computer einbezogen wird, und damit werden einige Fragen offenkundig, z. B. die Frage, woher das Bild kommt und auf welcher Ebene es existent ist, als digitalisiertes Bild oder als photographisches Bild.

„Supercluster" von John Kahrs steht für eine ganze Gattung computergenerierter Bilder aus 3D-Daten. Das Bild hat zu tun mit 3D-Modelling, es hat zu tun mit dem Material, es verwendet künstliches Material für ein Bild und verwendet das Bildmaterial weniger prozeßorientiert, sondern eher als Momentaufnahme. Bei diesem Werk existiert weder ein offensichtliches Konzept noch eine formale Komposition, aber es stellt eine Aussage zur Computergraphik dar und dazu, wie sie aussehen sollte, nämlich weniger wie eine Computergraphik. In diesem Fall ist es ausschließlich die Qualität des Rendering und der Lichtführung, die den Unterschied ausmacht.

involved, and it poses some questions as to where the image comes from and on which level the image exists: as a digitised image or as a photographic image.

"Supercluster" by John Kahrs represents a whole class of computer-generated images derived from 3-D data. It has something to do with 3-D modelling, it has to do with the material; it uses artificial material for a picture, applying picture material in a still rather than in a procedural manner.

There is no obvious concept or formal composition, but it makes a statement about computer graphics and how it needs to look less like computer graphics. Thus it is strictly the quality of the rendering and the lighting that makes the difference here.

PRIX ARS ELECTRONICA

BEGRÜNDUNG DER JURY FÜR COMPUTERANIMATION
STATEMENT OF THE COMPUTER ANIMATION JURY

Während der ersten Durchgänge war es leicht, nur in den Schlußrunden fiel die Entscheidung der Jury äußerst schwer. Die Jury mußte sehr intensiv beraten, um einen Gewinner der Goldenen Nica zu ermitteln. Die Entscheidung, den Preis zu teilen und ihn zwei unterschiedlichen Einreichungen zuzuerkennnen, resultierte aus der grundlegenden Spannung zwischen den möglichen Wegen, hochqualitative Computeranimationen zu erreichen. Einerseits hatte die Jury „Jurassic Park" mit seinem gewaltigen Budget (und ILM als international anerkanntem Spitzenbetrieb der Filmtechnologie) ausgewählt, andererseits ein von der Jury als sehr kraftvoll eingeschätztes, von einem kleinen Team mit geringen Mitteln hergestelltes Stück, „K.O. KID".

Die Jury hat sich letzten Endes dazu entschieden, den Preis zu teilen und an zwei Firmen zu vergeben, die beide Arbeiten schaffen, die technisch sehr gut sind. Einmal ILM für „Jurassic Park", weil es ein technisch bahnbrechend komplexes Werk der Special-Effects-Anwendung des Computers im Film und auch kommerziell sehr erfolgreich ist, wobei dieser große Erfolg droht, die Bemühungen kleinerer Filmfirmen und Einzelpersonen völlig in den Schatten zu stellen. Es ist allerdings keineswegs Auffassung der Jury, daß die Arbeiten dieser Leute nicht vergleichbar gut sind. Es ist aber kaum möglich, „Jurassic Park" zu ignorieren, weil dieser Film ein wichtiger Schritt in der Geschichte der Computergraphik ist. Allerdings ist es auch wichtig, jene zu ermutigen, die keine solch gewaltigen Budgets für die Herstellung neuer Arbeiten zur Verfügung haben. Daher hat die Jury die zweite Goldene Nica an die Urheber von „K.O. KID" vergeben, die eine einzigartig dichte, beeindruckende und komplexe Arbeit geschaffen haben. In jeder Hinsicht, sowohl in technischer als auch in filmischer und inhaltlicher Hinsicht, ist dieser computergenerierte Film ein Kunstwerk, und deshalb hat die Jury damit ein Gegengewicht zur Special-Effects-Industrie und damit zu ILM geschaffen.

Die Anerkennungen gehen an die Filme „No

It was an easy choice all the way up to the final few rounds, when it became extremely difficult. The jury worked very hard together to pick a winner for the Golden Nica. The eventual decision to split the prize and award it to two different entries was a result of the fundamental tension between the different avenues available for creating high quality computer animation. On the one hand the jury was presented with "Jurassic Park", which had an enormous budget (and ILM is an acknowledged world leader in film-making technology), and on the other hand there was what the jury considered to be a powerful piece by a small team working with a small budget: "K.O. KID".

In the end it was decided to split the award in order to give it to two companies who are both creating work that is technically very well done. ILM wins one for "Jurassic Park" for the simple reason that it is a technically pioneering and complex example of special effects applications in films. As everybody knows, it is also very successful in the commercial sense, and this very success threatens to completely overshadow the efforts of many smaller film companies and individuals active in computer graphics - and the jury certainly does not believe that these people's work is not comparably good. It is hardly possible to ignore "Jurassic Park", because it represents an important step in the history of computer graphics, but it is very important that people who do not have tremendous resources to try to create new work should be encouraged.

That is why the other Golden Nica is awarded to the authors of "K.O. KID", who have created a singularly tight, impressive and complex work. In every technical, film-making respect as well as in terms of content, this computer-generated film is a work of art, and that is the reason the jury has honoured it as a contrast to the special effects industry represented here by ILM.

The Distinctions go to the films "No Sex" and "QUARXS", two very different works that illustrate two very important directions in computer graphics. Each was chosen for its

PRIX ARS ELECTRONICA

BEGRÜNDUNG DER JURY FÜR COMPUTERANIMATION
STATEMENT OF THE COMPUTER ANIMATION JURY

Sex" und „QUARXS", zwei sehr verschiedene Arbeiten, die zwei sehr wichtige Richtungen in der Computergraphik veranschaulichen. Beide wurden von der Jury ausgewählt, weil sie Inhalte transportieren. Obwohl „No Sex" in technischer Hinsicht nicht den letzten Stand der Technik repräsentiert und keine 3D-Arbeit im eigentlichen Sinn ist, meint die Jury, daß sowohl die technische Brillianz als auch die starke künstlerische Aussage eine Honorierung verdienen. Es ist zwar unüblich, daß das Werk nicht auf einem High-End-System erstellt wurde, diese Tatsache aber zeigt, daß es eben verschiedene Mittel und Wege gibt, Computeranimationen zu erstellen, und das Konzept dahinter ausschlaggebend ist. Die Arbeit besticht durch ihren Schnitt, durch die Choreographie und speziell durch das sehr gut konzipierte Zusammenspiel zwischen Bild, Ton und Inhalt. Jedes Bild, jeder Frame, kann als Graphik für sich alleine stehen. Das Werk durchbricht nicht nur übliche Stilkriterien und die zeitgenössische Clipkultur, sondern hat eine klare und starke Aussage.

„QUARXS" ist wahrscheinlich das schönste ausgewählte Werk. Die Arbeit ist eine gewaltige Leistung, was Modellierung und Rendering betrifft, und eine sehr realistische Darstellung nicht existenter Dinge – surrealer Lebensformen – unter Verwendung einer Technologie, die Wirkungen erlaubt, die in dieser Weise nicht durch andere Mittel erzielt werden können. So ist „QUARXS" ein sehr interessantes Beispiel, weil durch die perfekte Anwendung der Computergraphik hier eine Pseudo-Realität, eine pseudo-wissenschaftliche Untersuchung mit unzweifelhaftem Unterhaltungswert vorgegeben wird. Durch künstlerisch hochstehendes Design, exzellente Lichtführung und sein interessantes Konzept zeigt sich die technische Brillianz von „QUARXS" in der Art, daß sie gar nicht bemerkt wird. So wie auch bei „Jurassic Park", „K.O. KID" und „No Sex" ist die Verwendung des Computers als solchem in keiner Weise mehr vorrangig. Bei der Bewertung der Werke hat sich die Jury ausschließlich auf inhaltliche und formale Aspekte gestützt.

creative ability to express an idea.

Although "No Sex" does not represent state of the art technology or 3-D and cannot be considered 3-D graphics in the technical sense, the jury feels it is both a technically brilliant piece and a strong artistic statement and deserves to be honoured. It is unusual in that it was not done on a high end system, but it demonstrates that although there are different ways and means to create computer animation, it is the concept behind the work that makes all the difference. "No Sex" is distinguished by its editing, choreography, and in particular the very well-conceived interplay between picture, sound and content. Every image, every frame, stands as a graphic work in its own right. The work not only transcends traditional style and contemporary clip culture, but it also has a clear and strong message.

"QUARXS" is probably the most beautiful piece the jury selected. It is a powerful achievement in view of its modelling, rendering, and very realistic representation of non-existent things – surreal life-forms, to be exact – using the technology to create images that could not be achieved by any other means. In fact, what makes "QUARXS" such an interesting example is its perfect application of computer graphics to the representation of pseudo-reality – by portraying a pseudo-scientific investigation with undeniable entertainment value.

With its very artistic design, excellent lighting and interesting concept, the technical brilliance of "QUARXS" is such that it is not even noticeable. As with "Jurassic Park", "K.O. KID" and "No Sex", the actual use of the computer itself is no longer the main issue. These works were judged solely on the basis of form and content.

PRIX ARS ELECTRONICA

BEGRÜNDUNG DER JURY FÜR INTERAKTIVE KUNST
STATEMENT OF THE INTERACTIVE ART JURY

Die Jury für Interaktive Kunst hat entschieden, die Goldene Nica Christa Sommerer und Laurent Mignonneau für ihre interaktive Artificial-Life-Installation „A-Volve" zuzuerkennen. Die Jury faßte einstimmig den Beschluß, dieses Werk anzuerkennen, das dem neuesten Stand künstlerischer Möglichkeiten gerecht wird und sich mit dem neuen Gebiet des künstlichen Lebens befaßt, einer Richtung, die viele künstlerische Möglichkeiten bietet. Die Auszeichnungen gingen an Loren Carpenter für seine Arbeit „Kinoetic Evolution", die das Publikum in die Arbeit miteinbezieht, sowie an den Kunstverein TRANSIT für seine interaktive, an drei Orten gleichzeitig stattfindende musikalische Performance „Realtime". Beide Auszeichnungen gingen an Arbeiten, die viele Menschen in die Interaktion miteinbeziehen. Der Großteil interaktiver Arbeiten hingegen ist für einzelne Benutzer konzipiert; die Jury war daher besonders daran interessiert, jene Arbeiten auszuzeichnen, die neue Möglichkeiten einer computervermittelten Interaktion zwischen einer größeren Anzahl von Menschen eröffnen.

Die Kategorie Interaktive Kunst verzeichnet heuer eine große Anzahl von Einreichungen (mehr als 200), so daß der Wettbewerb um die Anerkennungen sehr hart war. Mehrere Werke, die Virtual-Reality-Technologie verwendeten, wurden in Betracht gezogen. Arbeiten dieser Art, die eine Anerkennung erhielten, waren die Installation für zwei Teilnehmer „PlaceHolder" von Brenda Laurel und Rachel Strickland sowie „Menagerie", die verspielte virtuelle Welt von Susan Amkraut und Michael Girard.

Heuer entschied sich die Jury, Anerkennungen für eine Reihe von Arbeiten zu vergeben, die Entwicklungen neuer Softwarewerkzeuge darstellen und dadurch eine hochwertige künstlerische Entwicklung ermöglichen. Solche Neuentwicklungen sind sehr wichtig, da die meisten Softwaresysteme entweder für kommerzielle, wissenschaftliche oder Zwecke der Massenunterhaltung erstellt werden und sich daher oft nicht besonders für künstlerische Arbeit eignen. Beispiele für solche Arbeiten,

The Interactive Art Jury awarded the Golden Nica award to Christa Sommerer and Laurent Mignonneau for their interactive artificial life installation "A-Volve". The Jury was unanimous in recognising this state-of-the-art work in the new field of artificial life, a direction which offers many artistic possibilities. The distinctions were awarded to Loren Carpenter for his audience participation work "Kinoetic Evolution" and to the group TRANSIT for their three site interactive musical performance "Realtime". Both of the distinctions were awarded to work which involves interactions with many people. Most interactive work is designed for single viewers; the jury was particularly interested in acknowledging work which exploited new possibilities from computer mediated interactions involving a number of participants.

This year the Interactive Art category received a large number of submissions – over 200 – so that the competition was very tough. Several works that involved virtual reality technologies were reviewed. Two works of this type received mention: the virtual reality installation for two participants called "PlaceHolder" by Brenda Laurel and Rachel Strickland, and the playful virtual world "Menagerie" by Susan Amkraut and Michael Girard.

This year the Jury chose to recognise with Honourable Mentions a number of works which represent the development of new software tools with potential for rich artistic development. These new developments are very important, since most software systems have been created for commercial, scientific or mass entertainment purposes and are often not well suited for artistic work. Examples of work recognised with Merits this year are "Video Streamer" by Edward Elliott, which provides a very effective way of displaying time sequences of video images in manipulable format; also the work "ALIVE" by Patti Maes – a virtual environment where a viewer can interact with artifical creatures; the computer visualisation system "Responsive Workbench" by Wolfgang Krüger. The Jury debated at some length about

PRIX ARS ELECTRONICA

BEGRÜNDUNG DER JURY FÜR INTERAKTIVE KUNST
STATEMENT OF THE INTERACTIVE ART JURY

die heuer mit Anerkennungen bedacht wurden, sind z.B. „Video Streamer" von Edward Elliott, die eine sehr wirkungsvolle Möglichkeit, Zeitsequenzen von Videomaterial in manipulierbare Formate umzuwandeln, darstellt. Auch die Arbeit „ALIVE" von Pattie Maes – eine virtuelle Umwelt, in der ein Zuschauer mit künstlichen Lebewesen interagieren kann –, sowie Wolfgang Krügers „Responsive Workbench", ein computergestütztes Visualisierungssystem, zählen dazu. Die Jury setzte sich lange damit auseinander, wo denn die Grenzen zwischen innovativen Softwarewerkzeugen und künstlerischer Arbeit anzusiedeln seien, entschied aber dann, daß Arbeiten dieser Art von solchem künstlerischen Interesse sind, daß ihre Einteilung in Kategorien zweitrangig ist.

Die Jury möchte bemerken, daß eine bedeutende Anzahl von Künstlern, denen Preise zuerkannt wurden, österreichischer Herkunft sind oder in Österreich arbeiten. Dies spricht für den Erfolg des Prix Ars Electronica und des Festivals Ars Electronica als Anregung an österreichische Künstler, sich mit diesem Bereich zu beschäftigen. (Roger F. Malina)

where the boundary between innovative software tools and artistic work might be, but finally decided that these kinds of works were of such artistic interest that their categorisation was secondary.

The jury notes this year the significant number of Prize and Merit winners who are from Austrian backgrounds or work in Austria. This can only be a tribute to the success of the Prix Ars Electronica and the Festival in inspiring Austrian artists to work in this area. (Roger F. Malina)

PRIX ARS ELECTRONICA

BEGRÜNDUNG DER JURY FÜR COMPUTERMUSIK
STATEMENT OF THE COMPUTER MUSIC JURY

Der diesjährige Wettbewerb verzeichnete mit 45 Prozent mehr an eingereichten Kompositionen einen Zuwachs, der aufhorchen ließ. Die Jury hörte 341 Stücke von 231 Komponisten aus 26 Ländern.

Ein Teil der Zunahme ist auf die stärkere Beteiligung von Frauen und ein verstärktes lokales Interesse zurückzuführen. Dies läßt sich an der großen Anzahl von Einreichungen österreichischer Künstler ablesen und ist unzweifelhaft auf das besondere Engagement der Organisatoren zurückzuführen, die sich bemüht haben, Informationen über den Prix Ars Electronica so weit wie möglich und so früh wie möglich zu verbreiten.

Ein Jahr nach dem Tod des Komponisten John Cage scheint die Verwendung aufgezeichneter Naturklänge in allen Arten von Arbeiten akzeptiert und abgesichert zu sein. Besonders gerne wird auch eine raffinierte Manipulation klanglichen Materials eingesetzt, zumal die dafür notwendige leistungsfähige Signal-Processing-Software allgemein zugänglich geworden ist.

Algorithmische Kompositionen waren in geringerem Maß vertreten, feinsinnige Interaktion zwischen Live-Interpreten und Computersystemen dagegen stärker. Hier sind zwei französische Systeme hervorzuheben, nämlich das IRCAM Signal Processing und GRM Syter. Der erste Preis in der Höhe von öS 150.000 ($ 12.500) wurde dem jungen deutschen Komponisten Ludger Brümmer für seine Arbeit „The Gates of H." zuerkannt, in der er als Quelle Klänge eines bulgarischen Frauenchors, weitgehend verändert und jenseits ihrer Wiedererkennbarkeit, verwendet. Das Stück zeigt eine Führung formalen Aufbaus über einen langen Zeitraum, eine klare technische Logik, die auf binärer Gatterlogik beruht, und hat trotzdem einen starken emotionalen Eindruck hinterlassen. Brümmer, der in Essen und Stanford studiert hat, hat außerdem sehr effektvolle Bandkompositionen auf der Grundlage von Zitaten aus Ravels Klavierzyklus „Miroirs" produziert.

Eine Auszeichnung erhielt der schwedische

This year's competition saw a startling 45% increase in the number of music compositions entered. The jury heard 341 pieces entered by 231 composers from 26 contries. Part of the increase was due to the greater participation of women composers, and also to increased local interest, with many Austrian works being submitted, undoubtedly due to the staff's special effort to disseminate advance information about the Prix competition.

One year following the death of composer John Cage, the use of recorded natural sounds in all types of work seems now to be accepted and assured. There is also an emphasis on the sophisticated manipulation of sound materials, as powerful signal processing software has become widely available.

Algorithmic composition is much less in evidence. Sophisticated interaction between live performers and computer systems, dominated by two French systems, the IRCAM signal processing workstation and the GRM Syter, was also much in evidence.

The first prize of öS 150,000 ($ 12,500) was awarded to the young German composer Ludger Brümmer for the work "The Gates of H." which used as a source the sounds of a Bulgarian women's choir, but largely transformed beyond recognition. The piece exhibited a command of formal construction over a long time scale and a lucid technical logic, based on gating procedures, yet had a powerful emotional impact. Brümmer, who has studied at Essen and Stanford, also has produced very effective tape compositions based on quotations from Ravel's piano cycle "Miroirs".

The second prize was awarded to the Swedish composer, Åke Parmerud, for his work "Strings & Shadows" for harp and tape. This delicate, meditative essay employs the computer to expand the sound world of the instrument in subtle and surprising ways, yet succeeds in allowing the natural lyricism of the instrument to speak. Born in 1953, he now teaches at the Music Conservatory of Gothenburg and is internationally established as one of his country's leading electroacoustic composers.

PRIX ARS ELECTRONICA

BEGRÜNDUNG DER JURY FÜR COMPUTERMUSIK
STATEMENT OF THE COMPUTER MUSIC JURY

Komponist Åke Parmerud für sein Werk „Strings & Shadows" für Harfe und Tonband. Dieser feinfühlige, meditative Essay verwendet den Computer in subtiler, überraschender Weise, um die instrumentale Klangwelt zu erweitern, und verhilft damit der natürlichen Lyrik des Instruments zu einem besonderen Ausdruck. 1953 geboren, unterrichtet Parmerud am Musikkonservatorium von Göteborg und ist, auf internationaler Ebene anerkannt, einer der führenden Komponisten seines Landes auf dem Gebiet der Elektroakustik.

Die zweite Auszeichnung erhielt der in London lebende Komponist und Trompetenvirtuose Jonathan Impett für sein Werk „Mirror-Rite". Das Werk ist für „Meta-Trompete", Computer und Elektronik instrumentiert und manipuliert die Verarbeitungsprozesse von Instrumentenklängen oder voraufgezeichnetem Material mit den unterschiedlichsten Mitteln. Unter anderem werden Instrumentenhaltung, der Hand- und Atemdruck und unterschiedliche Ventilpositionen herangezogen, um im Zuge der Life-Aufführung eine multidimensionale Interaktion herbeizuführen. Impett hat eine Reihe zeitgenössischer Trompetenwerke uraufgeführt (BBC Proms, IRCAM...), ist aber ebenso als Interpret von Barock-Trompete und Kornett sowie als Mitglied des Orchestra of the Eighteenth Century und des Amsterdam Baroque Orchestra bekannt. Die Trompeten-Schnittstelle baute der in Den Haag lebende Bert Bongers. (Charles Amirkhanian)

The other second prize was awarded to the London-based composer and virtuoso trumpet player, Jonathan Impett, for his work "Mirror-Rite". The work is scored for "meta-trumpet", computer and electronics, and manipulates processing of the instrumental sounds and pre-recorded material by various means. The tilt of the instrument, hand and breath pressure, and various valve positions, among other things, are used to create a multi-dimensional interaction in the course of live performance. Impett has premiered many contemporary trumpet works (BBC Proms, IRCAM...) and is also well-known for his work as a Baroque trumpeter and cornetto player, a member of the Orchestra of the Eighteenth Century and the Amsterdam Baroque Orchestra. The trumpet interface was built by Bert Bongers who resides in Den Haag. (Charles Amirkhanian)

C O M P U T E R G R A P H I K

COMPUTERGRAPHIK

MICHAEL JOAQUIN GREY

Michael Joaquin Grey (USA), geb. 1961, lebt und arbeitet als Künstler und Wissenschafter in New York. Bachelor of Science in Genetik und Bachelor of Arts an der University of California/Berkeley, Graduate der University of California/Davis und Master of Fine Arts an der Yale University, New Haven, Connecticut. Zahlreiche Einzel- und Gruppenausstellungen in den USA, Japan und Europa.

■ «Ich habe drei eng verwandte Arbeiten eingereicht: ‚Jellylife', ‚Jellycycle' und ‚Jelly Locomotion'. Das sind 3D-Animationen von der Entwicklung neuraler Netzwerke und genetischer Algorithmen. Gerechnet wurden sie auf einem Stardent Supercomputer. Design wurden sowohl die genetischen Algorithmen als auch die neuralen Netze von uns selber; die Visualisierung beruhte auf einer wissenschaftlichen Visualisierungssoftware, die von Stardent entworfen worden war. Die Standbilder wurden auf einem Tectronic-Drucker ausgedruckt. Das Verhalten der Information wird hier als Animationsstandbilder, Kohlenstoff-Täfelchen und lithographische Modelle in 3D dargestellt. Die 3D-Modelle haben durch ein von Quadrax entwickeltes Verfahren Gestalt angenommen, bei dem man Dateien mittels eines UV-Lasers in flüssiges, lichtempfindliches Harz druckt. ‚Jellycycle' z.B. hat mehr als eine Viertelmillion Entwicklungsstufen hinter sich, genug, um ‚à la cinéma verité' in voller Länge gezeigt zu werden. Wir aber haben uns dazu entschlossen, 56 Standbilder von Entwicklungsstadien zu zeigen (so daß man mit einem Blick die Gesamtentwicklung des Zyklus überschauen kann). Diese Stücke sind also sowohl Computergraphik als auch Computeranimation. Die Bilder zeigen 3D-Formen, selbstorganisierende Systeme, die entscheidende morphologische Veränderungen im Wachstum der Netzwerke repräsentieren. Das Netzwerk wird als einfache Ausgangsform aufgezeichnet, und sein Wachstum hängt ab von der Veränderung seiner Umgebung (Zufallszahlengenerator). Der

Michael Joaquin Grey (USA), born 1961, lives and works in New York as an artist and scientist. B.S. (Genetics) and B.A., University of California, Berkeley; Graduate Program, 1988 University of California, Davis; M.F.A., 1990 Yale University, New Haven, Connecticut. Numerous solo and group exhibitions in USA, Japan and Europe.

■ «I have included three highly related works, 'Jellylife', 'Jellycycle' and 'Jelly Locomotion'. They are 3-D animations of the development of neural networks and genetic algorithms. They were processed by a Stardent supercomputer. We designed the neural nets and genetic algorithms ourselves, the visualization was on scientific visualization software designed by Stardent. The cels were printed on a Tectronics printer. The behavior of the information is visualized here as animation cels, graphite tablets, and 3-D stereo lithographic models. The models are solidified by drawing the 3-D files with a UV laser in a liquid UV sensitive resin, a process developed by Quadrax Corp.
As an example, 'Jellycycle' has over a quarter million stages in its developmental cycle, enough to present it as a full length film, 'à la cinéma verité', however we choose to present it as 56 stages, each a still image (so as to be able to see the complete development of the cycle all at once). All these pieces are both computer images and computer animations.
The images represent 3-D forms, self-organizing systems, representing crucial morphological changes in the growth of the networks. The network is mapped onto a platonic form to begin with, and its growth is dependent on the variation in the environment (random number generator). The supercomputer supports our random number generator which feeds the neural networks (the number generator is partly based on the computer clock, it could, however, be any data generator; it is random only because it attempts to create a control model for observing variation in form and behavior). The

C O M P U T E R G R A P H I K

MICHAEL JOAQUIN GREY

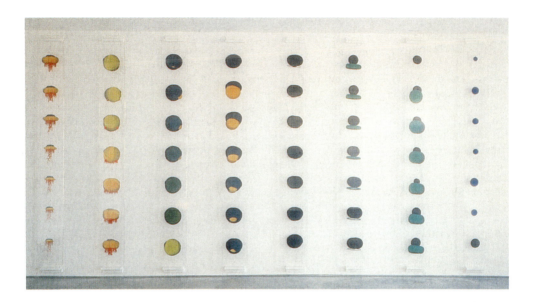

Goldene Nica
Jellylife, 1991/92
HW: Stardent Supercomputer
SW: Artist's Proprietary (Genetic Algorithms)

COMPUTERGRAPHIK

MICHAEL JOAQUIN GREY

Supercomputer unterstützt unseren Zufallszahlengenerator, der das neurale Netzwerk speist (unser Zahlengenerator stützt sich zum Teil auf die Computeruhr, könnte jedoch genausogut irgendein Datengenerator sein. Die Zufälligkeit ist nur deswegen nötig, weil versucht wird, ein Kontrollmodell zur Beobachtung von Veränderungen in Form und Verhalten herzustellen). Die jeweils unverwechselbare Entwicklung der Netzwerke wird durch Veränderungen im Zufallszahlengenerator, im Design des Netzwerks und der Algorithmen erreicht. Die neuralen Netzwerke und genetischen Algorithmen sind einzigartigerweise fähig ‚etwas zu bewältigen', ‚zu lernen' und in dieser kernigen Umgebung ‚zu leben'.

Wir haben bestenfalls versucht, frühe Beobachter und Beschreiber des Verhaltens von Information in einer Größenordnung zu sein, die erst beginnt, erforscht zu werden. Als frühe Beschreiber und Beobachter neuen Verhaltens und neuer Formen haben wir (im Gegensatz zu den unvermeidlichen Interpreten und Ausbeutern) die historischen Modelle eines Leeuwenhoek, eines Audubon oder Kepler herangezogen und, in unserer Befangenheit, auch unsere eigenen Neigungen und Geschichten bei der Entdeckung ‚künstlichen Lebens' berücksichtigt.

Die drei ausgewählten Stücke stellen drei spezifische Verhaltensweisen dar. ‚Jellycycle' ist ein dreidimensionales neurales Netzwerk, entstanden aus knapp 254.000 Iterationen. Es entwickelt sich aus einer einfachen Kugel zu einer hochdifferenzierten, selbstorganisierenden Form. Die Ontogenese der Information ahmt in vielerlei Beziehung frühe Entwicklungsstufen wirbelloser Meeresbewohner nach. Das vorliegende 3D-Modell ‚Jellylife' hat eine hochkomplexe innere Anatomie; es unterteilt sich in vier Entwicklungsstufen und benötigt mehr als ein Gigabit Speicher für ein einziges 3D-Bild oder plastisches Modell.

3 x 16 Syntax (als Palindrom angelegt) und Carbone Codex 16 x 16 sind jeweils genetische Algorithmen und neurale Netzwerke. 3 x 16 Syntax (Palindrom) ist ein Auszug aus Carbon

unique development of the networks is created by the variation in the random number generator and the design of the networks and algorithms. The neural networks and genetic algorithms are uniquely able to 'cope' and 'learn' and 'live' in this robust environment.

At best, we were attempting to be early observers and describers of the behavior of information on an order of magnitude only recently beginning to be explored. As early observers and describers of new behavior and form (in contrast to the inevitable explainers and exploiters), we took the historical models of Leeuwenhoek, Audubon or Kepler and considered self-consciously our own biases and narrative in discovering 'Artificial Life'.

The three pieces chosen exhibit three specific behaviors. 'Jellycycle' is a 3-D neural network which has a full cycle of close to 254,000 iterations. It develops from a single sphere to a highly differentiated self-organizing form. The ontogeny of information mimics many stages of early development of marine invertebrates. The actual 3-D model, 'Jellylife', has a highly complex internal anatomy; it is divided into 4 stages and holds over a gigabit of memory for the single 3-D image and sculpture.

3 x 16 Syntax (Palindrome) and Carbon Codex 16 x 16 are both a genetic algorithm and neural network. 3 x 16 Syntax (Palindrome) is an excerpt of the Carbon Codex, 3 of the 16 lines created in the time period (T: June 6, 1992, 12:06 to 12:32 PM). Each iteration represents one character, and there is a 16 character long syntax which is repeated 16 times. Every cycle, the character evolves and becomes more 'gothic' in its structure, with increased variegation and branching off of the main stalk of the character. The 16 characters seem to be consistently present as a palindrome 8, then 8 backwards, stereoscopic 'isomers' or 3-D 'mirror' images. A palindrome is a formal syntactical strategy employed by actual genetic material to preserve its tertiary structure when being decoded to reduce translation error.

'Jelly Locomotion' ('Cancerhead') is a fully developed neural network which wanders

C O M P U T E R G R A P H I K

MICHAEL JOAQUIN GREY

Goldene Nica
Jellylife, 1991/92
HW: Stardent Supercomputer
SW: Artist's Proprietary (Genetic Algorithms)

COMPUTERGRAPHIK

MICHAEL JOAQUIN GREY

Codex, nämlich drei der 16 Zeilen, die am 6. Juni 1992 (zwischen 12.06 und 12.32) erstellt wurden. Jede Iteration entspricht dabei einem Buchstaben einer 16 Zeichen langen Befehlszeile, die 16 Mal wiederholt wird. Mit jedem Durchlauf entwickelt sich das Zeichen und wird wesentlich ‚gotischer' in seiner Struktur, variiert immer mehr, und der Hauptstrang des Zeichens verzweigt sich zunehmend. Die 16 Zeichen scheinen ständig als das Palindrom gegenwärtig zu sein, mit acht Vorwärts- und acht Rückwärtsschritten, als dreidimensionale ‚Isomere' oder 3D-Spiegelbilder. Ein Palindrom stellt eine formale, syntaktische Strategie dar, die von tatsächlichem genetischem Material verwendet wird, um bei der Decodierung seine Tertiärstruktur zu erhalten und Übersetzungsfehler zu verringern.

‚Jelly Locomotion' (‚Cancerhead') ist ein vollständig entwickeltes neurales Netzwerk, das aufgrund einer leichten Neigung zur nicht ganz so starken Zufälligkeit im Zufallsgenerator herumwandert. Das selbstorganisierende dreidimensionale Modell, das einer Qualle sehr stark ähnelt, wird von drei vorteilhaften Standpunkten aus abgebildet: von oben, als Vorderansicht und von unten. Die Darstellung seiner Fortbewegung wurde visualisiert, um die klassische Muybridge'sche Verhaltens- und Bewegungsdarstellung nachzuahmen.» (Michael Joaquin Grey)

about because of slight biases with a particular not so random number generator. The 3-D self-organizing system, which seems to very much resemble a jellyfish or medusa, is visualized from three vantage ponts: above, straight portrait, and below; the presentation of its locomotion was visualized to mimic the classic Muybridge presentation of behavior and movement.» (Michael Joaquin Grey)

COMPUTERGRAPHIK

MICHAEL JOAQUIN GREY

Goldene Nica
Jellylife, 1991/92
HW: Stardent Supercomputer
SW: Artist's Proprietary (Genetic Algorithms)

COMPUTERGRAPHIK

KEITH COTTINGHAM

Keith Cottingham (USA), geb. 1965, lebt und arbeitet als Künstler in San Francisco. Ausbildung an der San Francisco State University, u. a. bei Lynn Hershman (Photographie und Video), an der Suite 3D des Center for Computer Arts, San Francisco, und am San Luis Obispo Polytechnic, San Luis Obispo, Kalifornien. Zahlreiche Einzel- und Gruppenausstellungen in den USA und in Europa.

■ «Keith Cottinghams Arbeit ‚Fictitious Portraits' nagt an zwei der grundsätzlichen Mythen des Modernismus: an der ‚wissenschaftlichen Objektivität der Photographie' und an der ‚kreativen Echtheit der Subjektivität'. Sein photographisches Triptychon führt vor Augen, daß beide Vorstellungen nur gesellschaftliche Konstrukte sind.

Erst die Computertechnik macht Cottinghams Forschungstätigkeit technisch möglich. Durch die Methoden elektronischer Bilderstellung hat er seine Photographien buchstäblich von jener Kette befreit, die sie an die ‚Wieder-Gabe' einer räumlich-zeitlichen Konstellation durch lichtempfindliches Material – kurz das, was die Modernität als ‚Wirklichkeit' bezeichnet – bindet. Cottingham hat die Nabelschnur zur Moderne durchtrennt und ist in den imaginären, virtuellen Raum jenseits des ‚Wirklichen' eingetreten.

Doch das Aufregendste an ‚Fictitious Portraits', das, was sie von der billigen Illusion der Massenware abhebt, in der der Effekt zum verführerischen Eskapismus wird, ist die Tatsache, daß sich diese Virtualität auf die ebenso schillernden wie erschreckenden Geheimnisse der ‚modernen' Gesellschaft bezieht.

Indem ‚Fictitious Portraits' geschickt die darstellende Photographie nachahmt, zeigt sich jedoch, daß der Begriff ‚Realismus' sich als erstaunlich dehnbar erweist und daß Photographen, genauso wie Maler, Regeln und Schemata entwickeln, um ihre visuellen Zeichen zu hinterlassen. Photographien garantieren genausowenig Realität, wie die Malerei es tut. Wie es

Keith Cottingham (USA), born 1965, lives and works as an artist in San Francisco. He studied at San Francisco State University, including special study with Lynn Hershman (Photography and Video), and at the Center for Computer Arts, San Francisco, and at the San Luis Obispo Polytechnic in San Luis Obispo, California. Numerous solo and group exhibitions in the U.S. and Europe.

■ *«Keith Cottingham's work 'Fictitious Portraits' gnaws away at two of the foundational myths of Modernism: the scientific objectivity of the photograph, and the creative authenticity of subjectivity. His photographic triptych demonstrates that both notions are merely social constructions.*

Computer technology makes Cottingham's exploration technically possible. Through the techniques of electronic imaging he has literally loosened his photographs from their tether to a light-sensitive material's re-production of a spatio-temporal constellation – to what Modernity has labeled 'reality'. Cottingham has cut the umbilical cord to the Modern and has entered into the imagined, virtual space which lies beyond the 'real'.

Yet, what is most exciting about 'Fictitious Portraits', what sets it apart from manufactured make-believe where effect serves as seductive escapism, is that this virtuality is folded back upon the mysteries – both glamorous and terrifying – of 'Modern' society.

Yet, by mimicking representational photography so craftly, 'Fictitious Portraits' demonstrates that as a label 'realism' is remarkably elastic, and that just like painters, photographers invent rules and schemata for laying down visual signs. Photographs no more guarantee reality than paintings do. In the words of E.H. Gombrich, photography as well as painting is 'something akin to visual hallucination'.

We find, then, that Cottingham's concern is not with 'realism', but with what he calls

COMPUTERGRAPHIK

KEITH COTTINGHAM

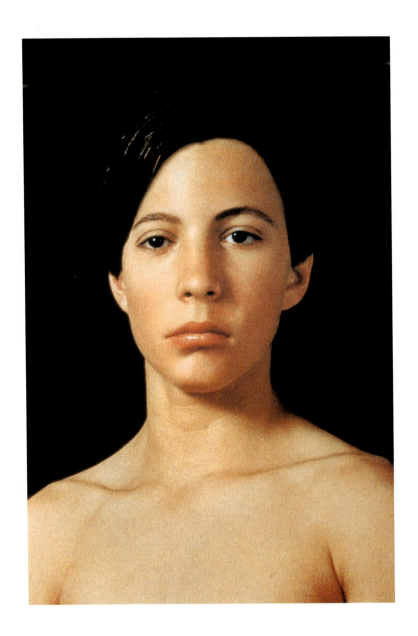

Auszeichnung
Fictitious Portraits, 1992
HW: Macintosh II
SW: Adobe Photoshop

C O M P U T E R G R A P H I K

KEITH COTTINGHAM

E. H. Gombrich sagte: Photographie, ebenso wie die Malerei, sei ‚etwas, das einer visuellen Halluzination verwandt' sei.

Wir sehen also, daß Cottinghams Anliegen nicht ‚Realismus', sondern, wie er es nennt, ‚konstruierter Realismus' ist. ‚Der Realismus in meiner Arbeit dient als enthüllender Spiegel für uns selbst und unsere Erfindungen, die ebenso charmant wie ekelerregend sind. Die Technik dient einfach der Projektion der imaginären Realität.'

Mit der elektronischen Reproduktion zapft Cottingham das, was er sich vorstellt, an und überschreibt damit die Wirklichkeit. Die Illusion photographischer Authentizität erlaubt es ihm, ansonsten eigenständige, ja sogar konkurrierende Konstellationen miteinander zu kombinieren. Doch das Kunstwerk wird nicht zur Collage eines Bildes, sondern zur Collage der Wirklichkeit. Die Fähigkeit, die Essenz der Wirklichkeit heraufzubeschwören und sich deren Inhalt vorzustellen, ist das, was Cottinghams Arbeiten ihre beunruhigende Kraft verleiht.

In ‚Fictitious Portraits' kann Cottingham dank der Möglichkeit zur elektronischen Reproduktion den Mythos der Photographie gebrauchen und mißbrauchen, kann den privilegierten Anspruch auf das Wirkliche, auf das, was er ‚die wichtigste Erfindung der modernen Zeiten – das Subjekt' – nennt, kritisch hinterfragen. Das ‚Selbst', der moderne Begriff des Menschseins, ist das, was Cottinghams photographisches Triptychon in Frage stellt.

Cottingham stellt sich Körper vor, indem er sie nicht als Wesen abbildet, sondern sich selbst mit anderen vermischt, indem er Gestalten aus Ton, aus anatomischen Zeichnungen, aus zahllosen Photographien von verschiedenen Rassen, Geschlechtern und Altersgruppen formt. Diese scheinbar normalen photographischen Portraits stellen die menschliche Wirklichkeit als Konstrukt in den Vordergrund, als das Produkt bedeutungsvoller Aktivitäten, die auf den Körper anspielen. Wie Cottingham peotisch sein Bild beschreibt: ‚Da ist diese leblose äußere Schale, mit ihrer Schuld, und hinterfragt zornig

'constructed realism': 'The realism in my work serves as a revealing mirror into ourselves and into our inventions, both charming and nauseating. Technique simply serves to project the imaginary reality'.

Through electronic reproduction Cottingham draws on what is imagined and writes it upon the real. The illusion of photographic authenticity, then, allows him to combine otherwise discrete and even competing contexts. Yet, the artwork becomes not a collage of an image, but a collage of reality. This ability to construct the essence of the real and imagine its content is what gives Cottingham's work its unsettling power.

In 'Fictitious Portraits', electronic re-production allows Cottingham to use and abuse photography's myth, its privileged claim to the real; to critique what he calls 'the most important invention of modern times – the subject.' The self, the Modern notion of personhood, is what is being called into question by Cottingham's photographic triptych.

By hybridizing himself with others, by creating characters out of clay, anatomical drawings and numerous photographs of different races, genders, and ages, instead of re-presenting subjects, Cottingham imagines bodies. These seemingly formal photographic portraits foreground human reality as construction, as the product of signifying activities which play upon the body. As Cottingham poetically describes the image: 'There's the lifeless, external shell with its guilt, angrily questioning the viewer's responsibility, leaving body, blank eyes. Breath. Older, hard, intense – younger, innocent, relaxed. Unaware. Flux of warning, guilt, worried questioning. In the blink of an eye, the movement between life and stagnation.' Through the construction of bodies, made possible by electronic reproduction, Cottingham shows that selves, like 'Fictitious Portraits', are mental collages made from numerous images from the past, future, and the imagined. By creating a portrait as multiple personas, the 'self' is exposed not as a solidified being, but as the product of social and interior interaction.

COMPUTERGRAPHIK

KEITH COTTINGHAM

die Verantwortlichkeit des Betrachters, den Körper verlassend, leere Augen, Atem. Älter, hart, ernst – jünger, unschuldig, entspannt. Unwissend. Flux der Wärme, Schuld, besorgt fragend. Einen Augenblick lang, die Bewegung zwischen Leben und Stillstand.'
Mit seinem Zusammenstellen von Körpern, das erst durch elektronische Reproduktion möglich wird, zeigt Cottingham auf, daß unser aller ‚Selbst‘, genauso wie ‚Fictitious Portraits‘, nichts anderes ist als eine geistige Collage aus zahlreichen Bildern der Vergangenheit, der Zukunft und der Phantasie. Indem er ein Portrait aus mehreren Persönlichkeiten zusammensetzt, wird das ‚Selbst‘ als ein nichteinheitliches Wesen, als Produkt von gesellschaftlicher und innerer Wechselwirkung entlarvt. Cottingham veranschaulicht, daß eine Auseinandersetzung damit die Anpassung des ‚Ich‘ und des ‚Du‘ an ein Idealbild beinhaltet und sich der Betrachter durch diese Art von Bildern selbst findet.» (Greg Grieve/Keith Cottingham)

Cottingham shows that discourse involves the 'match' of the signifiers 'I' and 'you' to ideal representation, and that it is through those representations that the subject finds itself.»
(Greg Grieve/Keith Cottingham)

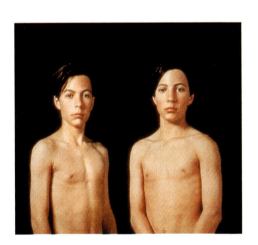

Auszeichnung
Fictitious Portraits, 1992
HW: Macintosh II
SW: Adobe Photoshop

COMPUTERGRAPHIK

JOHN KAHRS

John Kahrs (USA) ist Chefanimator der Firma Blue Sky Productions in Ossining, nördlich von New York. Schon als Halbwüchsiger interessierte er sich für Animation, verwandelte Schundhefte in Flipbooks und experimentierte mit Super-8-Filmen. Zum Master of Fine Arts promovierte er am Nova Scotia College of Art and Design, Kanada. In jüngster Zeit hat er damit begonnen, computergenerierte Arbeiten bei kleinen Veranstaltungen in Manhattan zu zeigen.

■ «Das Bild ‚Supercluster' wurde mit ‚cgiStudio' erstellt. Das ist ein Software-Paket, das derzeit von Blue Sky Productions in Ossining, New York, entwickelt wird. Diese Software verwendet eine eigene Computersprache (‚Studio's'), die an die Computersprache ‚C' erinnert und sich bei der Erstellung von Graphiken stärker auf die Geometrie von Festkörpern und binäre Modelle als auf Vieleckgeflechtberechnung stützt. Da die Software von Festkörpern ausgeht, eignet sie sich besonders gut zum ‚Raytracing', eine von ‚Studio's renderer' begründete, sehr robuste Technik zur Erzeugung von Computerbildern.
‚Supercluster' (5000 Kugeln) wurde unter Verwendung der Computersprache ‚Studio's' erstellt. Ihre Fähigkeit, mit einfachen Programmen komplexes Bildmaterial zu formen, gefiel mir, und da ich keine Erfahrung im Programmieren hatte, wurde die Herstellung der Cluster-Bilder für mich zum Lernprozeß. Das Programm produziert mehrere Tausend Kugeln, die es clusterförmig um zufällig im Raum verteilte Punkte anordnet.
Gerendert wurde das Bild mit ‚Radiosity', ein hochentwickeltes Lichtführungsmodell, das Lichtreflexionen zwischen diffusen Oberflächen wiedergibt. Ein gutes Beispiel dafür wäre etwa ein Sonnenstrahl, der auf eine rote Bodenfläche fällt und den ganzen Raum rötlich überhaucht. Meines Erachtens ist die Fähigkeit, diese Feinheiten gegenseitiger Beeinflussungen des Lichts wiederzugeben, die spannendste

John Kahrs (USA) is Senior Animator at Blue Sky Productions in Ossining, north of New York City. His animation career started with his use of paperbacks for flipbooks, and experiments with Super-8 film. He received a Fine Arts degree from the Nova Scotia College of Art and Design, a small art school in northeastern Canada. He has recently started showing computer generated work in small shows around Manhattan.

■ *«The 'Supercluster' image was created with cgiStudio, a proprietary software package in development at Blue Sky Productions in Ossining, New York. The software uses its own programming language which is reminiscent of the C language, and it relies more heavily on solid geometry and Boolean modeling than polygonal meshes to create images. Because it is based on solids, the software is particularly well suited for raytracing, a very robust technique for creating CG (computer generated) imagery, which is the foundation of Studio's renderer.*
'Supercluster' (5000 spheres) was modeled using Studio's language. Studio's ability to model complex imagery using simple programs appealed to me, and as I had no previous experience in programming, creating the cluster images was a way of learning. The Studio program creates several thousand spheres that are clustered around randomly distributed points.
The image was rendered using radiosity. Radiosity is an advanced lighting model that reproduces the interreflection of light between diffuse surfaces. A good example of this would be a sunbeam shining on a red floor in a room, causing the whole room to take on a red hue. In my view, the ability to recreate this subtlety of light interaction is the most exciting thing to happen to CG imagery since people started using computers to make pictures, and it pushes the realism and beauty of computer pictures into a new realm.
As soon as one starts to work with radiosity, the

COMPUTERGRAPHIK

JOHN KAHRS

Auszeichnung
Supercluster (5000 Spheres), 1994
HW: Hewlett-Packard HP-735
SW: cgiStudio (Blue Sky Productions' Proprietary)

COMPUTERGRAPHIK

JOHN KAHRS

Angelegenheit im Bereich der Computerbilder, seit Menschen mit der Herstellung von Bildmaterial mittels Computer begonnen haben, und es eröffnet den Computerbildern sowohl in Bezug auf Realismus als auch auf Schönheit neue Dimensionen.
Sobald man mit ‚Radiosity' arbeitet, werden herkömmliche Methoden der Lichtführung mit dem Computer obsolet. Beispielsweise ist es nicht mehr nötig, Umgebungslicht zur optischen Balance der Bilder einzusetzen. Hier wird das Umgebungslicht richtig und automatisch berechnet. ‚Radiosity' liefert viele der fehlenden visuellen Vorgaben, wodurch Computerbilder erst jetzt tatsächlich photorealistisch aussehen. Mit ‚Radiosity' wird es sogar möglich, auf alle bisher üblichen Beleuchtungstechniken zu verzichten und sie durch ‚Boxes' oder Kugeln mit spezifischer Eigenhelligkeit oder ‚innerer' Farbgebung zu ersetzen. Diese hellen Objekte werfen ihr Licht auf andere, und ihre Lichtqualität ist dabei häufig sehr weich und schön, ganz im Gegensatz zu den harten Lichtern aus punktförmigen Lichtquellen, die man oft in der Computergraphik sehen kann. In ‚Supercluster' erfolgte die Beleuchtung, indem die Szenen von hellen Objekten beschienen wurden. Die Cluster treiben in einer Box mit offener Oberseite, und die Helligkeit des Hintergrunds ‚schimmert' hinunter ins Innere der Box und beleuchtet so die Kugeln. Licht im herkömmlichen Sinn wurde bei diesem Bild nicht verwendet.
Wenn man sich die letzten Absätze durchliest, dann scheint es, als müßte ein Künstler einen unglaublich verschlungenen Weg gehen, bevor er überhaupt ein Bild herstellen kann. Angesichts des ganzen Prozesses ist die Tätigkeit des Künstlers eigentlich nur darauf beschränkt, der Software Befehle zu erteilen. Meine Rolle sehe ich darin, auf hohem Niveau Anweisungen zu geben, Programme aufzubauen und zu speichern, Modelle zu erstellen und die Parameter zu verändern. Es ist eine Arbeitsweise, die zu endlosem Editieren und Manipulieren anregt. Derzeit verwende ich die Vorgaben und Modelle von ‚Supercluster' in einer neuen Serie

traditional methods of lighting with computers become obsolete. For instance, it is no longer necessary to use ambient light to make images look balanced: the ambient is calculated correctly and automatically. Radiosity provides many of the missing visual cues that prevented CG imagery from appearing truly photorealistic. With radiosity, it is even possible to avoid using traditional lights altogether, substituting them with boxes, spheres, etc. that have a brightness, or 'inner' color. These bright objects cast light onto other objects, and the quality of light can often be very soft and beautiful, in contrast to the hard edged point source lights often seen in CG images. This use of bright objects to light scenes is the way 'Supercluster' is lit. The clusters are floating in a box with an open top, and the brightness of the background 'shines' light down into the interior of the box, illuminating the spheres. There are no lights used in the image.
Reviewing the last few paragraphs, it must seem like an incredibly convoluted path for an artist to have to travel before he/she can produce an image. In terms of the entire process, the artist's job is limited to providing instructions to the software. My role is one of high-level direction, building and saving programs, making models and changing parameters. It's a way of working that invites endless editing and manipulation. Currently, I'm using the ideas and models from 'Supercluster' in the next series of images. The part of the process that is tedious and repetitive is, as usual, done by the software itself and the computers.
I feel comfortable now with it as a legitimate tool, like a pencil or paintbrush, because, for the first time, the richness of the imagery rivals that of other media.
The question of why I use computers to make images has a few different answers. I work as a CG animator every day at Blue Sky, so I'm constantly using computers. I'm always aware of the capabilities, the possiblities of the emerging technology, and I want to push the technology to see how far I can take it.
The most personal reason I have for using a

COMPUTERGRAPHIK

JOHN KAHRS

von Bildern. Das Langwierige und immer Wiederkehrende dabei übernehmen wie üblich die Software und der Computer.

Ich bin zufrieden damit, weil ich den Computer für ein legitimes Werkzeug ansehe – so wie Pinsel und Bleistift –, denn zum ersten Mal tritt damit das reichhaltige Bildmaterial aus dem Computer mit dem anderer Medien in Wettstreit.

Auf die Frage, warum ich den Computer dazu verwende, Bilder zu erzeugen, gibt es mehrere verschiedene Antworten. Zum einen arbeite ich tagtäglich als Computergraphik-Animator bei Blue Sky, d.h., ich verwende dauernd Computer. Und ich bin mir daher ständig der Fähigkeiten und Möglichkeiten dieser neu entstehenden Technologie bewußt, möchte sie vorantreiben, um zu sehen, wie weit ich damit komme.

Ein eher persönlicher Grund für den Einsatz von Computern ist schon schwieriger zu erläutern. Ich glaube, es hat damit zu tun, kleine Welten zu erschaffen und sie zu erforschen. Es hat schon etwas Magisches, ja Mystisches an sich, eine Szene zu erschaffen, die nur aus vergänglichen Befehlen und Zeichen, aus flüchtigen Nullen und Einsern besteht, und sie dann Pixel für Pixel vor Augen erscheinen zu sehen. Zuzusehen, wie sie durch Licht und Schatten an Festigkeit gewinnt. Jedes Mal, wenn ich eine ‚Supercluster'-Szenerie von einem anderen Standpunkt aus betrachte oder die Konfiguration der Cluster verändere und dann das fertige Bild sehe und die komplexen Raumverhältnisse überblicke, habe ich ein Gefühl wie ein Entdecker oder Forscher. Wenn das Rendering beginnt, dann tritt der Künstler in den Hintergrund und wird zum Beobachter. Der kreative Prozeß ruht, wenn die Software die Szene zeichnet, die Schatten in einer Art und Weise setzt, die man schwerlich voraussagen hätte können, und dabei das Verhalten der Wirklichkeit nachahmt. Der Künstler betrachtet das Bild und reagiert darauf. Diesen Dialog zwischen Mensch und Maschine finde ich sehr ermutigend, und er treibt mich dazu, Bilder zu schaffen, wie eben kein anderes Medium, das ich mir vorstellen kann.» (John Kahrs)

computer is more difficult to describe. I think it has something to do with creating little worlds and exploring them. There is something very magical, almost mystical about creating a scene that exists as ephemeral instructions and scripts, fleeting 1's and 0's, and seeing that world drawn, pixel by pixel, before your eyes. To see it given solidity with shadows and light. Each time I view the 'Supercluster' scene from a different location or change the cluster configuration, I always get the feeling of discovery and exploration when I see the image finished and survey the complex topologies. When rendering begins, the artist stands back and watches, the creative process rests as the software draws the scene, filling in the shadows in ways one never could have predicted, mimicking the behavior of reality. The artist views the image and responds. This dialogue between artist and machine is one I find particularly encouraging, pushing me to make images like no other medium I can think of.»
(John Kahrs)

COMPUTERGRAPHIK

LINDA DEMENT

Linda Dement (AUS), geb. 1960, 1988 Bachelor of Fine Arts am City Art Institute/Sydney, 1989 Postgraduate Studium am Sydney College of the Arts, 1993 Master of Fine Arts an der University of New South Wales. Arbeitet dort als Lehrbeauftragte für Photographie und Computergraphik und als freie Designerin im Multimediabereich.

■ «Der Inhalt meiner Arbeiten ist sehr persönlich und körperbezogen. Er bezieht sich auf meine eigenen Erfahrungen, Erinnerungen, Aggressionen, Fleisch, Lust, Verrücktheit, Blutrausch und Phantasie. Ich folge darin der Logik der Träume und Halluzinationen und erzeuge damit unter die Erde und unter die Haut gehende Geschichten persönlicher Symbole.

Um zu arbeiten, lege ich streng kontrollierte technologische Rahmenbedingungen fest, innerhalb derer ich dann loslegen kann. Über die Medien, die ich auswähle, übe ich faschistische Kontrolle aus. Diese Kontrolle gestattet mir, selber außer Kontrolle zu geraten und die Kunst sich selbst zu überlassen. Ich kann so mit Dingen arbeiten, die ich nicht kontrollieren kann: mit Verrücktheit, Unvernunft, den dunklen, verschwommenen, nebulosen Bereichen. Die Kreativität erlaubt mir, meine nihilistischen, zerstörerischen Tendenzen einzusetzen und mich in beide Richtungen über die Grenzen der Vernunft zu bewegen.

Der Computer verarbeitet und speichert Information. Meine Informationen. Und er gibt sie mir zurück, in der Reihenfolge und unter den Rahmenbedingungen, wie ich sie haben will. Es geht um Gedächtnis und darum, Gedächtnis zu verändern. Ich kann einen Wust von Lügen und Bildern in den Computer eingeben, mit ihnen irgendwo da draußen in einem nicht existenten Computer-Raum arbeiten und sie dann auf dem Bildschirm erscheinen sehen. Im klaren Licht der Tatsachen, der Technologie und des Geldes.» (Linda Dement)

Linda Dement (AUS), born 1960. M.F.A. College of Fine Arts University of NSW 1993; Post Graduate study Sydney College of the Arts 1989; B.A. (Fine Art) City Art Institute 1988. An exhibiting artist since 1984, with a background in photography, writing, film and animation, now working with computer based interactive installations and computer manipulated 2D imagery. Currently lecturing in photography and computer imaging at the College of Fine Arts, UNSW and working as a freelance multi-media designer.

■ «The content of my work is highly personal and corporeal. It has to do with my own experience, memories, aggression, flesh, desire, madness, bloodlust and fantasy. I follow the logic of dream and hallucination to create a subterranean, subcutaneous narrative of personal symbols.

In order to work, I establish a tightly controlled framework of technology within which I can let go. I always exercise fascistic control over the mediums I choose. Being in control allows me to lose control and so let the art take care of itself. This lets me work with that which I cannot control: madness, unreason, the dark areas, indefinite and nebulous. Creativity allows me to use my abrogative, destructive tendencies, to wander over both sides of the line that marks out 'reasonable'. There is value, knowledge and danger in the unreasonable, in madness, and in pain. In making art, I can use that which threatens me and in doing so, decrease the threat by working through it. There is something about creativity that sustains.

The computer processes and stores information, my information, and gives it back to me within the order and framework I have demanded. It is about memory and about altering memory. I am able to enter into the computer a confusion of lies and pictures, work on them, out there in non-existent computer space, then see it appear on the screen with the weight of fact, technology and money.» (Linda Dement)

COMPUTERGRAPHIK

LINDA DEMENT

**Anerkennung
Fur Gash, 1993
HW: Macintosh
SW: Adobe Photoshop**

COMPUTERGRAPHIK

PASCAL DOMBIS

Pascal Dombis (F), geb. 1965; Künstler, lebt und arbeitet in Paris. 1983–88 Ausbildung zum Ingenieur am INSA, Lyon. Abschlußgrad als CAD/CAM-Ergonom. 1987–88 Museum School of Fine Arts, Boston, USA. Ausstellungen bei Art+, Enghien 1992 und Salon de Montrouge 1993.

Pascal Dombis (F), born 1965; artist, lives and works in Paris. Museum School of Fine Arts, Boston USA, 1987–1988; Engineer INSA, Lyon, 1983–1988; Degree in Mechanical Engineering (DAD/CAM-ergonomics). Group exhibitions: Salon de Montrouge, Montrouge, 1993; Art+, Enghien, 1992.

■ «Meine Arbeit besteht darin, computergenerierte, fraktale Strukturen in Malerei einzufügen. Ich benütze diese Bilder als Ausgangspunkt, um einen Bildraum zu erarbeiten, in dem ich mich mit Polaritäten auseinandersetze: Struktur/Strukturlosigkeit, Gleichgewicht/Ungleichgewicht, Einfachheit/Komplexität. Wenn ich ein interessantes Bild ausgewählt habe, vergrößere ich es auf Leinwandgröße und drucke es auf mehreren Blättern aus, bis die gesamte Fläche gefüllt ist. Zusammengesetzt werden die Blätter mit Harz. Ich verwende Reispapier, mit dem ich Transparenzeffekte erziele, die die räumliche Qualität und die intermediäre Dimension verstärken. Die Transparenz ermöglicht mir, mehrere Blätter mit unterschiedlichen Entwicklungsstadien der fraktalen Strukturen übereinanderzulegen – ein Effekt, der Räumlichkeit und Dynamik verstärkt. Da mein künstlerischer Anspruch mit der Erforschung des bildlichen Raumes relativ klassisch ist, bemühe ich mich nicht, wunderschöne fraktale Bilder wie auf den Titelseiten der Wissenschaftsmagazine zu produzieren. Meines Erachtens handelt es sich dabei um eine eher anekdotische Seite fraktaler Bilder. Für mich ist es interessanter, an kargeren, mehrdeutigeren fraktalen Strukturen mit echtem Ausdruckspotential zu arbeiten.

Was meine Arbeit betrifft, so gestatten mir fraktale Formen abstrakte, geometrische Bilder ohne jedwede figurative, gestische oder illusionistische Hintergedanken auf einem Komplexitätsniveau zu erstellen, das der Mensch nie erreichen wird. Außerdem sind sie Stücke eines Raums, der sich jenseits des Bilderrahmens fortsetzt.» (Pascal Dombis)

■ «My artwork consists of using computer generated fractal structures to integrate them into paintings. I use these pictures as starting points to elaborate a pictorial space in which I deal with different tensions: structure-destructure, balance-unbalance, simplicity-complexity. Once I have selected the image I am interested in, I scale it to the canvas size and print it on different sheets to cover it entirely. These printings are assembled with resins. I use rice paper sheets which allow me to play on transparency effects, strengthening this intermediate dimension-space notion. The transparency obtained allows me also to superpose different sheets of paper describing different states of the fractal structure. This creates a more dynamic and growing space. Hence my artwork aim is relatively classical, because it consists of exploring the pictorial space of the canvas. I do not look forward to producing beautiful fractal images that can make the cover of scientific magazines. In my opinion, this anecdotal side of the fractal imagery shows very little interest from an artistic point of view. It seems to me more interesting to compose on more austere, more ambiguous fractal structures, yet still with a true potential of expression.

As far as my work is concerned, fractal forms allow me to create totally abstract geometric images without any figurative, gestural or illusionist implications, and that at a complexity level unreachable by man. They are also pieces of space that continue beyond the canvas frame.» (Pascal Dombis)

C O M P U T E R G R A P H I K

PASCAL DOMBIS

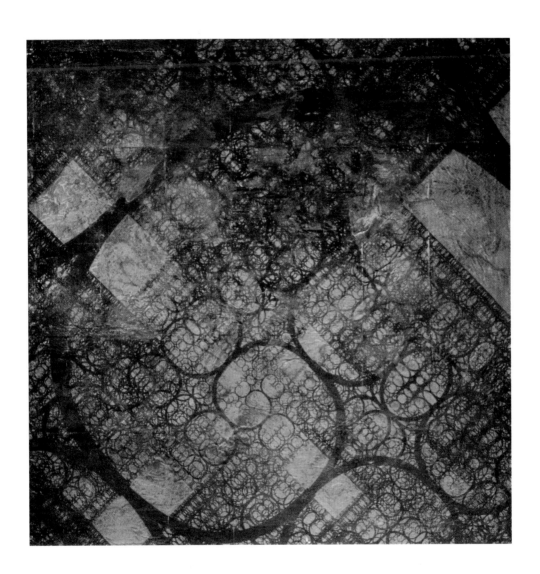

**Anerkennung
Untitled, 1993/94
HW: PC
SW: PostScript Language**

C O M P U T E R G R A P H I K

MOGENS JACOBSEN

Mogens Jacobsen (DK), geb. 1959, ist freischaffender Journalist für Technikmagazine. Studierte Mathematik in Aarhus und Film in Kopenhagen. Mitwirkung in einem experimentellen Orchester und Gründung des „Basedofv"-Labels für experimentelle Vokalmusik. Teilnahme an internationalen Computerkunstfestivals (u. a. Prix Ars Electronica 93).

■ «Heute Computergraphiken zu machen, ist nur schwer zu rechtfertigen. Jedermann macht Computergraphiken oder betreibt Desktop-Publishing. Ich suche nach Formen von Computerbildern, bei denen der Computer nicht als Ersatz für Stifte, Pinsel oder Spraydosen herhalten muß. Der Computer eröffnet dem neuen Künstler eine ganze Reihe von Möglichkeiten, z. B. Interaktivität, Kommunikation, Informationsverarbeitung, neue, vertiefende Technologien, Simulationen – und die Fähigkeit im schlimmstmöglichen Moment abzustürzen.

Da wissenschaftliche und soziale Trends unser Bild von der Realität verändern, muß sich die Kunst damit auseinandersetzen. Es ist ein Bild unserer Wirklichkeit entstanden, das diese als gewaltiges Informationsverarbeitungssystem begreift. Sprache (und Kunst) werden als ein System von Codes gesehen, in der Mathematik hat ein Wandel vom Umgang mit Zahlen, Raum und Logik hin zu einem Umgang mit Information stattgefunden. Das gegenwärtig beliebteste Werkzeug zur Erforschung von Information ist der Computer, und darum arbeite ich damit, obwohl der Großteil der graphischen Computer-„Kunst" an einem feindseligen Blick vom Elfenbeinturm auf die Welt leidet. Vielleicht ist wirklich das Medium die Botschaft, aber Information und Informationsverarbeitungssysteme spielen eine wichtige Rolle in der Formung unserer Gesellschaft. Daher sollten sie sorgfältig erforscht werden, sowohl von jenen Künstlern, die mit Pinsel und Bleistift arbeiten, als auch von jenen, die Kunst mit Harddrives und Chips machen.» (Mogens Jacobsen)

Mogens Jacobsen (DK), born 1959, is a freelance journalist for technical magazines. Studied mathematics in Aarhus and Film in Copenhagen. He was involved in an experimental orchestra, in the founding of the "Basedofv" record label for experimental vocal music, and has participated in international computer art festivals (e.g.: Prix Ars Electronica 93).

■ «Doing graphics on computer these days is really hard to justify. Everybody is doing computer graphics or desktop publishing. But I seek a form of computer images where the computer is not a replacement for pencils, brushes or spraycans. The computer has many things to offer the new artist: e.g. interactivity, communication, advanced information processing, new immersive technologies, simulations – and the ability to break down at just the worst possible moment.

As social and scientific trends change our view of reality, art must deal with these trends. A view of reality as a giant information-processing system has emerged in my time. Language (and art) are seen as systems of codes; a change in the understanding of mathematics as dealing with numbers, space or logic towards a new math dealing with information has evolved. The current popular tool for exploring information is the computer – so, of course, I work with computers, even though most computer generated graphic 'art' suffers from a very hostile ivory-tower-view of the world. Perhaps the media really is the message, but information and information processing systems play a major role in the forming of our society and should be carefully explored both by the artists using pencils and brushes as well as the artists using hard drives and chips.» (Mogens Jacobsen)

C O M P U T E R G R A P H I K

MOGENS JACOBSEN

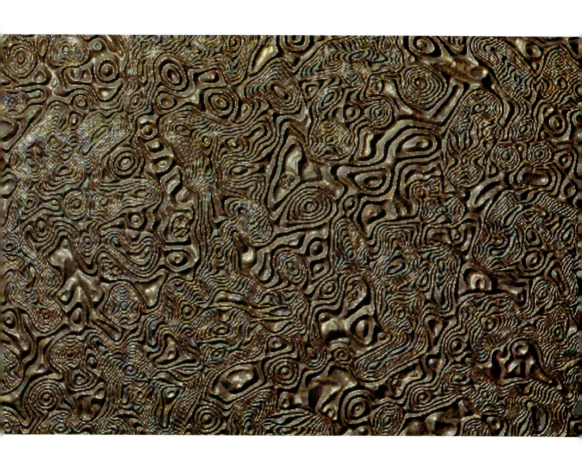

**Anerkennung
untitled #4 from the Heat Series, 1994
HW: 80386 PC
SW: Artist's Proprietary and Autodesk 3-D Studio**

COMPUTERGRAPHIK

RONALDO KIEL

Ronaldo Kiel (BRA), geb. 1958, hält Vorlesungen am Art Departement des Brooklyn College, New York, und arbeitet als freischaffender Werbedesigner und Multimedia-Entwickler in New York. 1985 Bachelor of Fine Arts in Brasilien; 1991 Master of Fine Arts am Brooklyn College der City University of New York.

■ «Ich nenne ‚D'Invenzione' gerne ein ‚soft-media'-Stück – eine mit dem Computer umgesetzte künstlerische Idee, die in jedem passenden Medium, wie im vorliegenden Fall als Druck oder als Video, realisiert werden kann. ‚D'Invenzione' stellt das Paradoxon von einem unendlichen, vom Menschen geschaffenen Gebilde unter Verwendung einer Ton/Bild-Schleife in den Raum. Der Ton wurde unter Verwendung der (nach dem Psychologen Roger Shepard benannten) Shepard-Notenskala erzeugt. Das Bildmaterial basiert auf den ‚Le Carceri'-Drucken von Giovanni Battista Piranesi (1720–1778). Alle Renderings wurden mit virtuellen Lichtquellen und Objektiven vorgenommen, um so das mit Texturen gemappte dreidimensionale Modell (eine imaginäre Architektur) aufzunehmen.
Der graphische Output: Eine Serie von 10 Ausdrucken wurde mit Electric Image Animation System als 32bit-Graphik (2048 x 1366 Pixels) gerendert und als 10" x 6,67" goße CMYK-Datei mit einer Auflösung von 300 Pixels/Zoll in Adobe Photoshop abgespeichert. Alle Dateien wurden auf einem Iris Ink Jet Printer ausgedruckt.
Der Video-Output: Die ursprünglichen Aufnahmen wurden auf einer Panasonic AG-7750 SVHS Maschine mit einer AG-F 700 Timecode-Karte und unter Verwendung des TrueVision NuVista Bildpuffer/Codierer sowie der DQ-Animaq DiaQuest Bildsteuerung durchgeführt. Die 90 Sekunden lange Animationsschleife wurde auf einem Macintosh IIci Computer in einem Bildformat von 640 x 480 Pixels in NTSC mit 30 Bildern pro Sekunde gerendert.» (Ronaldo Kiel)

Ronaldo Kiel (BRA), born 1958, is a Lecturer at the Art Departement at Brooklyn College, New York, freelance Advertising Designer and Multimedia Developer in New York. 1985 B.F.A. at Universidade Federal do Rio Grande do Sul, Porto Alegre, Brazil; 1991 M.F.A. at Brooklyn College, New York.

■ «I like to call 'D'Invenzione' a 'soft-media' piece – a computer-generated art idea to be outputted in any suitable medium – presented here in print and on video.
'D'Invenzione' stages the paradox of an endless man-made construction employing an audio/visual loop. The audio was generated by using the Shepard-tone scale (named for psychologist Roger Shepard), and the images were based on Giovanni Battista Piranesi's (1720–1778) 'Le Carceri' prints. All renderings were created using synthetic lights and lenses to shoot the 3D model mapped with textures (an imaginary architectural structure).
The graphic output: A series of 10 prints were rendered in Electric Image Animation System as 32 bit (2048 x 1366 pixels) images and saved as 10" x 6.67" CMYK files at 300 pixels per inch resolution in Adobe Photoshop. All files were printed as 13.5" x 20" on a Iris Ink Jet printer between March and November 1993.
The video output: the preliminary recordings were performed on the Panasonic AG-7750 SVHS deck with the AG-F700 time code reader generator card, using the True Vision NuVista + frame buffer/encoder and the DQ-Animaq DiaQuest frame controller. The 90-second animation loop was rendered over a period of 20 days on a Macintosh IIci computer (with 8 MB RAM) in a 640 x 480 frame format at NTSC 30 frames/second rate.» (Ronaldo Kiel)

C O M P U T E R G R A P H I K

RONALDO KIEL

Anerkennung
D'Invenzione #04, 1993
HW: Macintosh IIci
SW: EIAS and Adobe Photoshop

COMPUTERGRAPHIK

DON MacKAY

Don MacKay (CDN), geb. 1937, Bachelor of Fine Arts an der Mt. Allison University, Master of Fine Arts an der Cornell University, ist bildender Künstler und hat seit 1970 Zeichnen, Malen, Siebdruck und Bildhauerei unterrichtet, seit 1983 auch Computergraphik. In den letzten 10 Jahren sind seine Malereien von Computerkunst abgelöst worden.

■ «Auf einem Computer mit einfacher zwei- und dreidimensionaler Graphiksoftware, baue, modelliere, färbe und beleuchte ich Umrißformen und wandle sie in Objekte um, die ich schließlich zu Bildern organisiere, wie zum Beispiel jenes Bild, das ich ‚Bell' genannt habe. Am meisten interessieren mich einfache Beziehungen zwischen Formen, Farben und Texturen im zwei- und dreidimensionalen Raum. Am liebsten erkläre ich meine Computerbilder, indem ich mich auf meine frühere Malerei beziehe und Worte verwende wie: Balance, Eleganz und Mysterium.
Gesellschaftliche Kommentare, versteckte Inhalte oder Symbolismen sind üblicherweise nicht Bestandteile meines bildlichen Vokabulars, und obwohl ich mir manchmal vorstelle, wie es denn wäre, durch die Welten, die ich gestaltet habe, zu wandern, sind meine Überlegungen im allgemeinen eher praktischer Natur. Der Prozeß, durch den ich meine Bilder entwickle, ist ebenso einfach. Ich beginne mit einem offenen Raum und konstruiere ein Objekt. Ich verändere die Form, baue andere dazu, füge Lichter, Farben und Texturen ein und bewege und verändere Einheiten solange, bis die Komposition interessant erscheint. Ich speichere das Bild und lade es in den dreidimensionalen Bildraum, den ich geschaffen habe, um darin weitere interessante Aspekte zu entdecken. Sobald das Geheimnisvolle des Raums verblaßt, ist das Werk vollendet, bis zu jenem Zeitpunkt in der Zukunft, zu dem ich wieder in den Raum eintrete und den Prozeß weiterführe.» (Don MacKay)

Don MacKay (CDN), born 1937, B.F.A. from Mt. Allison University, M.F.A. from Cornell University, is a visual artist and professor of Fine Arts at the University of Waterloo, where he has taught drawing, painting, screenprinting and sculpture since 1970, and computer imaging since 1983. Over the past ten years his paints have been replaced by the computer.

■ «On a PC, with basic two and three dimensional painting and drawing software, I construct, model, colour, light and develop shapes into objects that I eventually organize into images such as the one I named 'Bell'.
Simple relationships of shapes, colours and textures in two and three dimensional space interest me most. I prefer to explain the pictures I make on the computer in terms I associate with my earlier paintings, with words such as balance and elegance and mystery.
Social comment, hidden content or symbolism are not regularly part of my visual vocabulary and, although occasionally I imagine what it would be like to wander through the environments I make, my concerns are usually practical ones.
The process I use to develop my images is also simple. I begin with open space and construct an object. I change the form, build others, add colours and lights and texture, and move and vary units until the composition looks interesting. I save the image, and then move into the three dimensional picture space that I have created to discover other intriguing views. I continue to add, remove, change forms and save images. When the mystery of the space fades, the work is complete until some future time when I return to move into the space again and continue the process.» (Don MacKay)

COMPUTERGRAPHIK

DON MacKAY

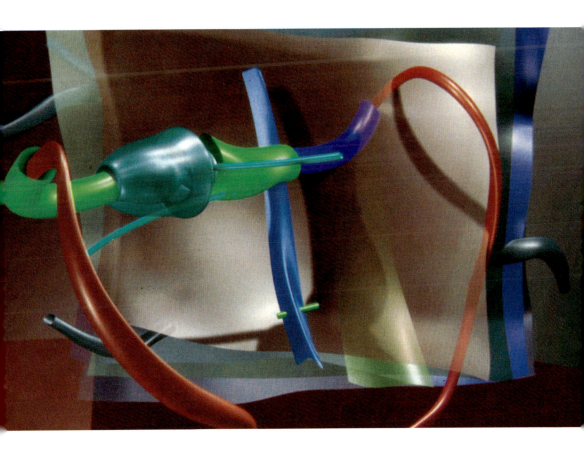

**Anerkennung
Bell, 1993
HW: 80486/50 PC
SW: Crystal 3-D and Photostyler**

COMPUTERGRAPHIK

STEWART McSHERRY

Stewart McSherry (USA), geb. 1961, Mitbegründer des Computergraphik-Labors am Design-Institut der UCLA und am Art Center College of Design. 1986–87 Konsulent, Laboratoriums-Manager und Instruktor an der UCLA und 1987–88 Manager des Graphik-Laboratoriums am ACCD. Zur Zeit studiert er am Silicon Graphics Corporate Center. Teilnahme an zahlreichen Ausstellungen, u.a. Prix Ars Electronica 92 (Auszeichnung), Osaka CG 1993 (erster Platz), Golden Platter 94, Japan CG Grand Prix (erster Platz).

■ «Ich beschäftige mich mit der Herstellung von Bildmaterial aus abstrakten dreidimensionalen Strukturen, die im allgemeinen unterschiedlich durchscheinend sind und in ihrem Aussehen eine gewisse Verwandtschaft zu gläsernen Objekten zu haben scheinen.
Quarz → Silizium (Chips) → Quarzglas, das erscheint mir ein interessanter Kreislauf zu sein.
Ich verwende relativ hochentwickelte Techniken, da ich versuche, eine gewisse photorealistische Abstraktion, einen ‚abstrakten Computerrealismus' zu erreichen, einen Zustand, in dem ein abstraktes, physikalisch nicht-existentes Computerbild real erscheint. Ich strebe dieses Ziel an, weil ich es für das fruchtbringendste Gebiet halte, nämlich die Tatsache, daß Computer anscheinend den Abgrund zwischen Realität und Abstraktion zunehmend verkleinern.
Meine Arbeit weist insofern eine Verwandtschaft mit Skulpturen auf, als ich interaktiv die Formen modelliere, die ich sichtbar zu machen versuche, und ich verändere und manipuliere sie, indem ich Farbabstimmungsprozesse anwende. Dieser Zugang behagt mir mehr als das ‚reine' Programmieren, weil es mir zumindest mehr Kontrolle über die Form einräumt.»
(Stewart McSherry)

Stewart McSherry (USA), born 1961, has been helping organize the current computer graphic labs in the UCLA Design Department and at Art Center College of Design. He served as consultant, lab manager and instructor at UCLA 86–87 and manager of the graphics lab at ACCD 87–88. Currently he studies at the Silicon Graphics Corporate Center.
Exhibitions: Prix Ars Electronica 92 (Distinction), Osaka CG 1993 (1st place), Golden Platter 94, Japan CG Grand Prix (1st place).

■ «I am involved with creating imagery consisting of abstract three-dimensional structures usually with varying translucency – in appearance seeming to be related to glass sculpture. Silica→Silicon→Silica, an interesting cycle.
I use fairly advanced techniques in an attempt to achieve a sort of photo-realistic abstraction, that is, 'computer abstract realism', a state whereby an abstract, and physically non-existent, computer image appears real. It is towards this goal that I strive, for I find this the most fertile target, the gulf between abstraction and realism that computers seem destined to increasingly shorten.
My work is related to sculpture, in that I interactively model the forms I am trying to visualize, and apply procedural shaders to modify and manipulate these. I prefer this approach to 'pure' programming, as for me, at least, it allows more control over form.»
(Stewart McSherry)

C O M P U T E R G R A P H I K

STEWART McSHERRY

**Anerkennung
red heart yellow bile, 1994
HW: SGI Indigo R4000
SW: Alias**

COMPUTERGRAPHIK

GAVIN MILLER/NED GREENE

Gavin Miller (USA), Staff Scientist bei Apple Computer. Ph.D. in Computergraphik und computerunterstützter Fertigung, Universität Cambridge. Gemeinsame Animationsprojekte mit Ned Greene und Michael Kass.
Ned Greene (USA), Mitglied der Advanced Technology Group bei Apple Computer. Master of Science an der New York University. Zahlreiche Beiträge zum Technischen Programm von SIGGRAPH und zum Electronic Theatre.

■ «‚Santa Clara Falls' ist ein Standbild aus der Animation ‚Flow', die wir 1993 im SIGGRAPH Electronic Theatre gezeigt haben und die sich mit der Abbildung von Flüssigkeiten in allen möglichen Formen beschäftigt. Beispiele dafür: Wolken, ein Geysir, ein Fluß und ein Wasserfall. Der Titel bezieht sich auf das Santa-Clara-Tal, das auch als ‚Silicon Valley' bekannt ist und in dem der Apple-Computer seinen Ursprung hat.
Wir haben dazu gemeinsam mit Michael Kass unsere eigene Simulations- und Renderingsoftware geschrieben. Wasser wird darin simuliert, indem wir ein maschengitterartiges Flüssigkeitsdynamiksystem mit einem interaktiven Teilchensystem kombinieren. Am Anfang der Simulation füllt das Wasser, dargestellt durch ein Maschengitter, ein Bassin oben am Wasserfall. An der Abbruchkante erreicht es eine Schwelle, an der es in einzelne Partikel umgewandelt wird und so nach unten fällt, um am Grund des Wasserfalls wieder in die Maschengitterform überzugehen.
Die Animation nahm etwa 20 Minuten pro Frame auf einer SGI-Crimson-Workstation in Anspruch. Rund 700.000 Einzelpartikel konnten wir mit einem 60MB-Hauptspeicher simulieren. Die Schatten der Einzelpartikel wurden jeweils selbsttätig berechnet und mit einem Massen-Renderingverfahren namens ‚splatting' wiedergegeben. Die Geländehöhenstufe wurde mit einem interaktiven Zeichenprogramm erstellt.» (Gavin Miller/Ned Greene)

Gavin Miller (USA) is a staff scientist at Apple Computer. Ph.D. in Computer Graphics and Computer Aided Manufacture at Cambridge University, England. Several animation projects with Ned Greene and Michael Kass.
Ned Greene (USA) is a member of the Advanced Technology Group at Apple Computer, M. Sc. from New York University. Numerous contributions to the SIGGRAPH technical program and to the Electronic Theater.

■ «'Santa Clara Falls' is a still from 'Flow', an animation from the 1993 SIGGRAPH Electronic Theatre, which depicts fluid flow in various forms – clouds, a geyser, a stream, and a waterfall. The title jokingly refers to the Santa Clara Valley, also known as Silicon Valley, where Apple Computer is based.
We wrote our own simulation and rendering software, building on a program that was originally written for the 1990 animation 'Splashdance', done with Michael Kass. Water was simulated by combining mesh-based fluid dynamics with an interacting particle system. At the beginning of the simulation, water represented as a mesh fills a basin at the top of the falls. At the lip of the cliff, the water reaches a slope threshold and is converted to particles which descend over the falls. At the base of the falls, particles are converted back to mesh representation.
The animation took about twenty minutes a frame on an SGI Crimson workstation. With 60 MB of main memory, we were able to simulate 700,000 particles. The particles are self-shadowing and were rendered with a form of volume rendering called 'splatting'. The terrain height field was painted with an interactive paint program. Terrain colors were taken from a photograph of Bryce Canyon in Utah.» (Gavin Miller/Ned Greene)

COMPUTERGRAPHIK

GAVIN MILLER/NED GREENE

**Anerkennung
Santa Clara Falls, 1993
HW: SGI Crimson and Macintosh Quadra 950
SW: In-House Code**

COMPUTERGRAPHIK

ANNA GABRIELE WAGNER/ADELHARD ROIDINGER

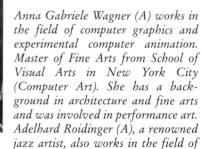

Anna Gabriele Wagner (A) arbeitet auf dem Gebiet der Computergraphik und experimentellen Computeranimation. Master of Fine Arts an der School of Visual Arts in New York City (Computer Art), außerdem Studium der Architektur (TU Graz).
Adelhard Roidinger (A), neben Tätigkeit als Jazzkünstler auch Arbeit auf dem Gebiet der experimentellen Photographie, Computergraphik und Computermusik. Seit 1982 eigenes Computer Art Studio ACROASIS. Er studierte Architektur, Kontrabaß und Jazzkomposition.

■ «Unser künstlerisches Interesse richtet sich auf die kreative Auseinandersetzung mit morphologischen Wechselbeziehungen. Mittels Photographie gelangen wir zunächst zu makroskopischen Szenarien des Realen in belebter und unbelebter Natur: Mineralien, Kristallisationen, Blätter, Fließformen und objets trouvés. Für die Herstellung dieser Aufnahmen verwendeten wir unter anderem eine dafür entwickelte Dunkelfeld-Makrophotographieeinrichtung. Als nächsten Schritt komponieren und manipulieren wir die Bilder im Computer in mehreren Schichten, wobei die Komputation für uns eine künstlerische Sprache und ein Medium der Entdeckung darstellt und weniger als Produktionsmittel dient. Die Ergebnisse zeigen, daß eine organische Struktur mehr beinhaltet, als sich dem Auge unmittelbar zeigt.
Durch das Addieren und Subtrahieren von Pixelwerten von zwei oder mehreren Bildern und das Anwenden von komplexen Algorithmen ent-decken wir eine bislang unsichtbare Formen- und Farbenwelt. Die so emergierenden neuen Bildwelten werden in einem zusätzlichen Prozeß der kontinuierlichen Koordinatentransformation deformiert. Diese Vorgangsweise führt uns zu einer schrittweisen Verknotung sich überschneidender Relationsfelder, zu einer Morphologie der Mehrdimensionalität.» (Anna Gabriele Wagner/Adelhard Roidinger)

■ «Our artistic collaboration is based on a creative exploration of morphological relationships. First, photography provides us with macroscopic scenarios of the 'real' in animate and inanimate nature: minerals, crystallisations, leaves, flow forms and objets trouvés. For the production of these photographs we use our own specially developed dark field macrophotography equipment.
As a next step we manipulate and compose these images in the computer in multiple layers, using computing as an artistic language and a means of discovery, rather than a production tool. This shows that there is more to an organic structure than what immediately meets the eye. We reveal invisible – but inherent – hidden layers of images from the 'real world'. We search for similarities in different dimensions and compare similar structures by using image processing techniques. Through adding and subtracting pixel values from two or more different images or applying algorithms on those values, we literally dis-cover the unseen virtual beauty. In an additional step the emerging new images are distorted through continuous transformation of the coordinates. This procedure leads us to a step by step linking of overlapping fields of relation and to a morphology of multidimensionality.» (Anna Gabriele Wagner/Adelhard Roidinger)

COMPUTERGRAPHIK

ANNA GABRIELE WAGNER/ADELHARD ROIDINGER

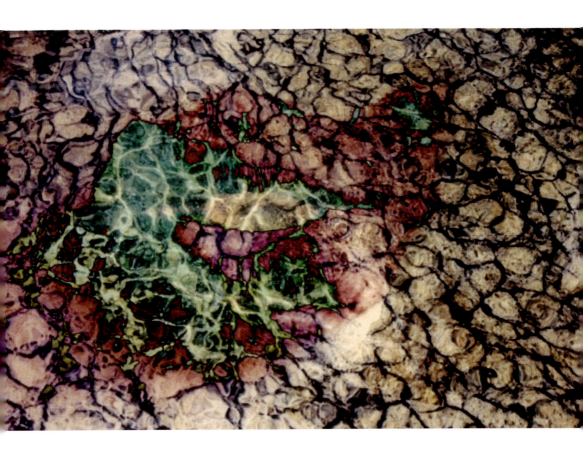

Anerkennung
Undine, 1994
HW: Macintosh and SGI
SW: Adobe Photoshop and Softimage (Eddie)

C O M P U T E R   A N I M A T I O N

A

COMPUTERANIMATION

DENNIS MUREN/MARK DIPPÉ/ILM

Dennis Muren (USA), Senior Visual Effects Supervisor bei Industrial Light & Magic. Er hat sieben Oscars für Visual Effects erhalten. Er ist für Design und Entwicklung neuer Techniken und Ausrüstung zuständig.
Mark A. Z. Dippé (USA) arbeitet seit 1988 als Assistant Visual Effects Supervisor bei Industrial Light & Magic und war 1988–90 Lektor für Computergraphik an der University of California in Berkeley. Mitarbeit an zahlreichen Filmen, diverse Werbespots und Publikationen.
ILM/Industrial Light & Magic ist eine Abteilung der LucasArts Entertainment Company in San Rafael, Kalifornien, die sich auf die Herstellung von Special Effects in Spielfilmen mittels Computeranimation spezialisiert hat. Mitarbeit unter anderem an „The Abyss", „Terminator II", „Death Becomes Her", „Jurassic Park". Zahlreiche internationale Auszeichnungen: Ehren-Nica beim Prix Ars Electronica 92 für „Terminator II", Academy Award (Oscar) für „Death Becomes Her" 1993.

■ «Die computeranimierten Dinosaurier in ‚Jurassic Park' sind der Gipfel einer Entwicklung aus Experiment und Fortschritt, die begonnen hatte, als George Lucas vor 14 Jahren die Abteilung Computergraphik bei Industrial Light & Magic gründete. Nun ist diese Abteilung das maßgebliche Werkzeug kreativen Schaffens innerhalb der Gesellschaft. Die mit ‚Jurassic Park' geleistete Arbeit ist aber mehr: Sie ist ein Quantensprung nach vorne, der die Art und Weise, Filme zu machen, für immer verändern wird.
Spielberg trat schon früh im Verlauf dieser Arbeit an ILM heran, nachdem er schon bei einer ganzen Reihe seiner früheren Filme mit dieser Effekteschmiede zusammengearbeitet hatte. Und Dennis Muren, der siebenfache Oscar-Preisträger und Effects Supervisor von ILM wollte unbedingt an ‚Jurassic Park' mitarbeiten. Weil aber Spielberg ursprünglich vorhatte, mit vollmechanischen Dinosaurier-Modellen in Originalgröße zu arbeiten, war

Dennis Muren (USA) is the Senior Visual Effects Supervisor at the Industrial Light & Magic. Recipient of seven Academy Awards for Best Visual Effects, Muren is actively involved in the design and development of new techniques and equipment.
Mark A. Z. Dippé (USA), 1988 – present: Industrial Light & Magic, Assistant Visual Effects Supervisor; 1988–1990: U.C. Berkeley, Lecturer in Computer Graphics. Several commercials and publications.
ILM/Industrial Light & Magic is a division of LucasArts Entertainment Company in San Rafael, California, specializing in computer animation for film production. Collaboration on films like "The Abyss", "Terminator II", "Death Becomes Her", "Jurassic Park". ILM has won numerous international awards, for instance the "Honorary Nica" at Prix Ars Electronica 92 for "Terminator II", Academy Award (Oscar) for "Death Becomes Her" 1993.

■ «The computer graphic dinosaurs in 'Jurassic Park' are the culmination of experimentation and progress that began at Industrial Light & Magic 14 years ago, when George Lucas set up the computer graphics department. It is now their most potent creative tool. Yet, the work in 'Jurassic Park' is more than that: it is a quantum leap forward, forever changing the way films will be made.
Spielberg consulted with ILM early in the process, having collaborated with this effects house on previous films. ILM's effects supervisor, Dennis Muren, a seven-time Academy Award winner, was anxious to participate in 'Jurassic Park', but since Spielberg hoped to use full scale dinosaurs and Go-Motion, Dennis was unclear about ILM's role in the project.
Muren had the ILM computer graphics team begin experimenting with an idea for 'Jurassic Park' – they built the dinosaur bones and skeleton in a computer, and from that, they created a herd of Gallimimus dinosaurs and a walking T-Rex.

COMPUTERANIMATION

DENNIS MUREN/MARK DIPPÉ/ILM

sich Dennis über die Rolle, die ILM innerhalb dieses Projekts spielen sollte, nicht ganz klar.
Er ließ das Computergraphik-Team von ILM mit einem Vorschlag für ‚Jurassic Park' zu experimentieren beginnen – und zwar wurden Dinosaurierknochen und -skelette im Computer zusammengebaut. Daraus wurden dann eine Herde von Gallimimus-Dinosauriern und ein aufrecht gehender Tyrannosaurus Rex.
Beeindruckt von ILM's Testergebnissen, gab Amblin Entertainment bald grünes Licht für weitere Testaufnahmen, darunter eine Stampede und eine ganze Reihe von Weitwinkelaufnahmen mit einer Herde von Sauriern in einer weitläufigen Landschaft.
Als Muren das nächste Mal zu Amblin kam, verblüffte er die Filmemacher mit einer computergenerierten Sequenz, in der ein T-Rex bei Tageslicht umherspazierte. Es schien, als würde der herkömmliche Trickfilm mit vollbeweglichen Modellen angesichts des Aufstiegs computergenerierter Filme auch bald aussterben.
Ein Team von über 100 Technikern und Künstlern brachte in den folgenden 18 Monaten die Computergraphik auf Höchstform und steuerte letztendlich mehr als 50 Dinosaurierszenen zum Film bei.
Eine der heikelsten Aufgaben, mit der sich die Techniker dabei konfrontiert sahen, war sicherzustellen, daß sich die Dinosaurier natürlich bewegten. Man wollte erreichen, daß sie als echte Tiere über die Leinwand kamen und nicht als Filmmonster im herkömmlichen Sinn. Die Dinosaurier waren nicht bloß computergene-

Impressed with ILM's test results, Amblin Entertainment soon gave ILM the green light to take on several additional test shots, including a stampede and several wide-angle scenes that illustrate a herd of dinosaurs against a sweeping vista. When Muren next returned to Amblin, he astounded the filmmakers with a computer-generated sequence of the T-Rex walking in daylight. It appeared that with the advent of computer-generated images, Go-Motion might soon be extinct.

Over the next 18 months, a team of over a hundred ILM creative and technical artists brought computer graphics to new heights, ultimately contributing over fifty dinosaur shots.

One of the most critical tasks the ILM team faced was making sure these dinosaurs moved naturally. They wanted them to come across as real animals, not movie monster stereotypes. The dinosaurs were not just computer-generated beasts, they were real characters with heart and soul and a distinctive attitude. To accomplish this, the ILM team, under the guidance of Dinosaur-Supervisor Phil Tippett, studied animal behavior, including the movements and body language of elephants, alligators, ostriches and lions. ILM's animators received special training, including movement lessons, so their animation would capture these behavioral nuances. In addition, Phil Tippett's shop in Berkeley supplied animation for over a dozen of ILM's 'Jurassic' shots.

'People will never believe our dinosaurs were made in a computer. Notice that as the bigger

Goldene Nica
Jurassic Park, 1993
HW: SGI Image
SW: Alias, Softimage, Parallax, Pixar (RenderMan)

COMPUTERANIMATION

DENNIS MUREN/MARK DIPPÉ/ILM

rierte Bestien. Sie alle waren echte Persönlichkeiten mit Herz, Seele und charakteristischen, individuellen Verhaltensweisen. Um das zustandezubringen, studierte das ILM-Team unter der Leitung des Saurier-Supervisors Phil Tippett tierische Verhaltensweisen, u. a. Bewegungen und Körpersprache von Elefanten, Alligatoren, Straußen und Löwen. Die Animatoren erhielten ein spezielles Training und Unterricht in Bewegungslehre, damit ihre Animationen diese Verhaltensnuancen einfangen konnten. Darüber hinaus besorgte Phil Tippetts Betrieb in Berkeley die Animationen für mehr als ein Dutzend der ‚Jurassic'-Einstellungen.

‚Die Leute werden niemals glauben, daß diese Dinosaurier in einem Computer entstanden sind', erklärte Muren. ‚Schauen Sie sich an, wie bei den größeren Tieren die Bäuche unter ihrem eigenen Gewicht hin- und herschwingen. Wenn sie laufen, dann wird mit jedem Schritt ihr ganzer Körper erschüttert. Achten Sie auf die Kleinigkeiten, darauf, wie der Velociraptor seinen Körper anspannt, wenn er aufgeschreckt wird. Er schaut richtig aufgeweckt und intelligent.'

Und schließlich meint Dennis Muren: ‚Die Arbeit an ‚Jurassic Park' war für mich die spannendste und herausforderndste in meinen ganzen Jahren als Visual Effects Supervisor. Die Ergebnisse, die wir damit erzielt haben, haben meine wildesten Spekulationen übertroffen. Es war ungeheuer befriedigend, mit Computern zu arbeiten und damit Wesen zu schaffen, die genauso aussehen, sich genauso bewegen und genauso verhalten wie richtige Dinosaurier. Der schlagendste Beweis für unseren Erfolg aber ist, daß die Zuschauer diese Wesen nicht für computergeneriert halten.» (Industrial Light & Magic)

animals walk, their bellies sway to and fro from the weight. When they run, their entire body reverberates with each footstep', Muren explains. 'Look for subtleties in the way the velociraptor tenses her body when she is startled. She looks alert and intelligent.'

'Working on 'Jurassic Park' has been the most exciting and challenging experience I've had in all my years as a visual effects supervisor', concludes Muren. 'The results we achieved on this film exceeded my wildest expectations. Using computers to create full-motion dinosaurs – creatures that look, move and behave like real dinosaurs – was immensely satisfying. The fact that viewers can not tell these creatures were computer-generated is the strongest evidence of our success.'» (Industrial Light & Magic)

Goldene Nica
Jurassic Park, 1993
HW: SGI Image
SW: Alias, Softimage, Parallax, Pixar (RenderMan)

COMPUTER ANIMATION

DENNIS MUREN/MARK DIPPÉ/ILM

Goldene Nica
Jurassic Park, 1993
HW: SGI Image
SW: Alias, Softimage, Parallax, Pixar (RenderMan)

COMPUTERANIMATION

MARC CARO

Marc Caro (F) begann seine Karriere als Comics-Zeichner für französische und amerikanische Magazine (Métal Hurlant, Charlie-Hebdo, Hara-Kiri, L'Écho des Savannes und Raw). Wechselte in der Folge das Metier und produziert seit 1981 Kurzfilme, Video-Clips und Jingles, u. a. gemeinsam mit Jean-Pierre Jeunet. Kurzfilmpreise (Grand Prix du Festival de Lille, Prix à Grenoble). 1991 gemeinsam mit Jean-Pierre Jeunet Buch und Regie zum Spielfilm „Delicatessen".

■ «‚K.O. KID' zeigt einen rhythmischen Boxkampf zwischen einem bestialischen Monster und einem Schwächling mit Spitznamen K.O. KID. In drei Runden gewinnt K.O. KID unerwartet durch K.O. über seinen korpulenten Gegner.
Grundprinzipien
Es ist ein Boxkampf, der wie ein Zeichentrickfilm behandelt wird. Aber anstelle gezeichneter Figuren handelt es sich um reale Personen, die alle typischen Veränderungen des Cartoons durchmachen. Vorbild für diese Cartoons ist Tex Avery.
Die Geschichte
Es sind Auszüge aus einem Boxkampf mit den Highlights einer jeden Runde. Der Kleine verhält sich wie eine glitschige Seife, und der Dicke zerstört den ganzen Ring, Schiedsrichter inbegriffen, indem er versucht, ihn zu schlagen. Das Ausweichen des Kleinen wird durch alle 3D-Möglichkeiten der Personen wiedergegeben. Am Ende gewinnt der Kleine durch K.O..
Die Regie
Die Erzählweise ist rhythmisiert, jeder Schlag ein Effekt: ein Boxkampf à la Charlie Chaplin, David gegen Goliath.
Die Personen:
– Der Böse: Die Bestie.
– Der Nette: Klein, mager, ängstlich, zitternd versteckt er sich hinter dem Schiedsrichter. Er verbringt seine Zeit mit dem Versuch, der Bestie zu entkommen, indem er alle Möglichkeiten ausschöpft, die ihm der Ring bietet. Er

Marc Caro (F) began his career as a comics artist for French and American magazines (Métal Hurlant, Charlie Hebdo, Hara-Kiri, L'Écho des Savannes and Raw). Subsequently changed profession and has been producing short films, music videos and jingles since 1981, some in collaboration with Jean-Pierre Jeunet. Short film prizes (Grand Prix du Festival de Lille, Prix à Grenoble). Co-wrote screenplay for and co-directed the feature film "Delicatessen" (1991) together with Jean-Pierre Jeunet.

■ «'K.O. KID' shows a rhythmic boxing match between a bestial monster and a weakling with the nickname K.O. KID. In three rounds K.O. KID wins an unsuspected victory over his mighty opponent.
Summary
A boxing match straight out of a cartoon. But instead of painted figures, we see real people going through all the typical sight gags of a cartoon, taking Tex Avery as a model.
The Story
These are excerpts from a boxing match with the highlights from each round. The little one is a slippery customer; to get at him the big one has to smash up the ring – referee included. To render the Kid's dodging, the characters are put through every three-dimensional possibility. In the end, the Kid wins by a Knockout.
The direction
The narrative style is on the rhythmic side, every punch cues an effect. It is a boxing match à la Charlie Chaplin; David vs. Goliath.
The characters:
– The baddie: the big brute.
– The goodie: small, thin, timid, trembling, he hides behind the referee and spends his time trying to escape the brute by any means the ring can offer him. He is astonishingly good at escaping and has a certain skill with his fists which allows him to place his punches.
Introduction
Moving, blood-red silken material fills the

COMPUTERANIMATION

MARC CARO

besitzt eine erstaunliche Fertigkeit im Ausweichen und eine gewisse Kompetenz im Boxen, die es ihm erlaubt, seine Schläge zu plazieren.

Einleitung

Close-up auf einen seidigen, blutroten Stoff, der sich bewegt. Kameraauffahrt, wodurch der Titel ‚K.O. KID', gestickt mit weißer Seide, erscheint. Blitzlicht.
Man bemerkt, daß der Titel des Films im Grunde genommen auf dem Bademantel des Boxers steht, der sich unter den Blitzlichtsalven der Photoapparate in Richtung Ring entfernt. Man findet unseren Boxer wieder, wie er zwischen den Seilen des Rings durchklettert, deren Vibrationen die Baßlinien der Filmmusik anheben lassen.
Schwenk, der den Gegner ins Bild bringt: einen Goliath mit Verbrecherfratze in der anderen Ecke des Rings. Im Vordergrund erscheint der Schiedsrichter, der das von der Decke hängende Mikrophon nimmt, um die beiden Gegner anzukündigen.
Unsere zwei Boxer haben ihre Bademäntel abgelegt und kommen in die Mitte des Rings, wo ihnen der Schiedsrichter die Kampfregeln erklärt. K.O. KID scheint ziemlich beunruhigt durch die Drohgebärden der Bestie.
Großaufnahme der zwei Handschuhpaare, die sich treffen werden. Übergang zum Gong der ersten Runde.

screen. The camera pulls back to reveal the title 'K.O. KID', embroidered in white silk. Camera flashbulbs go off.
We see that the title of the film is written on the robe of a boxer, who is on his way to the ring under a hail of camera flashes.
We rejoin our boxer as he climbs through the ring ropes, which can be seen vibrating with the bass-lines of the score.
The camera pans to reveal the adversary in the opposite corner of the ring, a Goliath with the features of a thug. The referee appears in the foreground and uses the microphone suspended from the ceiling to announce the two rivals.
Our two boxers have taken off their robes and stepped to the middle of the ring where the referee explains the rules to them. K.O. KID seems rather unsettled by the brute's threats.
Close-up on the two pairs of gloves that are going to meet. Transition gong to the first round.

Round One
Observation phase.
The fierce beast. The floor shakes with every step. K.O. KID evades, ducks and flees (à la Charlie Chaplin). He ends up taking a punch, but is saved by the gong.
K.O. KID washes his mouth out while his opponent looks daggers. Transition by means of

Goldene Nica
K.O. KID, 1993, 3.20 min
HW: Arnault Lamorlett
SW: Buf Software

COMPUTERANIMATION

MARC CARO

Erste Runde
Beobachtungsphase.
Wildes Gehabe der Bestie. Mit jedem Schritt zittert der Boden. Ausweichen und Flucht von K.O. KID (à la Charlie Chaplin). Dieser bekommt schließlich einen Schlag, wird aber durch den Gong gerettet.
K.O. KID spült sich den Mund, während sein Gegner die Augen funkeln läßt. Übergang durch eine Kamerazufahrt in das blaugeschlagene Auge von K.O. KID. Das Spiegelbild des Gegners, das sich bedrohlich nähert, ist der Übergang zur zweiten Runde.

Zweite Runde
K.O. KID wird in seinen Täuschungsmanövern und in seinem Ausweichen immer sicherer. Er besticht mit wunderbarer Beinarbeit. Sein Gegner, der immer wütender wird, hat Schwierigkeiten, ihn zu erreichen, obwohl seine Schläge Teile des Rings zerstören.
Das Ende der zweiten Runde läßt unsere Bestie total entkräftet zurück. Er stillt seinen Durst im Kübel neben seinem Hocker. Zufahrt ins trübe Wasser auf dem Kübelgrund, Übergang zur dritten und letzten Runde.

Dritte Runde
Dieses Mal greift K.O. KID an. Eine Serie von Haken und Uppercuts macht seinem Gegner schwer zu schaffen. Mit einer letzten, rechten Geraden schickt er schlußendlich die riesige Bestie B.O. auf die Bretter.

Finale
Unter dem Applaus und dem Knistern der Blitzlichter erklärt der Schiedsrichter K.O. KID zum Sieger durch K.O. Eine Kamerabewegung nach hinten läßt uns die Zuschauer entdecken, die mit Boxhandschuhen frenetisch unserem Champion applaudieren.
Ablaufender Nachspann mit Überblendung.» (Marc Caro)

a camera movement into K.O. KID's black eye. The mirror image of his ominously looming opponent takes us into...

Round Two
K.O. KID becomes more self-assured in his bluffs and dodges. He charms us with magnificent legwork. His ever more furious adversary has difficulty reaching him, even though his punches destroy parts of the ring.
The end of round two leaves our brute completely drained of power. He quenches his thirst in the bucket next to his stool. From the murky water in the bottom of the bucket, a transition takes us to the third and final round.

Round Three
This time K.O. KID counters. A series of hooks and upper cuts forces his enemy to go on the defensive. With a final straight right he sends the enormous brute crashing to the canvas.

Finale
To cheers and a volley of flash bursts the referee declares K.O. KID the winner by a knockout. The camera tracks back to reveal the spectators wildly applauding our champion.
The rolling credits fade in.» (Marc Caro)

Goldene Nica
K.O. KID, 1993, 3.20 min
HW: Arnault Lamorlett
SW: Buf Software

COMPUTERANIMATION

MAURICE BENAYOUN

Maurice Benayoun (F), geb. 1957, unterrichtet „Kunstvideo und neue Bilder" an der Universität Paris 1. Teilnahme an Forschungsarbeiten über Spezialeffekte und den Beitrag der neuen Technologien zur audiovisuellen Produktion und zum künstlerischen Schaffen am Centre de Recherche et d'Édude sur le Cinéma et les Arts Audiovisuels (CRECA) und des Centre de Recherche sur l'Image (CRI). 1993 Preisträger der Villa Medicis Hors Les Murs des Außenministeriums für sein Projekt „A.M.E.", einer zeitgenössischen Kunstsammlung in Virtual Reality. Zahlreiche Videos über Kunst.

■ «Am Anfang hat sich Gott geirrt!
Das war der Ausgangspunkt für QUARXS: Die Idee, daß das Computerzeichnen Mittel in die Hände des Menschen legte, die es ihnen ermöglicht, sich eine viel bessere oder viel schlechtere – auf jeden Fall andere – Welt vorzustellen. Eine Welt, für die die großen Prinzipien der Physik, der Biologie, der Optik sich verhöhnt, verneint, in ihr Gegenteil verkehrt finden. Und wenn diese Welt, die dem widerspricht, was die Wissenschaft und die Erfahrung uns lehren, mit der unseren zusammenstoßen würde? Wenn diese Wesen, die sich entwickeln, wachsen und sich kraft dieser paradoxen Gesetze vermehrten, sich mit unserem alltäglichsten, banalsten Umfeld konfrontiert fänden? Dann würden sie dazu gebracht werden, Erklärungen zu liefern für eine große Anzahl jener Vorfälle, die unser Leben säumen, und jener kleinen Zwischenfälle, die manchmal unerklärt bleiben; dann müßten sie jene Vorkommnisse erklären, die keinerlei völlig rationale Erklärung verdienen, und auch jene Phänomene, die dabei gewinnen, wenn man sie neu interpretiert.
Dieses Wieder-Lesen der Welt spürt die Eindeutigkeiten auf und ruft manchmal ebenso existentielle wie belanglose Interpretationen hervor. Die treibenden Kräfte, die das Benehmen der ‚Quarxs' lenken, sind trotz allem dieje-

Maurice Benayoun (F), born 1957, teaches "Art Video and New Images" at the University of Paris. Participation in research projects about special effects and the contribution of new technologies to audio-visual production and to artistic creativity within the Centre de Recherche et d'Étude sur le Cinema et les Arts Audiovisuels (CRECA) and the Centre de Recherche sur l'Image (CRI). 1993 prize-winner of the Villa Medicis Hors Les Murs of the Foreign Ministry for his A.M.E. project, a contemporary art collection in virtual reality. Numerous videos about art.

■ «In the beginning God made a mistake!
That was the starting point for QUARXS – the idea that computer graphics gave mankind a means for conceiving a world much better or much worse than our own, but a different world in any case. A world in which the great principles of physics, biology and optics find themselves ridiculed, negated, transformed into opposites of themselves. And what if this world, which contradicts everything science and experience have taught us, were to collide with our own? What if these beings that evolve, breed and multiply under these paradoxical laws found themselves confronted with this most everyday, most banal of universes? Then they would serve as an explanation for many of the little incidents and accidents which shape our lives but tend to remain unexplained; things which do not merit any totally rational explanation but are increasingly being re-interpreted.
This new conception of the world is on the lookout for certainties, and in the process it sometimes comes up with interpretations that are just as existential as they are futile. After all, the driving forces behind the Quarxs' behavior are the same ones that control real life: how to feed, how to reproduce, how to hide from predators (man, the scientist?), eventually to disappear. Maybe even this disappearing is not final, for in this case (as elsewhere) no truth

COMPUTERANIMATION

MAURICE BENAYOUN

nigen, die auch das Lebendige lenken. Wie sich ernähren, sich vermehren, vor den Verfolgern verstecken (dem Menschen, dem Wissenschafter?), um letztlich unterzugehen? Vielleicht ist dieser Untergang gar nicht endgültig, denn hier (wie anderswo) ist keine Wahrheit endgültig. Das ist vielleicht ein Zugeständnis, das man den Gesetzen des Genre machen muß.

Inzwischen sind sie aber da! Bis jetzt haben wir gut auch ohne sie gelebt, sie könnten uns jedoch helfen, eine oftmals zu absurde Welt zu ertragen, indem sie uns vollkommen unzufriedenstellende Nicht-Erklärungen vorschlagen. Der Realismus des Bildes verstärkt noch zusätzlich die Pseudo-Glaubwürdigkeit der Demonstration und der Beobachtung. Das Dekor stellt die beunruhigende Wunderlichkeit her, die dem Phantastischen so lieb ist. Aber hier keine Angst! Der Zuschauer fällt auf die Täuschung nur herein, weil er diese neue Übereinkunft, die Darstellung betreffend, akzeptiert, die das Computerbild auf halbem Weg zwischen dem photographischen Bild (dem des Kinos und des Videos) und der traditionellen Zeichentrickfilmtechnik situiert. Hier handelt es sich nicht um eine Welt des Cartoons. Niemals werden die ‚Quarxs' ein menschenähnliches Benehmen haben, auch nicht ein karikaturenhaftes. Sie behalten vom Menschen nur jene Grundmotivationen, die ihn dem Tierreich annähern.

Die ‚Quarxs' sind aus dem Wunsch heraus entstanden, ein Programm zu gestalten, dessen Personen direkt der Funktionalität des 3D-Computerbildes entsprungen sind. Der ‚Elastofragmentoplast' und der ‚Spatio Striata', zum Beispiel, führen häufig binäre Rechenvorgänge (Schnittpunkt des Volumens) aus, ebenso benutzt der ‚Polymorpho Proximens' synthetische Interpolationen (Verwandlung eines Objektes in ein anderes), um sich zu verstecken, und der ‚Mnemochrom', ein Bakterium mit hoch entwickeltem Sozialleben, scannt die Bilder der Meister, Punkt für Punkt, Zeile für Zeile, nach Art der Elektronenbündel, die den Video- oder den Computerschirm abtasten.

is final. Maybe that in itself is a concession to the laws of the genre.

Anyway, here they are! We've managed fine without them so far, but they might be able to help us cope with a world that is all too often absurd, by offering us completely unsatisfactory non-explanations.

The realism of the picture strengthens the pseudo-credibility of demonstration and observation. The decor inspires the unsettling strangeness that is so important to fantasy. But not to worry! The viewer only falls for the illusion because he accepts this new convention of representation, which places the computer image half-way between the photographic image (that of the cinema and video) and traditional animation. This is not about a cartoon universe. 'Quarxs' behavior will never be anthropomorphic or a caricature. All they have in common with humans are basic motivations like those found in the animal kingdom.

The 'Quarxs' were born from the desire to build a program around characters that owe their very existence to the functionality of 3-D computer graphics. The 'Elastofragmentoplast' and the 'Spatio Striata', for instance, continuously carry out Boolean operations (intersection of volumes) just as the 'Polymorpho Proximens' uses synthetic interpolation (metamorphosing one object into another) to conceal itself, and the 'Mnemochrom', a bacterium with a highly developed social life, scans the paintings of the masters – dot by dot, line by line, the same way cathode rays sweep across a video or computer screen.

Can Computer Life-Forms Move Like Real Ones?

In the traditional approach, a person is animated using observations of real movement: I examine a slow-motion film of a moving animal, derive phases of animation from it, modify them to amplify their expressive character and make them easier for the viewer to 'read'. The animation keys are subsequently used to simulate a typical animal movement

COMPUTERANIMATION

MAURICE BENAYOUN

Auszeichnung
QUARXS, 1993, 20.33 min
HW: SGI
SW: Softimage

COMPUTERANIMATION

MAURICE BENAYOUN

Können sich Computerwesen wie andere Wesen bewegen?
Nach dem traditionellen Ansatz entsteht die Animation der Person aus der Beobachtung von echten Bewegungen. Ich beobachte ein im Zeitraffer gefilmtes Tier, ich leite davon Animationsphasen ab, die ich verändere, um deren expressiven Charakter zu verstärken und ihre Lesbarkeit zu verbessern. Die Animationsschlüssel werden anschließend benutzt, um Bild für Bild eine typische Tierbewegung zu simulieren.
Für die Schaffung von einigen ‚Quarxs' haben wir den Prozeß verändert, um ihren besonderen Charaker zu berücksichtigen. Die so geschaffene Animation entsteht nicht durch die Beobachtung der Wirklichkeit, sondern durch die Anwendung von EDV-Prozessen.
Beim Beispiel des ‚Spatio Striata' bildet man einen Torus (einen Schwimmreifen …), man multipliziert ihn, um eine Serie von aneinandergereihten, regelmäßig verschobenen Tori zu bilden. Das Ganze gleicht also einem kannelierten Rohr … Jeder Torus wird dann mit einer vollkommen regelmäßigen Rotationsbewegung versehen (360° pro Sekunde zum Beispiel).
Das anfängliche ‚Rohr' scheint sich dann auf zyklische Art zusammenzuziehen (die Ringe machen abwechselnd horizontale und vertikale Phasen durch). Aber wenn man eine regelmäßige Zeitverschiebung in die Drehung von einem Ring zum folgenden einführt, erhält man eine Wellenbewegung, die der eines Regenwurms täuschend ähnelt, obwohl wir nie den Umriß seiner Fortbewegung nachgemacht haben. Wir haben ganz einfach auf experimentelle Art die Fortbewegungslogik nachgebildet. Hier ist es die Bewegung, die Form schafft!
Man kann nicht sagen, daß solche Prozesse in der traditionellen Zeichentrickfilmtechnik nicht auswertbar wären, aber sie eignen sich besonders gut für die numerische Animation.»
(Maurice Benayoun)

frame by frame.
For the construction of some 'Quarxs' we modified the style of movement to take their inherent character into consideration. The animation created by this method is not based on observations of reality, but by the application of data processing methods.
For instance, to make 'Spatio Striata' we create and multiply a lifebelt shape to form a series of identical, regulary spaced segments. The whole thing then resembles a rippled tube … Each segment is then put through a perfectly regular rotation movement (e.g. 360° per second).
The initial 'tube' then appears to contract in a cyclic fashion (the rings go through alternate horizontal and vertical phases). But if we introduce a regular time shift in the rotation from one ring to the next, we achieve a wave motion strikingly similar to that of an earthworm, without even having imitated its means of propulsion. We have quite simply reconstructed its means of propulsion by experimental means.
Here it is movement that creates the form!
It can not be said that such processes can not be used in traditional animation methods, but they are particularly well suited to animation by computational methods.» (Maurice Benayoun)

COMPUTERANIMATION

ERIC COIGNOUX

Eric Coignoux (F) lebt und arbeitet seit 1991 als Computeranimateur bei Mikros Images in Paris. Ausbildung an der Videoabteilung der École Nationale Supérieure des Arts Décoratifs/Paris. Spezielles Interesse am Mischen verschiedener Techniken wie Video, Animation, zweidimensionale Computergraphik (Harry, Paintbox), Typographie und Klang.

■ «Eric Coignoux fängt wieder an. Nach ‚Trashdance', der computergraphischen und donnernden Fassung von ‚Flashdance', kommt nun ‚No Sex', sommerlich-technische post-Aids-Raserei, elektronisches Ballett des Strandboys und der Bademeister, die unter heftigen erotischen Trieben leiden. Leider ist es in diesen Zeiten der Abstinenz angebracht, seine niedrigen Instinkte zu unterdrücken. Unsere Helden werden es auf ihre Kosten erlernen. Eine verführerische und in Verzückung geratene Nixe, bekleidet mit einem roten Badeanzug, verbreitet Schamlosigkeit und Verlangen auf dem Strand ... aber sie verweigert ihnen hartnäckig ihre Gunst. Zweifellos zeugt es von Vorsicht, sich mit seinem Strandzubehör zufriedenzustellen, mit Kübeln, Schaufeln, Schwimmreifen, Drachen. Zweifellos ist es gesünder, auf den Fang von Miesmuscheln, Austern und Seesternen zu gehen (ihrerseits exquisite vaginale Symbole).
Sie werden nebenbei auch die hohe Meisterschaft der Graphik und Animation, die perfekte Mischung von Video und numerischen Techniken, die Vorzüglichkeit der Montage und des Rhythmus (eine seltene Kenntnis bei Computergraphikern), ebenso wie die Feinheit der Illuminationen bemerken. For bitchboys only.» (Jean-Yves Barbichon)

«Ich habe bei der Gestaltung von ‚No Sex' versucht, die neuen Technologien auf eine andere Weise zu benützen – nämlich ohne jene Überfülle von Spezialeffekten –, indem ich den Computer als ein einfaches, graphisches und betastbares Ausdrucksmittel betrachtet habe.

Eric Coignoux (F) lives and works as a computer-animator at Mikros Images in Paris. Education at École Nationale Supérieure des Arts Décoratifs/Paris, video section. Especially interested and involved in "mixing" techniques: video, animation, 2-dimensional graphics/painting, typography and sound.

■ «Eric Coignoux is at it again. Following 'Trashdance', the thundering, computer graphics version of 'Flashdance', here comes 'No Sex', the frenzied techno-summer, post-aids electronic ballet featuring a beach warden and beach boys struggling with powerful erotic urges. In these times of abstinence, sadly, it is more prudent to keep one's base instincts under control, as our heroes will learn to their cost. A seductive siren in a red bathing outfit spreads shamelessness and desire across the beach ... but she obstinately denies them her favors. It would probably make more sense to be content with beach accessories – with buckets and spades, swimming tires, kites. No doubt it would be healthier to go fishing for mussels, oysters and starfish (equally exquisite vaginal symbols).
Along the way you will notice the impressive mastery of graphics and animation, the perfect mix of video and numerical techniques, the excellence of editing and rhythm (a skill seldom found in computer graphics artists), as well as the finely detailed painting. For bitchboys only.» (Jean-Yves Barbichon)

«In realizing 'No Sex' I have tried to use new technology in a different way, without overdoing the special effects, using the computer as a simple, graphic, tactile means of expression. It lets me 'mix' images from divese sources (video, photos, drawings, typography...).
I work in a different optical style than is usually associated with 'computer graphics': the image is dirtied, the animation is jerky, the rhythm nervous and the intention aggressive. The traditional narrative is sidelined in favour of an audio-visual experience in rhythm and editing,

COMPUTERANIMATION

ERIC COIGNOUX

Er erlaubt mir, Bilder aus verschiedenartigsten Quellen zu ‚mixen' (Video, Photo, Zeichnung, Buchdruck ...).
Ich arbeite mit einer anderen Optik, als man allgemein unter ‚Computergraphik' versteht: Das Bild ist verschmutzt, die Animation ruckartig, der Rhythmus nervös, die Absicht aggressiv. Die traditionelle Erzählweise lasse ich beiseite. Es sind eher die audiovisuellen Erfahrungen über den Rhythmus und die Montage, die Beziehungen zwischen den Farben, die den Bildern ihren Sinn geben.
‚No Sex' ist eine graphische und rhythmische Suche über die Themen Kommunikation/Nichtkommunikation, Frustration/Verlangen, Haß/Liebe, Erwachsener/Kind, Mann/Frau. Die Darstellung des Körpers ist der rote Faden. Die Körper werden behandelt, verformt, eingesperrt in den Rahmen des Videobildschirms. Sie werden ihn nicht verlassen können.
Die Figuren auf diesem Strand werden gequält, begehren sich, spielen, schreien, tanzen, bekriegen sich, aber letzten Endes kämpfen sie für nichts. Kommunikation wird nicht stattfinden.» (Eric Coignoux)

with color relationships making sense of the images.
'No Sex' is a graphic and rhythmic investigation of themes such as communication/non-communication, frustration/desire, hate/love, adult/child, man/woman. The representation of the body is the central theme. The bodies are treated, distorted, trapped in the frame of the video screen where they can't get out.
The characters on the beach are mistreated, they desire each other, they play, shout, dance, make war on each other, but in the end they are fighting in vain. Communication will not take place.» (Eric Coignoux)

Auszeichnung
No Sex, 1992, 5.00 min
HW/SW: Harry-Paintbox

COMPUTERANIMATION

ERIC COIGNOUX

**Auszeichnung
No Sex, 1992, 5.00 min
HW/SW: Harry-Paintbox**

COMPUTERANIMATION

BÉRIOU

Bériou? Das war ein Bergbewohner, der in einem verlorenen Tal in den Alpen lebte. Einen Teil seines Lebens verbrachte er damit, gemeinsam mit Freunden nach Gold zu graben. Eines Tages entdeckte er, daß seine Ader nur eine Mischung aus Kupfer und Eisen enthielt, das „Gold der Narren". Also verkaufte er, schlau wie er war, seine Goldmine an einen aus dem Flachland. Aber vorsichtig wie er ist, gräbt er noch immer selbst weiter. Seitdem gräbt Bériou Bild-Labyrinthe und baut Hügelgräber, um zu sich selbst zu finden.

■ «‚Tableau d'Amour' beginnt mit einer grauen Landschaft, über die sich ein Raster gelber Linien zieht. Das Schlußbild zeigt ein üppiges Design organischer Materie und enthüllt ein Modell labyrinthischer Körperstrukturen. Zwischen diesen beiden Sequenzen entspinnt sich eine Liebesgeschichte.
Dieser Übergang beinhaltet neun Szenen, die durch neun getrennte Inkarnationen führen, die jeweils neun erotische Posen oder Gefühlsstimmungen darstellen. Neun Mal Liebe, trotzdem nur eine Liebe.
Ein Mann und eine Frau, voneinander abgegrenzt durch Körperkonturen, die aus der Bildsprache der abendländischen Malerei entnommen sind, werden in andauernder Veränderung gezeigt, entweder interagierend oder fast wie sich am Himmel über der Landschaft paarende Fische. Und dann plötzlich bahnen sich ihre Einheiten zu einer erotischen Pose.
Die Infrastruktur beinhaltet ein Betrachtungsgerät, das durch die Anwesenheit eines Suchers und eines Augenpaares, die durch verschiedene Öffnungen in der Landschaft spähen, konkret repräsentiert wird. Dieses Betrachtungsgerät erzwingt eine zweifache Entwicklung. Einerseits sind die Liebenden eingefrorene Stanzen, Modelle für spätere labyrinthische Körperstrukturen, andererseits werden beide in Objekte mit unauslöschlichem Erdbezug transformiert, die dann in das Farbmuster des Schlußbildes eingearbeitet werden.» (Bériou)

Bériou? He was a mountain guy who used to live in a lost valley in the Alps. He spent part of his life with his friends digging for gold in a mine. One day he realised that the seam he was working on was just a mixture of copper and iron – "fools' gold". So, crafty as he was, he sold the mine to someone from the flatlands. But, careful as he is, he keeps on digging himself. Ever since then Bériou has been digging at the labyrinths of images and building rockpiles in order to find himself.

■ *«'Tableau d'amour' opens on a grey, desert-like landscape with an overlay of yellow grid lines. The final tableau displays a rich design of organic matter and reveals a module of labyrinthian body structures. Between those two sequences, a love story has unraveled.
This transition comprises nine scenes leading through nine separate incarnations which are also nine erotic poses or sentimental variations. Nine loves, one single love.
A man and a woman, defined with body frames retrieved from the corpus of Western painting, are shown in constant mutation, interactive and otherwise, reminiscent of two fish mating above a landscape. Suddenly, their entities strike out some erotic pose.
This infrastructure includes a viewing device which is concretized by the presence of a viewfinder and eyes peering through various landscape ports. The viewing device forces a dual development. On one hand, the lovers are frozen cut-outs which will be used as modules for future labyrinthian body structures. On the other hand, both characters are transformed into objects with indelible earth connotations which will be integrated to the color spotted final tableau.» (Bériou)*

COMPUTERANIMATION

BÉRIOU

**Anerkennung
Tableau d'Amour, 1993, 5.25 min
HW: Hewlett-Packard
SW: Synthetic Video 4**

COMPUTERANIMATION

PETER CALLAS

Peter Callas (AUS), geb. 1952, Bachelor of Arts an der University of Sydney. Bild- und Tonassistent bei ABC Television, Sydney. 1980 Abschluß des Kunststudiums am Sydney College of the Arts. 1982–90 Lehrbeauftragter für Videokunst am City Art Institute, Sydney College of the Arts; NSW Institute of Technology, Sydney; School of Art, University of Tasmania, Hobart. 1986 Video Artist in Residence am Marui Department Store, Tokio.

■ «‚Bilderbuch für Ernst Will' ist die Übertragung einer proto-televisionären Ikonomanie auf ein elektronisches Medium: nämlich die Schaffung von wahllos hergestellten, privaten Sammelbüchern für Bilder, ‚Bilderbüchern'. Diese Bücher hatten das mystische Vermögen, auf wundersame Art den Bodensatz und die einsamen Überbleibsel der Hochzeit der Buchdruckerkunst in der zweiten Hälfte des 19. Jahrhunderts auf das Prächtigste zu verwandeln.
Oft konnte die Zusammenstellung eines Buches zu einem anderen Zeitpunkt von einem anderen Menschen unter Einschluß anachronistischen Bildmaterials wieder aufgenommen werden. Dieser Typ eines prä-literarischen/post-verbalen und oft intrapersonellen Grundgedankens konnte zur Entstehung visueller Ausdrucksformen von erstaunlicher Klarheit führen, die der Frage nach dem Zweck bei der Herstellung von ‚Sinn' ausweichen und zur Entwirrung einer Art Rätsel, eines rätselhaften Codes führen, der das Private im Umgang mit dieser Unmenge von aus Massenproduktion stammenden, öffentlichen Bildern von fernen Szenen, Ereignissen und Menschen sichtbar macht. Die zufällige Zusammenstellung von Stadtansichten, Forschungsreisen, Katastrophen, Schlachtenszenen und königlichen Porträts wird zur Magie in den Händen eines begnadeten Schnipslers wie Hans Christian Andersen oder jenes unbekannten Schöpfers des ‚Bilderbuchs für Ernst Will' im Wien der Kriegszeit.» (Peter Callas)

Peter Callas (AUS), born 1952, B.A. Honours, University of Sydney. 1975–78 Assistant film editor, sound editor, ABC Television, Sydney. 1980 Diploma in Art, Sydney College of the Arts. 1981–90 Lecturer for Video Art, City Art Institute, Sydney College of the Arts, NSW Institute of Technology, Sydney; School of Art, University of Tasmania, Hobart. 1986 Video Artist in Residence, Marui Department Store, Tokyo.

■ «'Bilderbuch für Ernst Will' is an electronic rendering of a form of proto-televisual iconomania: the creation of haphazardly sourced private pictorial scrap books or bilderbücher. Often intended for the surprise, delight and edification of grandchildren by grandparents, these books had the anagogical potential to become flamboyant transmogrifications of the detritus and sequestered oddments of the great age of print in the latter half of the 19th century.
Often the composition of a book might be re-entered at a later date by another hand with the inclusion of parachronic imagery. This type of pre-literate/post-verbal, and often intrapersonal, animus could lead to the creation of visual tropes of astonishing clarity. Such tropes beg the question of intention in the creation of 'meaning' and suggest the unravelling of a kind of rebus or enigmatic code which reveals the extremely private within the use of the plethora of mass-produced public images of distant scenes, events and people.
The fortuitous collocation of views of towns, voyages of exploration, catastrophes, battle scenes and royal portraits become mantic in the deft hands of an expert snipper such as Hans Christian Andersen or the unknown creator of Ernst Will's picture book in war-time Vienna.» (Peter Callas)

COMPUTERANIMATION

PETER CALLAS

Anerkennung
Bilderbuch für Ernst Will – A Euro Rebus, 1993, 11 min
HW/SW: Quantel Harriet, Fairlight CVI+

COMPUTERANIMATION

CASSIDY J. CURTIS

Cassidy J. Curtis (USA), Programmierer und Animator bei XAOS. Bevor er zu XAOS ging, arbeitete Curtis bei R/Greenberg and Associates in New York als Animator und Programmierer. Er absolvierte die Brown University mit einem Bachelor of Arts in Mathematik mit Schwerpunkten Computergraphik und Kunst.

■ «XAOS bekam den Auftrag für die Gestaltung der Titelanimation und Graphik von ‚MTV Top 20 Video-Countdown', die derzeit beliebteste Sendung von MTV. Sie wird international von jedem angeschlossenen Sender ausgestrahlt und ist in 78 Millionen Haushalten zu sehen. Die computergenerierten Bilder sind seit Anfang 1994 im Programm und sind das Ergebnis von Tests, die der Programmierer Cassidy Curtis mit rücklaufenden Zahlen, eingebettet in einen mehrfarbigen, flüssigen Hintergrund, anstellte und an MTV einschickte. Laut MTV-Produzent Robert Jason sind sie das perfekte Gegenstück zur Aufmachung des Senders.
Cassidy Curtis entwickelte auch die Software, die er zur Erstellung brauchte. Das Ziel, so erklärt er, war es, das Aussehen einer Flüssigkeit wie Wasserfarbe oder Tinte zu simulieren, die an einer Glasscheibe hinunterläuft und dabei einen Schmierfilm hinterläßt. Zum Schluß erinnert die Animation an ein ‚Naturphänomen', was in der Computergraphik eine schwierige Vorgabe ist.
Die spezielle Technik, die er dabei anwendet, bezeichnet er liebevoll als ‚ichor' und beschreibt es mit ‚Blut eines übernatürlichen Wesens'. Diesen Stoff konnte er mit bestimmten Eigenschaften ausstatten und steuerte seine Bewegung durch ‚Zwangsmaßnahmen' und nicht mit spezifischen Befehlen. Diese kontrollierte Zufälligkeit, wie sie in vielen XAOS-Softwareprogrammen zu finden ist, ahmt Qualitäten nach, wie sie in der Natur vorkommen, und gibt dem Ganzen ein natürlicheres Erscheinungsbild.» (XAOS)

Cassidy J. Curtis (USA), programmer and animator at XAOS. Prior to joining XAOS, Curtis worked as an animator and programmer at R/Greenberg and Associates in New York. He holds a B.A. in Math, with an emphasis in Computer Graphics and Art, from Brown University.

■ «MTV commissioned XAOS, the San Francisco computer animation and design facility known for its non-traditional style, to create the opening animation and graphics for their Top 20 Video Countdown, which is currently the most widely seen show on MTV. It is broadcast by every international MTV affiliate and shown in over 78 million homes worldwide. In the U.S., the show airs Fridays at noon and 8:00 p.m. as well as Saturday mornings. The computer generated graphics, which have appeared since 1994, are the result of tests created by XAOS programmer Cassidy Curtis. XAOS sent these tests, which featured a countdown of numbers integrated into a fluid multi-color background, to MTV. According to Robert Jason, MTV's producer of the opening and packaging, they were the 'perfect counterpart' to the MTV design.
According to Curtis, who developed the software and created the graphics, the idea was to simulate the appearance of a liquid, such as watercolor or ink, that leaves behind a film as it slides down a glass surface. The final piece is 'reminiscent of a natural phenomenon', which is a difficult challenge in computer graphics.
Curtis affectionately refers to the technique he used in creating the software as 'ichor' which he describes as 'blood of a supernatural being'. He was able to create this substance with specific attributes, and he controlled its motion through coersion as opposed to specific commands. Inherent in much of XAOS software, this 'controlled randomness' mimics those qualities found in nature, creating a more naturalistic appearance.» (XAOS)

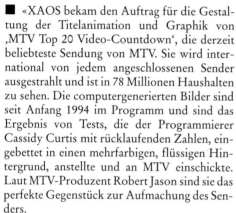

COMPUTERANIMATION

CASSIDY J. CURTIS

Anerkennung
MTV Top 20 Video Countdown Graphics, 1993, 0.45 min
HW: SGI Workstations
SW: XAOS Proprietary

COMPUTER ANIMATION

ERIC DARNELL/MICHAEL COLLERY

Eric Darnell (USA) ist Animator und Mitglied der Character Animation Group bei Pacific Data Images (PDI), Sunnyvale. Er graduierte am California Institute of the Arts zum Master of Fine Arts. Bevor er zu PDI kam, arbeitete er an einer Reihe von Animationen für Musikvideos und Werbespots sowie als Animationslehrer für High-School-Studenten.
Michael Collery (USA) ist Chefanimateur und Effects Supervisor bei PDI. Bevor er zu PDI kam, arbeitete er sieben Jahre bei Cranston-Csuri und wirkte an einer Reihe preisgekrönter Filme mit. Er ist Master of Fine Arts der Ohio State University.

■ «Weltweit hatten nun Erdlinge Gelegenheit, in eine außerirdische und doch irgendwie eigenartig wohlbekannte Welt zu blicken. Diese machte ihren Weg von den Computerbildschirmen des Computeranimations- und Special-Effects-Studios von Pacific Data Images (PDI) über Programmkinos, internationale Filmfestivals zu den öffentlich-rechtliche Fernsehstationen und MTV. ‚Gas Planet', bevölkert von pastellfarbenen, langschnäuzigen, ballonartigen Kreaturen, die eine bestimmte Pflanzenart fressen, was sich ähnlich auswirkt wie der Verzehr von Bohnen bei Erdlingen, ist eine Schöpfung von Eric Darnell.
Um den Eindruck einer händisch gezeichneten Animation entstehen zu lassen, entwickelte der Animator Michael Collery, der für diesen Film die Rolle des Technical- und Art-Directors innehatte, eine eigene Software. Und indem er mit einer ganzen Reihe von Bildbearbeitungstechniken experimentierte, entwickelte er dabei ein Aussehen, das die organischen Qualitäten eines handgezeichneten Bildes mit den Vorteilen dreidimensionaler Computeranimation in Einklang bringt.» (Eric Darnell/Michael Collery)

Eric Darnell (USA), animator and member of the Character Animation Group at Pacific Data Images (PDI), Sunnyvale. Master of Fine Arts from the California Institute of the Arts. Before joining PDI he worked on a series of animations for music videos and commercials as well as instructing high school students in animation.
Michael Collery (USA), senior animator and effects editor at PDI. Previously worked at Cranston-Csuri where his credits included a number of prize-winning animations. Master of Fine Arts from Ohio State University.

■ «From the computer screens of Sunnyvale based computer animation/special effects studio, Pacific Data Images (PDI) to the film screen of local art house cinemas and international film festivals to television screens tuned into public tv and MTV, earthling audiences worldwide have had the opportunity to take a look into an alien, yet comically familiar place. 'Gas Planet', filled with pastel colored, long snouted, balloon-like creatures ingesting a strange plant life which produces effects similar to those of bean eating earthlings, is the product of filmmaker Eric Darnell.
Animator Michael Collery, who served as the Art/Technical Director on the film, developed custom software to achieve the effects animation and also worked with Eric to achieve the hand-drawn look of the piece. Experimenting with a variety of image processing techniques, Michael developed a look which reflected the organic qualities of hand-drawn imagery while maintaining the three-dimensional advantages available through computer animation.» (Eric Darnell/Michael Collery)

COMPUTERANIMATION

ERIC DARNELL/MICHAEL COLLERY

Anerkennung
Gas Planet, 1992, 3.30 min
HW: SGI Personal Iris
SW: PDI Proprietary

COMPUTERANIMATION

YOICHIRO KAWAGUCHI

Yoichiro Kawaguchi (J), geb. 1952. 1978 graduierte er zum Master of Fine Arts an der Tokyo University of Education. Derzeit Associate Professor of Computer Graphics Art am Art & Science Lab, Department of Art, Nippon Electronics College, Tokio. 1975 erste Computerbilder, seit 1986 Forschungsarbeit zum High Definition TV (HDTV). Zahlreiche Preise, u. a. bei Eurographics 84; Grand Prix PARIGRAPH 87; erster Preis bei Imagina 91 und Eurographics 92.

■ «In dem Stück ‚Artificial Life Metropolis CELL' möchte ich dreidimensionale Computerbilder, also plastische Computerkunst, die auf dem Grundprinzip zellularer Modelle basiert, vom Standpunkt der Kunst aus darstellen. Die Selbstorganisation des dreidimensionalen Raums, der sich aus einer Masse von ‚Voxels' zusammensetzt, kann einen sich komplex ändernden Raum hervorrufen. Die Idee entspringt der Theorie der Selbstautomatisation im zweidimensionalen Raum. Ein Modell, das auf einem dreidimensionalen Zellmodell basiert, kann aus einer sehr einfachen Grundformel unvorhersehbare, zerbrechliche Vibrationen entstehen lassen.
Wir verwenden ein Gitternetz von Koordinaten, um Leben und Tod der Zellen im dreidimensionalen Raum zu simulieren. Den Begriff ‚Voxel' wenden wir für die Grundeinheit eines zellularen Würfels im Koordinatensystem an. Eine Gruppe von ‚Voxels' bildet dabei ein dreidimensionales Objekt, so wie Millionen von Zellen in der Natur lebendige Formen ergeben. Es handelt sich dabei um eine künstlerische Anwendung der dreidimensionalen Zellautomatisation. Der Erfolg des selbstorganisierenden Systems ist also abhängig von der Animation des dreidimensionalen Kunstwerks, die der Gegenstand der Experimente innerhalb des Kontexts des Voxel-Raums ist.» (Yoichiro Kawaguchi)

Yoichiro Kawaguchi (J), born 1952. Master of Fine Arts from Tokyo University of Education in 1978. Currently he is Associate Professor of Computer Graphics Art at Art & Science Lab, Department of Art, Nippon Electronics College, Tokyo. 1975 first computer images, since 1986 involved in research work for High Definition TV (HDTV). Numerous awards, e. g. Eurographics 84; Grand Prix PARIGRAPH 87; first Prize Imagina 91, first Prize – Art Eurographics 92.

■ «In the piece 'Artificial Life Metropolis CELL' I would like to present three-dimensional plastic art as represented by a computer image using the basic principle of a cellular model as seen from an artistic point of view. The self-organization of a three-dimensional space, which is composed of a mass of 'voxel', can generate complex evolving space. This idea is inspired by the theory of self-organizing automaton in two-dimensional space. A model based on a three-dimensional cell model is capable of inducing unpredictable, delicate and emergent vibration using one simple rule.
We use grid coordinates to simulate the life and death of a cell in three-dimensional space. We also use the term of 'voxel' as an elemental cube in the grid coordinates. A group of 'voxel' make up a three-dimensional object, just as millions of cells make up a natural life form.
The success of the self-organizing system of the voxel is correlative to the animation of plastic art, which is the object of experimentation within the context of voxel space.» (Yoichiro Kawaguchi)

COMPUTERANIMATION

YOICHIRO KAWAGUCHI

Anerkennung
Artificial Life Metropolis CELL, 1993, 4.03 min
HW: SGI Iris
SW: Improved 3-D Cell Algorithm by Yoichiro Kawaguchi

COMPUTERANIMATION

SABINE MAI/FRANK PRÖSCHOLDT

Sabine Mai (D), geb. 1965 in Miltenberg am Main. 1988–94 Studium der bildenden Künste in Nürnberg.
Frank Pröscholdt (D), geb. 1965 in Heide. Freier Programmierer. Zusammenarbeit am Projekt „Generative Systeme" seit 1991.

■ «Programm:
Das Projekt ‚Generative Systeme' untersucht die Entwicklung paralleler Automaten in geschlossenen Systemen.
Jeder Automat ist mit einer Reihe von Grundfunktionen ausgestattet. Diese enthalten Anweisungen zur spezifischen Interaktion mit anderen Elementen. Dazu gehören die Wahrnehmung benachbarter Felder (Umgebungsanalyse), die individuelle Entscheidung und eine Reihe von Aktionsmöglichkeiten zur Veränderung der Umgebung.
Die graphische Darstellung der Systeme ist die Bildschirmoberfläche. Jeder Pixel repräsentiert einen Automaten und zeigt dessen aktuelle Position.
Der Einflußbereich der Automaten umfaßt jeweils acht Nachbarfelder. In einem System befinden sich bis zu 81.920 Elemente nebeneinander, deren Aktionsfelder sich überschneiden und so im zeitlichen Ablauf einen vernetzten Wirkungskomplex bilden.
Prozeß:
Jeder Automat hat einen eng begrenzten Wirkungsradius, dessen Einfluß sich im zeitlichen Verlauf fortsetzt und so auf die Gesamtkonstellation einwirkt. Die Algorithmen sind determiniert, auf Zufall wurde verzichtet.
Intention:
Ziel der Arbeit ist es, eine generative Programmentwicklung zu betreiben. Die Systeme sind niemals auf einen Endzustand hin konzipiert. Eine Versuchsanordnung und die aus ihr gewonnenen Erkenntnisse dienen als Grundlage für eine erneute Dekonstruktion der algorithmischen Zusammenhänge. Der Programmkomplex wird dabei weiter differenziert und – wenn notwendig – von Grund auf neu festgelegt.» (Sabine Mai/Frank Pröscholdt)

Sabine Mai (D), born 1965 in Miltenberg am Main, studied visual arts in Nuremberg from 1988 to 1994.
Frank Pröscholdt (D), born 1965 in Heide, is a freelance programmer and has worked on the "Generative Systems Project" since 1991.

■ *«Program:*
The 'Generative Systems' project examines the development of parallel automatons in closed systems.
Every automaton is equipped with a number of basic functions. These contain instructions for specific interaction with other elements. That includes the perception of neighbouring fields (surroundings analysis), individual decision-making, and a number of possible actions for changing the environment.
The systems are depicted on the screen. Each pixel represents an automaton and shows its momentary position.
An automaton's sphere of influence comprises eight neighbouring fields. A system can include up to 81,920 elements with overlapping fields of action which, over a period of time, act as a networked, integrated active complex.
Process:
Each automaton has a narrow radius of influence which spreads its influence in the course of time, thus affecting the whole configuration. The algorithms are deterministic, nothing is left to chance.
Intention:
The object of this work is to operate a generative programming development. The systems are not conceived with a final state in mind; the arrangement and the knowledge acquired as a result serve as the basis for a renewed deconstruction of the algorithmic connections. In the process, the program complex is further varied and – if necessary – rebuilt from the ground up.» (Sabine Mai/Frank Pröscholdt)

COMPUTERANIMATION

SABINE MAI/FRANK PRÖSCHOLDT

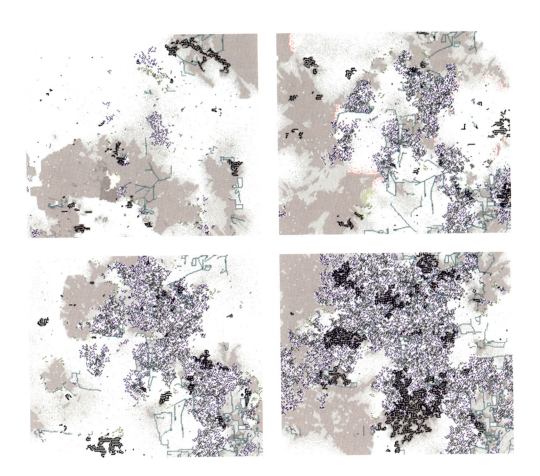

Anerkennung
Generative Systeme – System 2, 1994, 6 min
HW: Amiga 4000
SW: C++

COMPUTERANIMATION

JOHN TONKIN

John Tonkin (AUS), geb. 1963, ist bildender Künstler mit Schwerpunkt auf Film und Video. Mit der Computeranimation begann er 1986 nach seinem wissenschaftlichen und künstlerischen Studium. Seine Arbeiten wurden international ausgestellt, zuletzt auf der SIGGRAPH 93 und bei FISEA.

■ «‚these are the days' handelt vom Vergehen der Zeit, dargestellt anhand einer auf physikalischer Ebene angesiedelten Simulation von fallenden, weißen Papierblättern. Indem ich die mathematischen Modelle verschiedener physikalischer Phänomene wie Schwerkraft, Elastizität und Aerodynamik miteinander kombiniere, erstelle ich Simulationen der tatsächlichen Welt im virtuellen Raum. Obwohl die Simulationen relativ stark vereinfachen, ist die Bewegung, die sie darstellen, gleichzeitig komplex und naturalistisch. Neben den formalen Qualitäten, die in diesem Stück untersucht werden, bin ich auch an anderen Lesarten dieser Zusammenstellung interessiert.

Unser Leben wird in einer andauernden Flut von Papier dokumentiert. Jeder noch so kleine Übergang, jede Veränderung, wird auf einem Stück Papier vermerkt, von der Geburt bis zum Tod, von Zeugnissen bis hin zu Kassenzetteln aus dem Supermarkt.

Die Auswirkungen der Schwerkraft sind oft als eine Metapher für die Vergänglichkeit der Zeit verwendet worden: das Fallen der Blätter, der Sand, der durch eine Sanduhr rieselt, die Blätter, die von einem Abreißkalender abfallen.

Der endlose Strom fallenden Papiers wirkt wie ein meditativer Ausschnitt eines Wasserfalls, zeugt aber auch von Konsum und Verschwendung.» (John Tonkin)

John Tonkin (AUS), born 1963. Visual artist with a background in film and video making. Began working with computer animation in 1986 after studying science and visual art. His work has been exhibited internationally, most recently at SIGGRAPH 93 and FISEA.

■ «'these are the days' is about the passing of time. It is a physically based simulation of falling white paper.

By combining mathematical models of different physical phenomena such as gravity, elasticity and aerodynamics, I create simulations of real world systems in virtual space. Although these simulations are relatively simplistic, the motion they exhibit is both complex and naturalistic.

As well as the formal qualities that are explored in this work, I am interested in other readings suggested by the installation: our lives are documented by a continual stream of paper, every major and minor transition/transaction is marked on a piece of paper – from birth and death certificates to supermarket receipts.

The action of gravity has often been used as a metaphor for the passing of time; the falling of leaves, sands through the hour glass, pages blowing from a calendar.

The endless stream of falling paper suggests the meditative space of a waterfall, yet also speaks of consumption and waste.» (John Tonkin)

COMPUTERANIMATION

JOHN TONKIN

Anerkennung
these are the days, 1994, 1.40 min
HW: Commodore Amiga
SW: Artist's Proprietary

COMPUTERANIMATION

HIDEO YAMASHITA/EIHACHIRO NAKAMAE

Hideo Yamashita (J), Professor am Laboratorium für Elektrotechnik, Universität Hiroshima. Seine Arbeit betrifft v. a. Computergraphik und wissenschaftsorientierte Visualisierung. Eine seiner letzten Arbeiten, die im HDTV-Verfahren aufgezeichnet wurde, beschäftigt sich mit der Visualisierung der Verteilung von Elektromagnetismus in Induktionsmotoren.
Eihachiro Nakamae (J), Professor an der Abteilung Management und Informatik, Universität Hiroshima. Er studierte Computergraphik. Eine Reihe seiner Arbeiten wurden bei der SIGGRAPH in verschiedenen Kategorien gezeigt. Seine Arbeiten beschäftigen sich v. a. damit, Lichteffekte zu simulieren.

■ «Die Animation ‚Rhapsody in Light and Blue' simuliert Beleuchtungseffekte, wie sie in einem Hallenbad auftreten, das von mehreren Lichtquellen sowohl über als auch unter Wasser beleuchtet wird.
Eine Kombination verschiedenfarbiger Lichter, die sich ein- und ausschalten, aktivieren die Animation. Ein ganzer Reigen von Lichtern leuchtet da in ein nächtliches Hallenbad. Die verschiedensten Lichtcharaktere werden gesetzt, sowohl an die Wände des Bades als auch unter Wasser. Und jedes der Lichter schaltet sich auf seine eigene Art und Weise aus und ein. Reflexionen und Lichtbrechungen entstehen auf der Wasseroberfläche, werden vom Wasser zerstreut oder im Wasser absorbiert, Schatten werden auf die Wasseroberfläche geworfen.
Um photorealistische Bilder, die Wasserbereiche mit einschließen, zu rendern, bedarf es neuester Techniken, die auf optischen Phänomenen aufbauen, z. B. Streuung und Absorption von Licht.» (Hideo Yamashita/Eihachiro Nakamae)

Hideo Yamashita (J), professor in the Electric Machinery Laboratory at Hiroshima, working with computer graphics and scientific visualisation. Co-director of the computer animation "Rhapsody in Light and Bleu" which was shown at SIGGRAPH 93. One of his latest visualisation works, "Electromagnetic Distributions in an Induction Motor", was recorded in an HDTV format.
Eihachiro Nakamae (J), professor in the Hiroshima University Department of Management and Information Science. Studied computer graphics; a number of his works have been shown in various categories at SIGGRAPH. His works are mainly concerned with simulating light effects.

■ «The animation 'Rhapsody in Light and Blue' simulates the lighting effects in an indoor pool lit by multiple light sources both above and beneath the water.
The combination of various colors of light and the turning on and off of the light make this animation active.
A festival of light is held in an indoor swimming pool in the night. Various kinds of light are set both on the walls and under the water. Each light turns on and off in its own way.
The light is reflected and refracted on the surfaces of the water; the light is scattered and absorbed in the water, and shadows are cast on water surfaces.
To render photo-realistic images including water region, many latest techniques based on optical phenomena, such as scattering and absorption of light, are employed.» (Hideo Yamashita/Eihachiro Nakamae)

COMPUTER ANIMATION

HIDEO YAMASHITA/EIHACHIRO NAKAMAE

Anerkennung
Rhapsody in Light and Blue, 1993, 1.34 min
HW: SGI Iris and NEC EWS
SW: RAYSKY (In-House Software)

COMPUTERANIMATION

THOMAS ZANCKER

Thomas Zancker (D), geb. 1956; Studium der freien Kunst an der Hochschule für bildende Kunst in Hamburg bei Prof. Sigmar Polke und Prof. Fritz Heubach. Informatikstudium an der Uni Hamburg bei Prof. Schefe und Prof. Brunnstein. Seit 1991 Technischer Regisseur bei der Firma mental images in Berlin.

Thomas Zancker (D), born 1956, studied liberal arts at the Hochschule für bildende Kunst in Hamburg under Prof. Sigmar Polke and Prof. Fritz Heubach and computer science at the Universität Hamburg under Professor Schefe and Professor Brunnstein. Since 1991 he has been working at the mental images company in Berlin.

■ «In dem Film ‚Displaced Dice' (‚Verlegte Würfel'), erscheint ein Würfel ohne Augen im rotierenden Lichtkegel eines Scheinwerfers. Im weiteren Verlauf passiert dann Unerwartetes: Das Filmbild, das den Würfel im Licht des ihn umkreisenden Scheinwerfers wie in einem falsch gebauten Planetenmodell zeigt, verformt sich, während es nach hinten gleichsam in sich selbst hineinklappt. Während sich vor den Augen des Betrachters selten gesehene Formen entwickeln – wobei die Lichter als Höhen aus dem Bild herauswachsen –, wird das Filmbild selbst zur Landschaft und zur Form. Die zweidimensionale Projektion wird dreidimensional. Es entsteht eine neue Instanz im Film, in der nicht mehr der gefilmte Würfel, sondern der Film selbst, als wabernde Funktion seiner Helligkeiten, zum dargestellten Objekt wird. Diese Rückkopplung, in der der vorher berechnete Film selbst zum Ausgangsmaterial für eine neue Instanz wird, wiederholt sich noch zweimal, wobei das Chaos immer wilder zu werden scheint. Tatsächlich gibt es weder Zufallsgenerator noch ‚Chaosformeln' in der Berechnung der geometrischen Formen. Die sich abbildende Komplexität ist ausschließlich ein Ergebnis der sich rotierend verändernden Beleuchtung und der dreidimensionalen Interpretation der auftretenden Helligkeiten durch das verwendete Programm. Die Kamerafahrt am Schluß des Films führt dann in diese Landschaft und durch im Boden auftauchende Löcher (Augen) wieder zum Ausgangsmotiv, dem nächsten blinden Würfel.» (Thomas Zancker)

■ «In the film 'Displaced Dice', a die without eyes appears in a rotating beam of light from a spotlight. What follows is unexpected: the film image, showing the die in the light of the spotlight which is encircling it, re-forms itself, folding up into itself backwards at the same time. Rarely witnessed scenes develop in front of the eyes of the beholder, in which the lights protrude out of the picture as highs, and the picture itself becomes a landscape and a shape. The two-dimensional projection has become three-dimensional. A new thing takes shape in film, in which it is no longer the portrayed die, but the film itself which becomes the depicted object as a wab function of its brightness values/luminosity. This feedback, in which the previously calculated film itself becomes the raw material for a new instance, repeats itself twice, whereby the chaos seems to get ever wilder. In fact, there are neither random generators nor 'chaos formulae' in the calculation of the geometrical shapes. The self-representing complexity is exclusively a result of the emerging luminosity, of the rotating, changing lighting, and of the program used. The camera movement at the end of the film leads through this landscape and through the holes (eyes) appearing in the floor, back to the original motive, the next blind die.» (Thomas Zancker)

COMPUTERANIMATION

THOMAS ZANCKER

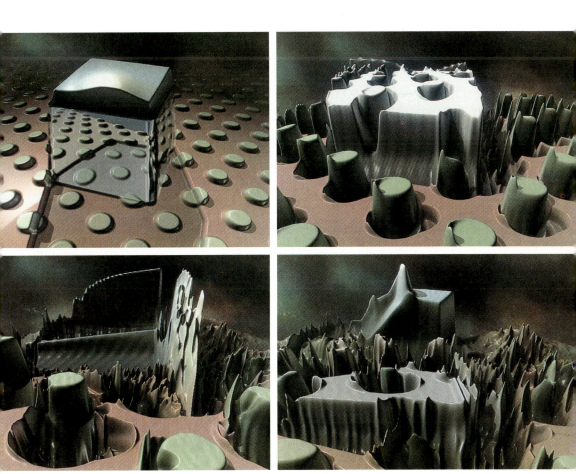

Anerkennung
Displaced Dice, 1994, 1.29 min
HW: Hewlett-Packard HP-735 (Cluster of 6)
SW: mental ray, Version 1.8

COMPUTERANIMATION

TAMÁS WALICZKY

Tamás Waliczky (H), geb. 1959, ist Animator und Maler, der seit 1986 Computer als künstlerisches Ausdrucksmittel verwendet. Zur Zeit erforscht er Computeranimation am Zentrum für Kunst und Medientechnologie in Karlsruhe. Seine Arbeiten wurden auf internationalen Festivals ausgestellt (SIGGRAPH 91 und 93, Imagina 90, 91 und 93, Prix Ars Electronica 88, 89 und 90). Auszeichnungen: u. a. Goldene Nica beim Prix Ars Electronica 89, 3. Preis bei Imagina 91 und World Graph Prize in Locarno 91. Zahlreiche Ausstellungen, Publikationen und Vorlesungen.

■ «‚Der Wald' ist eine Animation eines Waldes in schwarz-weiß, der sich entlang der x-, y- und z-Achse endlos erstreckt. Die Bewegung innerhalb des Waldes kann vorwärts, rückwärts, nach rechts und nach links erfolgen, ohne daß jemals ein Ende erreicht wird.
Es gibt keinen Startpunkt und kein Ziel. Es gibt keinen Himmel, keinen Boden, keinen Horizont. Es gibt keine Möglichkeit, keine Zeichen, sich im Raum zu orientieren. Nur die immer gleichen Bäume, wieder und wieder.
Die Animation ist eine fast fünf Minuten lange Reise innerhalb dieses seltsamen Waldes. Der Soundtrack suggeriert, daß der Betrachter sich in einem Zug befindet. Es reist noch jemand mit: Eine Frauenstimme wiederholt immer wieder dieselben Strophen eines deutschen Kinderliedes. Vielleicht versucht sie, ihr Kind in den Schlaf zu singen.
Die ganze Situation ist so seltsam und still. Falls man darauf aus ist, das Ende des Waldes zu erreichen oder die eigene Position zu orten, wird sie zum Alptraum. Wenn man aber einfach den Trip als solchen genießt, kann die Endlosigkeit des Waldes, das Rattern des Zuges und die Stimme des Mädchens den Betrachter zur Ruhe kommen lassen.» (Tamás Waliczky)

Tamás Waliczky (H), born 1959, is an animator and painter who has been using the computer as an artistic medium since 1986. Presently he is Computer Animation Researcher at the Zentrum für Kunst und Medientechnologie, Karlsruhe. His works have been shown internationally at such events as SIGGRAPH 91 and 93; Imagina 90, 91 and 93; Prix Ars Electronica 88, 89 and 90. Awards include the Golden Nica at Prix Ars Electronica 89, the Third Prize at Imagina 91 and the World Graph Prize at Locarno 91. Many international exhibitions, publications and lectures.

■ *« 'Der Wald' ('The Forest') is a monochrome animation of a forest which extends to infinity along the x, y, and z axes. Movement within the forest can take place forwards, backwards, leftwards and rightwards without ever reaching an end.*
There is no origin and no destination. There is no sky, no ground, no horizon. There is no basis, no reference points for spatial orientation. Just the very same trees over and over again.
The animation is an almost five minute journey through this peculiar forest. The soundtrack gives the viewer the impression of being on a train. The traveler is not alone: over and over again, a woman's voice repeats the same verses from a German nursery rhyme. Perhaps she is trying to sing her child to sleep.
The whole situation is so strange and quiet. If one's aim is to reach the end of the forest or to find out one's position, it becomes a nightmare. But if one simply enjoys the trip for its own sake, then the infinity of the forest, the rattling of the train, and the woman's voice allow the viewer some peace.» (Tamás Waliczky)

COMPUTERANIMATION

TAMÁS WALICZKY

Anerkennung
Der Wald, 1993, 4.54 min
HW: SGI Indigo Elan
SW: Softimage

INTERAKTIVE KUNST

INTERAKTIVE KUNST

CHRISTA SOMMERER/LAURENT MIGNONNEAU

Christa Sommerer (A), geb. 1964, Studium der Botanik an der Universität Wien. 1985 Bildhauereistudium an der Akademie der bildenden Künste Wien, Mag.art.; Post Graduate Stipendium an der Städelschule Frankfurt, Institut für Neue Medien (Peter Weibel). 1993/94 Vorlesungen u. a. in der School of Arts, New York; EVL-University Chicago; School of Art & Design, Champaign/Urbana; Eldorado Festival, Antwerpen; interActiva, Köln.
Laurent Mignonneau (F), geb. 1967, studierte drei Jahre lang angewandte Kunst an der École Technique Angoulême, 1987 Studium an der Academy of Fine Arts, Angoulême, in den Abteilungen Video sowie Computergraphik am CNBDI (Centre Nationale de la Bande Dessinée et de l'Image, Angoulême). 1989 Master of Arts für Bildhauerei und 1991 für Plastischen Ausdruck.

■ «Im interaktiven Echtzeit-Environment ‚A-Volve' können Besucher virtuelle tierähnliche Kreaturen erzeugen, die in einem wassergefüllten Glasbecken schwimmen und mit den Besuchern interagieren.
Auf einem Touchscreen können die Besucher mit ihrem Finger oder einem Zeichenstift das Profil und den Umriß jeder beliebigen Form zeichnen. Diese zweidimensionalen Zeichnungen werden nun automatisch zusammengesetzt und in ein dreidimensionales künstliches Lebewesen umgewandelt, welches simultan im wassergefüllten Glasbecken schwimmt und auf die Reaktionen der Besucher wartet. Die Besucher können nun ihre Hände ins Wasser des Glasbeckens tauchen und versuchen, mit der Bewegung ihrer Hände im Wasser die künstlichen Tierchen anzulocken.
Diese werden jedoch alles tun, um den Handbewegungen der Besucher auszuweichen, damit sie nicht eingefangen werden; da die Form der künstlichen Tierchen wie bei einer dünnen, elastischen Haut sehr flexibel ist und sich sofort an die Umgebung anpassen kann, wird das Tierchen sein Aussehen ständig verän-

Christa Sommerer (A), born 1964. Studied botany at University of Vienna and sculpture at Academy of Fine Arts, Vienna, Master of Arts (1990). 1991–93 Fellow (post graduate) at Städelschule Frankfurt, Institut für Neue Medien (Peter Weibel). 1993–94 lectures at: School of Visual Arts, New York; Art Institute of Chicago; EVL-University of Chicago; School of Art & Design, Champaign/Urbana; Eldorado Festival, Antwerpen; interActiva, Cologne.
Laurent Mignonneau (F), born 1967, studied Applied Art (3 years) at technical school, Angoulême; 1987 studied video at Academy of Fine Arts Angoulême; studied at department of Computer Graphics at CNBDI (Centre National de la Bande Dessinée et de l'Image, Angoulême). 1989 National Diploma for Plastic Arts, "Master of Arts", 1991 National Diploma for Plastic Expression, "Master of Arts".

■ «'A-Volve' is an interactive environment where visitors interact with virtual organisms in the real space of a water filled glass pool. By drawing the profile and shape of any possible form with a sensor pencil onto a monitor screen, visitors will create three-dimensional organisms.
These organisms will be transferred and displayed simultaneously as three-dimensional creatures in the water of the pool.
By using a special editor, the visitors can create any kind of form with the drawing pencil and change and modify it in real time.
The three-dimensional forms will immediately be 'alive' and will move and swim in the water of the pool.
These virtual creatures are products of the rules of evolution, they are influenced by human creation and decision.
They are sensitive to the viewers's hand movements in the water; they react according to the viewer's behavior; the viewer can catch them, modify their forms and communicate with them in real time.

INTERAKTIVE KUNST

CHRISTA SOMMERER/LAURENT MIGNONNEAU

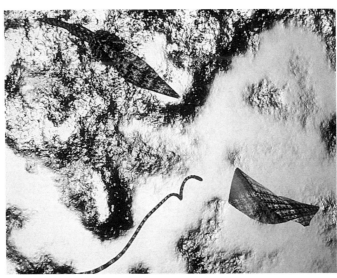

Goldene Nica
A-Volve, 1993/94
HW: SGI Onyx Reality Engine
SW: "A-Volve" by the Authors

INTERAKTIVE KUNST

CHRISTA SOMMERER/LAURENT MIGNONNEAU

dern und der Umwelt entsprechend reagieren: So kann das Tierchen zum Beispiel durch die Handbewegungen der Betrachter in die Enge getrieben werden, aber auch durch sie angelockt oder beruhigt werden. Es gilt also herauszufinden, wie die Tierchen reagieren und wie mit ihnen interagiert werden kann. Bis zu sechs Tierchen können gleichzeitig im Becken schwimmen und natürlich auch miteinander interagieren.

Die Individualität der künstlichen Tierchen manifestiert sich in erster Linie durch ihr Aussehen, ihr Verhalten wiederum konstituiert sich als Ausdruck ihrer Formen, d.h. das Verhalten und die Bewegung der Tierchen im Raum ist bestimmt durch ihre Form. Form ist somit als Anpassung an die Umgebung zu verstehen. Die Form an sich und die Art der Bewegung sind eng miteinander verbunden.

Wie bei einer Qualle können sich die Formen dieser fischähnlichen Lebewesen ständig verändern und an ihre Umgebung anpassen: Dies ist nur möglich durch ein neues System von Echtzeit-Neukalkulation, das einer steten Veränderung der Formen folgen kann. Diese flexiblen Algorithmen (programmiert von Laurent Mignonneau und Christa Sommerer) garantieren sehr lebensähnliche und natürliche Bewegungen, die gewisse Bezüge zu Schwimmbewegungen von Fischen oder Wasserlebewesen aufweisen.

Das Anliegen von ‚A-Volve' ist es jedoch nicht, Tiere oder Tierbewegungen zu imitieren, sondern einen Pool von künstlichen Lebewesen zu erzeugen, die ihre Eigenständigkeit besitzen, jedoch auf ihre Umgebung reagieren können. Das künstlerische Konzept hinter der Installation ‚A-Volve' liegt in erster Linie im Interesse an der Schaffung natürlich-künstlicher Systeme, die auf ihre Umgebung reagieren und offen für die Interaktion mit den Besuchern sind.

Ein Hauptaspekt der Arbeit ist das Einbeziehen der Individualität der Betrachter, die ihre individuellen Entscheidungen an die künstlichen Lebewesen weitergeben und damit deren künstliche Individualität mitbestimmen. Aus

If the viewer 'touches' a creature, it will avoid the viewer's hand and try to flee, or sometimes it will come back to the viewer in order to 'play' with him or her.

The movements and behavior of the organisms will depend mainly on their forms, on how the viewer has designed them on the drawing screen.

Each creature moves, reacts and evolves according to its form, creating unpredictable and always new life-like behavior. Since these organisms will capture the slightest movement of the viewer's hand in the water, the form and behaviour of these organisms will change constantly.

Specific algorithms developed by Mignonneau & Sommerer ensure that these creatures move very smoothly and animal-like, by changing and re-calculating their forms in real time.

None of the forms is pre-calculated, they are all 'born' in real time by visitor design and achieve their behavior through their movement in the environment of the real water.

If nobody is creating any forms or interacting with them, the creatures will die and disappear. These living and reacting organisms will also interact with other organisms in the pool, which have been created by previous visitors.

In order to bring about the 'birth' of a new organism, visitors try to bring two creatures of their choice together: With the movements of their hands in the water, visitors can 'merge' two organisms by trying to bring them close to each other. As soon as this succeeds, a new organism will be born.

It carries the characteristic look of both parents. This new creature will now also live in the pool and interact with its environment; it will be ready to merge and interact with other forms. Human decision in the creation of a new form and the rules of evolution and selection will create an environment that is open to all possible modifications and selections, following the laws of evolution and creation.

The visitor is part of the evolutionary system, she/he is a partner of the virtual organisms and gives them their 'artificial life'.

INTERAKTIVE KUNST

CHRISTA SOMMERER/LAURENT MIGNONNEAU

Goldene Nica
A-Volve, 1993/94
HW: SGI Onyx Reality Engine
SW: "A-Volve" by the Authors

INTERAKTIVE KUNST

CHRISTA SOMMERER/LAURENT MIGNONNEAU

der engen Kombination von Realität und künstlicher Realität entsteht ein komplexes System von künstlichem Leben, das sich im Pool ‚A-Volve' manifestiert.

Das künstliche Lebensbiotop ‚A-Volve' kann sich auch selbst fortpflanzen: Gelingt es zum Beispiel einem der Besucher, zwei Tierchen mit seinen beiden Händen in die Enge zu treiben und sehr nahe aneinanderzubringen, werden diese ihren genetischen Code austauschen und ein neues Lebewesen gebären: Dieses neue Lebewesen ist somit eine Kombination seiner Elternteile, die ihr Aussehen an ihren Nachfolger weitergeben. Die Möglichkeit zur Reproduktion und Fortpflanzung soll somit den Formenetat im Pool ‚A-Volve' auffrischen, indem es Neukombinationen des Erbmaterials ermöglicht.

Ein Kamera- und Sensoriksystem zeichnet die Handbewegungen der Besucher im Wasser auf und leitet sie an das Interfaceprogramm weiter. Diese Daten geben den Tierchen nun die Information, wo sich die Hand der Besucher befindet; damit können die Tierchen nun in Echtzeit auf die Hände der Besucher reagieren, mit ihnen spielen, sie vermeiden oder aber auch sich anlocken lassen.

Fünf bis zehn Besucher können gleichzeitig am Pool ‚A-Volve' partizipieren: Jeweils eine Person kann am Zeichenmonitor wieder ein neues Lebewesen kreieren, welches dann ebenfalls im Wasser des Pools schwimmt. Letztlich werden die Besucher also auch über die Tierchen miteinander interagieren, indem sie versuchen, das Verhalten der Tierchen zu beeinflussen und deren Aussehen mitzubestimmen.

‚A-Volve' ist somit also als ein Pool von künstlichen Lebewesen, die ihrer Umwelt gegenüber offen sind und mit dem natürlichen und künstlichen Environment interagieren, zu verstehen.» (Christa Sommerer/Laurent Mignonneau)

'A-Volve' is a pool of artifically living creatures that are open to outside influences by reacting to and interacting with their 'natural' and 'artifical' environment.

'A-Volve' reduces the borders between real and unreal, by connecting reality to 'non-reality'.

Water as the metaphor for birth and basic evolution is the medium for this artificial life 'pool' that is open to its real environment.

Both installations revel our perception of reality by interpolating between both constitutions of environments ('real' versus 'unreal'). Complex natural interfaces (like plants or water) provide a new approach to our way of perception, by asking the question: 'What is Life?'. Complex systems like 'human and plants' and 'human and animal-like creatures' are connected through living interfaces, producing a complex system of an 'artificial biotope' that represents the interaction between visitors and their environment.

Another important aspect of this work is the issue of 'individuality' as a main constituent of life. 'A-Volve' connects the individuality of the visitors to the individuality of the artificial creatures, creating a pool of artificial individuals that represent a complex system of interactions. The individuality of the virtual creatures is, so to speak, a direct interpretation of the relationship between visitors and their perception of artificial reality.

The creatures will always be different, depending on how the visitors create them and how they play with them.

The direct and simultaneous communications between creatures and visitors through the water creates a pool that could be considered as a 'living system' itself.

Since several visitors can interact at the same time with the different organisms, visitors themselves will also interact with each other.

One person at a time can use the drawing device to create a new form, but at the same time the other people can interact with the creatures in the pool.» (Christa Sommerer/Laurent Mignonneau)

INTERAKTIVE KUNST

LOREN CARPENTER

Loren Carpenter (USA) ist Erfinder und Präsident von Cinematrix. Ausbildung in Computerwissenschaft an der University of Washington, Seattle. 1966–80 bei der Boeing Company angestellt. Seit 1980 bei Lucasfilm. 1986 Mitbegründer von Pixar. 1989 Academy Award für den besten animierten Kurzfilm für „Tin Toy", 1993 Scientific and Technical Academy Award für hervorragende Verdienste um die Filmindustrie durch die Erfindung und Entwicklung des Bildsynthese-Softwaresystems RenderMan. Derzeit konzentriert sich Cinematrix auf die Entwicklung von Technologien zur interaktiven Publikumsbeteiligung.

■ «Intention des Werks ‚Kinoetic Evolution' ist die Erforschung des kreativen Potentials einer aktivierten Gruppenintelligenz. Das Publikum saugt allzuoft nur passiv die Ideen anderer in sich auf. Ein weites Forschungsfeld sind daher die Fähigkeiten eines sich konzentrierenden, alles unter Kontrolle haltenden Publikums.
Wir beginnen dabei notwendigerweise mit ganz einfachen, lustbetonten Spielen wie Ping-Pong oder Flugsimulatoren, um die Teilnehmer auf die Arbeitsweise des Systems zu trainieren. Die Zielsetzungen werden dabei für das Publikum immer komplexer und lohnender und führen schließlich zum eigentlichen Zweck, nämlich schöne, bisher noch nie gesehene, organisch-geometrische Formen zu generieren. Der kreative Prozeß geht dabei gemeinschaftlich und mit Hilfe eines Computers vonstatten, der aus alten Formen neue macht, und die Zuschauer die Formen auswählen, die sie gerne realisiert sehen möchten.
Dabei wird folgendermaßen vorgegangen: Dem Publikum werden einfache, geometrische Figuren gezeigt (Zylinder, Würfel, Kugel …). Jeder im Publikum bekommt vorher einen Zauberstab (‚wand'), einen etwa 3 cm breiten und 20 cm langen Streifen aus Holz, Pappe oder Plastik, der an zwei gegenüberliegenden Seiten eines Endes mit reflektierender Folie beklebt

Loren Carpenter (USA), is inventor and president of Cinematrix. Education in computer science at the University of Washington in Seattle. 1966 to 1980 employed by The Boeing Company. Since 1980 at Lucasfilm. 1986, Co-Founder of Pixar. Academy Award for best animated short for "Tin Toy" in 1989. 1993, Scientific and Technical Academy Award for fundamental contributions to the motion picture industry through the invention and development of the RenderMan image synthesis software system. Currently Cinematrix is focussing on the development of interactive audience participation technology.

■ «The intent of 'Kinoetic Evolution' is to explore the creative potential of an activated collective group intelligence. Audiences are far too often passive absorbers of other's ideas. The capability of a focussed, in control, audience is a vast new territory for exploration.
We necessarily begin with simple, fun games to train participants in the operation of the system, for example, ping-pong variants and flying an airplane. Their tasks become more complex and rewarding, finally leading them toward the goal of creating pleasing organic geometric forms never before seen. The creative process proceeds jointly, with the computer creating new forms from old, and the audience selecting the forms it wants to see developed.
The creation process is as follows: the audience is shown several images of simple forms (cylinder, cube, sphere, etc.). Each member of the audience is given a small reflective device, called a 'wand', consisting of an approximately 3 x 20 cm piece of wood or stiff cardboard or plastic with retroreflective tape affixed to opposite sides of one end. The reflective tape is typically red on one side of the wand and green on the other side. Audience members hold their wands comfortably in either hand so the reflective end is approximately eye level. They can see the video screen directly ahead and their wand off to one side. One or more video cameras are

INTERAKTIVE KUNST

LOREN CARPENTER

ist, auf der einen Seite rot, auf der anderen Seite grün. Die Zuschauer halten ihren Zauberstab bequem in einer Hand, und zwar so, daß sich das reflektierende Ende etwa in Augenhöhe befindet. Die Video-Projektionswand liegt direkt vor ihnen, ihren eigenen Zauberstab sehen sie seitlich. Im Hintergrund sind eine oder mehrere Videokameras so aufgestellt, daß damit das ganze Publikum in deren Blickfeld liegt. Außerdem ist jeder Kamera ein Scheinwerfer zugeordnet, der der Kamera ein Bild aus den reflektierenden Punkten der bestrahlten Zauberstäbe liefert. Das Videosignal der Kamera wird jetzt in Echtzeit analysiert, um die Farbe eines jeden Reflektors festzustellen. Und diese Information steuert den Computer, der die Videobilder erstellt.

Mit den Zauberstäben wählt das Publikum jene zwei Formen aus, die es zu kombinieren wünscht. Den Einsatz der Zauberstäbe betreffend gibt es mehrere Möglichkeiten. Entweder wird ein Leuchtzeiger verwendet, und das Publikum kann seinen Favoriten auswählen, oder die Bilder werden der Reihe nach einzeln gezeigt, und es wird jeweils abgestimmt. Wenn einmal die beiden Ausgangsformen ausgewählt sind, erstellt der Computer sechs neue. Das geht ziemlich schnell, in etwas weniger als zwei Sekunden. Dann wählt das Publikum wieder zwei Formen aus, die miteinander kombiniert werden.

Zumeist werden die Formen mit jeder Generation komplexer und bringen erstaunlich verschlungene organische Muster hervor.

Die Computerbestandteile des Systems bestehen aus einer Silicon Graphics Indigo und einem speziell konfigurierten Bildverarbeitungscomputer. Die Indigo erstellt das Videosignal, das dem Publikum zugespielt wird. Der Bildverarbeitungscomputer wertet die Videosignale der Kameras aus und übermittelt die Resultate an die Indigo. Die Indigo wird von einem Operator bedient, der die zu verarbeitenden Programme auswählt und das System betreut. Wenn das Publikum Hilfe braucht, kann der Operator jederzeit eingreifen.» (Loren Carpenter)

positioned so as to cover the entire audience from behind. There is a lamp next to each camera so that when the lamp is turned on, the camera sees an image consisting of reflected dots. The camera's video signal is analyzed in real time to determine the color of everyone's reflector. This information is used to control the computer making the projected video images. The audience uses the wands to choose the two forms they wish to combine. There are a number of ways the wands can be used to accomplish this. We can have a moving pointer and they can vote for their favorite, or we can show the forms one at a time and they can vote, and so forth. Once the two forms are chosen, the computer creates 6 new forms. This should be quite fast, probably less than 2 seconds. The audience then chooses two new forms to combine. Forms often become more complex with each succeeding generation, resulting in amazingly beautiful, intricate, organic shapes. The computational components of the system consist of a Silicon Graphics Indigo computer and a specially configured image processing computer. The Indigo produces the video signal which is viewed by the audience. The image processor analyzes the camera's video signal and passes the results to the Indigo. The Indigo is controlled by a human operator who selects which program to run and manages the operation of the system. Generally, the operator can intervene if the audience is in need of assistance.» (Loren Carpenter)

INTERAKTIVE KUNST

LOREN CARPENTER

Auszeichnung
Kinoetic Evolution: Collective Collaborative Computer-Mediated Creation, 1991
HW: SGI Indigo and Custom Image Processor
SW: Artist's Proprietary

INTERAKTIVE KUNST

TRANSIT

TRANSIT ist ein Verein zur Durchführung künstlerischer Projekte im elektronischen Raum, insbesondere im Raum der Massenmedien Radio und Fernsehen. TRANSIT lädt Künstler zu Medienkunstprojekten ein. Für das Projekt „realtime" waren dies folgende Künstler: Isabella Bordoni, Andres Bosshard, Kurt Hentschläger, Horst Hörtner, Michael Kreihsl, Roberto Paci Daló, Waldemar Rogojsza, Gerfried Stocker, Irene Strobl, Tamás Ungvary, Mia Zabelka. Technische Leitung: Hans Soukup.

■ «Drei baulich identische ORF-Landesstudios (Innsbruck, Linz, Graz) und die dichte Netzwerkstruktur (Bild-, Ton- und Datenleitungen) zwischen ihnen sollten als gemeinsamer Produktionsort für ein interaktives Live-Projekt für Fernsehen und Radio fungieren.
Elektronischer Raum als virtuelle Bühne für die realzeitliche Interaktion der Künstler. Ein telematisches Simultan-Event.
Gesendet wurde live, synchron in Radio und TV ('Kunstradio Live', 'Round Midnight').
Als Weiterentwicklung vorausgegangener telematischer Simultan-Projekte, insbesondere des 1992 bereits für TRANSIT realisierten Projekts ‚Chipradio' (siehe Prix Ars Electronica 93) sollte die Performance der auf die drei Landesstudios verteilten Künstler nun auch für das Medium TV umgesetzt und dem Fernsehzuseher gleichermaßen wie dem Radiohörer erschlossen werden.
Konfrontation der unterschiedlichen Medienqualitäten als Laborsituation für adäquate Kulturtechniken einer realzeitlich vernetzten Gesellschaft. Testfall für das kommunikative Potential von Massenmedien.
Schwerpunkt der mehr als sechsmonatigen Planungsphase war die Suche nach Strategien, um die einander diametral entgegenstehenden Anforderungen der linearen Einweg-Medien (vor allem TV) mit den Gesetzmäßigkeiten offener Kommunikations-Netzwerke zu verbinden, galt es doch – über eine bloße Fernseh-

TRANSIT is an association for staging artistic projects in electronic space, particularly in the radio and television domain. TRANSIT invites artists to participate in media art projects. The following artists were responsible for the "realtime" project: Isabella Bordoni, Andres Bosshard, Kurt Hentschläger, Horst Hörtner, Michael Kreihsl, Roberto Paci Daló, Waldemar Rogojsza, Gerfried Stocker, Irene Strobl, Tamás Ungvary, Mia Zabelka. Technical supervision: Hans Soukup.

■ *«Three architecturally identical studio centers of the Austrian Broadcasting Corporation (ORF) in Innsbruck, Linz and Graz, linked together by a dense network structure of video, audio and data links, were taken over for use as a common work site for an interactive 'live' project for television and radio; a unified, simultaneous performance by artists at all three centres. Electronic space as a virtual stage for real-time interaction between the artists. A telematic, simultaneous event.
Simulcast live on radio and television ('Kunstradio Live', 'Round Midnight').
As a further development of previous telematic, simultaneous projects, particularly TRANSIT's 'Chip Radio' of 1992 (see Prix Ars Electronica 93), the performance was to be staged for television as well as radio this time, to include the TV viewer as well as the radio listener.
The clash between the different media qualities presented a laboratory setting suitable for studying cultural techniques for a networked society. A test case for the communicative potential of the mass media.
The emphasis for the more than six month long planning phase was the search for strategies which connect the diametrically opposed demands of the linear one-way media (above all, TV) with the natural laws governing open communications systems, the essential task being to compose the image out of the network, to go beyond a mere TV documentary of the event itself.*

INTERAKTIVE KUNST

TRANSIT

Auszeichnung
realtime, 1993
HW: PC, Macintosh, Atari, Custom Interfaces (Data Gloves, Robot Instruments)
SW: Mostly Artists' Proprietary

INTERAKTIVE KUNST

TRANSIT

dokumentation des Geschehens hinaus –, auch die Bildebene aus dem Netzwerk heraus zu gestalten.
Der eingeschlagene Weg basiert auf einer weitgehenden Autonomie der Bild- und Tonebenen. Die beiden Kanäle des Radios (L–R) und der TV-Monoton wurden zu einer gemeinsamen dreikanaligen Projektionsfläche für die akustische Umsetzung der räumlichen Konstellationen (reale Räume – telematische Räume).
Die Zuhörer/-seher wurden dementsprechend aufgefordert, möglichst TV-Gerät und Radio gemeinsam zu verwenden, um diese erweiterte Empfangssituation nutzen zu können.
Für die Visualisierung der Interaktions- und Produktionsprozesse zwischen den an auseinanderliegenden Orten versammelten Akteuren wurden eigene Körperinterfaces und Roboter entwickelt und gebaut.
Die Möglichkeit, unmittelbar an den jeweils anderen Orten tele-präsent zu sein, in das dortige Geschehen eingreifen zu können, bestimmte die Auswahl der eingesetzten Technologie.
Die aus dieser Vorgehensweise entstehenden unterschiedlichen Versionen (Live-Situation in den drei Studios, Radio, TV, Radio + TV ...) sind jedoch nicht bloß Teilmengen des Geschehens, sondern, dem strukturellen Pluralismus vernetzten Handelns entsprechend, alle als vollgültig anzusehen.
Für die Vorbereitung der realen Räume (Foyers der Landesstudios) sowie des gemeinsamen virtuellen Netzwerk-Raumes standen drei Tage zur Verfügung.» (TRANSIT)

«Während die Fernsehregie unter der Leitung von Michael Kreihsl beschäftigt war, Kamerapositionen (12 Kameras) und Ausleuchtung der drei Studios abzustimmen und Andres Bosshard nach einer minutiösen Planung mit den ORF-Technikern über Interkom Lautsprecher und Mikros positionierte und so das akustische ‚tuning' der Räume vornahm, wurde die gesamte Interaktionsebene für Körperinterfaces und Roboter von Horst Hörtner, Martin

The chosen plan was based on considerable independence between the image and sound layers. The two channels for radio (L-R) and the single channel of television made up a common 3-channel projection surface for the acoustic interpretation of spatial constellations (real spaces – telematic spaces).
Accordingly, the listeners/viewers were called on to use both radio and television together, if possible, in order to take advantage of this extended reception situation.
For the visualisation of the interaction and production processes between performers gathered together in far-flung places, custom body interfaces and robots were developed and built.
The possibility of being immediately telepresent in any another other place, to be able to take part in the events taking place there, is determined by the choice of the technology used.
However, the different versions arising from this working method (i.e. the live setting in the studio, radio, TV, radio + TV) are not merely sub-sets of the event, but are all to be seen as fully valid in accordance with the structural pluralism of networked activity.
Three days were available for setting up the real spaces (the foyers of the three regional studio centers) and the common virtual network spaces.» (TRANSIT)

«'While TV technicians under Michael Kreihsl's direction were busy co-ordinating the 12 camera positions and lighting in the three locations, sound technicians were helping Andres Bosshard carry out the 'acoustic tuning', positioning the microphones and loudspeakers according to meticulous plans they had drawn up earlier via intercom. At the same time, Horst Hörtner, Martin Schiter and myself were integrating the entire interactive layer for body interfaces and robots into the network structure between the studios. We worked almost around the clock for three days and were all constantly connected by means of these networks.
We could see and hear each other all the time,

INTERAKTIVE KUNST

TRANSIT

Schiter und mir vor Ort in die Netzwerkstruktur zwischen den Studios implementiert.
Wir arbeiteten drei Tage lang nahezu rund um die Uhr und waren dabei auf diesen verschiedenen Netzwerkebenen miteinander verbunden. Wir konnten uns ständig sehen und hören, die Computer waren vernetzt, Software wurde über Modems ausgetauscht und weiterentwickelt.
Es ergab sich für uns eine einmalige ‚Laborsituation'. Keiner von uns hatte sich zuvor so lange ohne wesentliche Unterbrechung in einem solchen virtuellen Raum der unmittelbaren Telepräsenz aufgehalten.» (Gerfried Stocker)

the computers were networked, and software was exchanged via modem and developed further.
The result was a unique 'laboratory situation' for us. None of us had ever spent such a long time in almost continuous immersion in a virtual space of such immediate tele-presence before.'» (Gerfried Stocker)

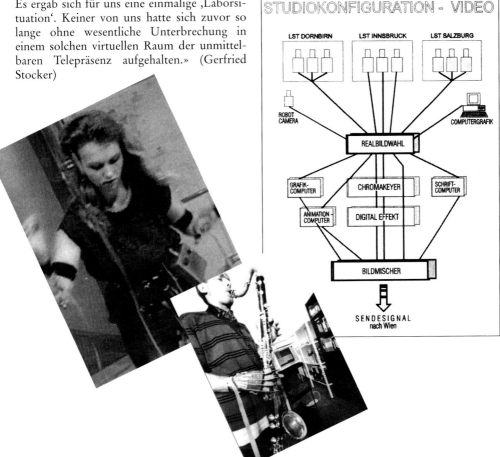

Auszeichnung
realtime, 1993
HW: PC, Macintosh, Atari, Custom Interfaces (Data Gloves, Robot Instruments)
SW: Mostly Artists' Proprietary

INTERAKTIVE KUNST

MAX ALMY/TERI YARBROW

Max Almy (USA), Video- und Medienkünstlerin mit internationalen Ausstellungen. Charakterisiert werden ihre Arbeiten durch die Verschmelzung von Bildmaterial mit experimentellen Strukturen und einer dem städtischen Leben gegenüber kritischen Erzählweise.
Teri Yarbrow (USA), Künstlerin mit starkem Bezug zu Design und Malerei. Beschäftigt sich vorwiegend mit Formen persönlicher und sozialer Kommunikation als Kommentar menschlicher Befindlichkeit. Ihre Arbeiten wurden national und international ausgestrahlt.

■ «‚Utopia' ist eine Multimedia-Installation, die die Lage der Umwelt, speziell die Krise der städtischen Umgebung, untersucht. Ihr Kernstück ist ein interaktives Videospiel, das unter Mitwirkung der Perfomancekünstlerin Rachel Rosenthal zustandegekommen ist und in dem der Betrachter ersucht wird, eine Reihe von Entscheidungen zu treffen: Himmel/Hölle, Macht/Ohnmacht, Fiktion/Realität, Utopie/Dystopie usw. Das sind die Dichotomien der Großstadt, speziell in Los Angeles, wo sich alle den Himmel wünschen und der Hölle möglichst nicht begegnen wollen, wo wir alle von der Hollywood-Vorstellung verführt worden sind, wir könnten alles haben – Reichtum, Schönheit, Paradies – und alles andere sei mit Scheitern gleichzusetzen.
Einerseits soll das interaktive Video den das Unterbewußtsein ansprechenden Charakter eines spannenden Videospiels haben, andererseits soll es aber gleichzeitig überzeugendes Videomaterial, Text, Begleitmusik und experimentelle Performance bieten. Angezogen wird der Zuschauer durch einen großen interaktiven Monitor, auf dem das Spiel stattfindet. In die Zange genommen vom Chor zweier daneben aufgestellter Monitore, greift der Zuschauer zu einer Laserpistole und beginnt, mit einem eigenartig bizarren, herausfordernden interaktiven Treiben gemeinsame Sache zu machen.» (Max Almy/Teri Yarbrow)

Max Almy (USA) is an internationally exhibited video and new media artist. Her works are characterized by compelling visual imagery, experimental structure and narrative which often critiques and satirizes contemporary urban life.
Teri Yarbrow (USA), artist with a strong background in design and painting. Started working with video as a way to move images in time and space. She is primarily concerned with communicating personal and social issues which comment on the human condition. Her work has been broadcast nationally and internationally.

■ «'Utopia' is a multi-media installation which explores the state of the environment and, specifically, the crisis of the contemporary urban environment. The core of the piece is an unusual interactive video game hosted by performance artist, Rachel Rosenthal, in which the viewer is asked to make a series of choices: heaven/hell, power/impotence, fiction/reality, utopia/dystopia...
These are the dichotomies of the city, particularly in Los Angeles, where we all desire Heaven and we don't want to confront Hell; where we are seduced by the Hollywood fiction that we can have Wealth, Beauty, Paradise, and that anything less is a failure.
The interactive video is designed to have the visceral, exciting quality of a video game while at the same time presenting compelling video imagery, text, sound score and experimental performance. Within the setting of the installation, the viewer is drawn toward the game on a large interactive monitor. Coaxed by a surrounding chorus on two additional video monitors, the viewer picks up a laser gun and enters into collusion with a strangely bizarre and challenging interactive activity.» (Max Almy/Teri Yarbrow)

INTERAKTIVE KUNST

MAX ALMY/TERI YARBROW

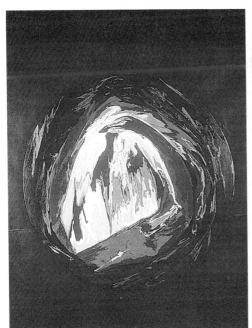 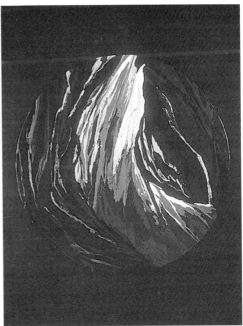

**Anerkennung
Utopia, 1994
HW: CDI, Video, Oil Paintings**

INTERAKTIVE KUNST

EDWARD ELLIOTT

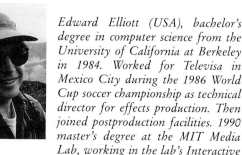

Edward Elliott (USA), 1984 Bachelor of Science in Computerwissenschaften an der University of California/Berkeley. Arbeitete 1986 während der Fußballweltmeisterschaft in Mexico City als technischer Leiter für Effekte bei Televisa. Anschließend Arbeit im Postproduktionsbereich. 1990 Mitarbeit in der Gruppe für interaktives Kino am Media Lab des MIT und Promotion zum Master of Science.

■ «‚Video Streamer' arbeitet in zwei einfachen Betriebsweisen: im Einspielmodus und im Betrachtungsmodus.
Im Einspielmodus wird die Bildquelle, entweder ein Fernsehprogramm, ein Video oder das Bild einer Standkamera, wie ein Flipbook Bild für Bild übereinander in einem dreidimensionalen Block gestapelt. Jedes neue Bild erscheint vorne und drückt damit die vorangegangenen Bilder in Richtung links oben auf dem Bildschirm zeitlich und räumlich nach hinten. Die Seiten dieses Blocks setzen sich aus den Rändern hunderter aufeinanderfolgender Video-Einzelbilder zusammen und verdeutlichen dadurch die zeitlichen Eigenschaften des Bildflusses. Einstellungswechsel und Schnittrhythmus sowie die meisten Kamerabewegungen lassen sich entlang der Blockseiten ablesen.
Durch Unterbrechung des Einspielmodus werden die Inhalte des Bildblocks abgefragt. Mit einer Maus oder einem Griffel werden die einzelnen Standbilder für die Wiedergabe ausgewählt. Jenes Bild, auf dessen Außenkante im Bildblock sich der Cursor befindet, wird einzeln angezeigt. Bewegungen des Cursors über mehrere Bildränder bringen die Bilder zum Laufen, ähnlich wie bei einem Flipbook.
Am Abspielmonitor wird der Inhalt des entsprechenden Bildes dabei mitsamt dem dazugehörigen Ton gezeigt. Von manchen wird dies mit dem in der Hip-Hop-Musik verwendeten ‚Scratchen' verglichen, nur ist hier neben dem Ton auch noch das Bild beteiligt.» (Edward Elliott)

Edward Elliott (USA), bachelor's degree in computer science from the University of California at Berkeley in 1984. Worked for Televisa in Mexico City during the 1986 World Cup soccer championship as technical director for effects production. Then joined postproduction facilities. 1990 master's degree at the MIT Media Lab, working in the lab's Interactive Cinema Group.

■ «The 'Video Streamer' works in two simple modes: flowing for capture and paused for review. When the Streamer is flowing, the video source, which can come from broadcast, from a camera, or from videotape, is arranged as a three-dimensional solid, stacking the picture frames in a block much like the pages in a flip book. As new frames enter, they push the older frames towards the upper left of the display, further away in distance and in time. The sides of this block, formed by the edges of hundreds of video frames, reveal a number of temporal attributes of the stream. Shot boundaries and editing rhythm are clearly visible along the sides of the block, as are many camera motions.
By pausing the Streamer, the user can review the contents of the block of frames. Using a mouse or a stylus, individual frames are selected for display by placing the pointer over the edges of those frames in the extrusion block. Moving the cursor quickly across many frames displays those frames in motion, similarly to thumbing through a flip book. As you stroke across each frame edge in the Streamer block, its image appears in the viewer, and its accompanying sound is played. Some people liken this to 'scratch' in hip-hop music, only here you are scratching across both pictures and sound.» (Edward Elliott)

INTERAKTIVE KUNST

EDWARD ELLIOTT

The configuration looks something like this:

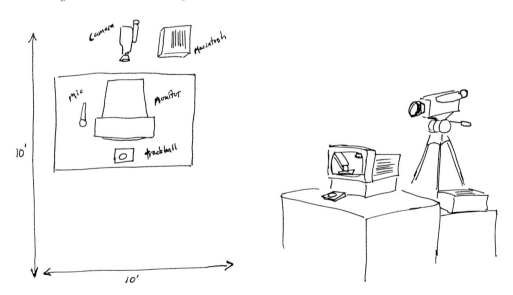

Anerkennung
Video Streamer, 1992/93
HW: Macintosh
SW: Custom Software

INTERAKTIVE KUNST

FRIEDRICH FÖRSTER

Friedrich Förster (D), geb. 1952, naturwissenschaftliches Studium, Diplom in Neurobiologie 1980. 1985–89 Arbeit am Max-Planck-Institut für biophysikalische Chemie in Göttingen. Seit 1990 selbständig, Realisierung intermedialer Projekte mit Musik, Laser und Projektionen. Künstlerische Zusammenarbeit u. a. mit dem Music Ensemble of Benares, Nederlands Dans Theater und dem KRONOS Quartett.

■ «Kern des Projektes ‚Das plastische Licht' bildet ein Lernmodell auf Neuronenebene: Die Bahnung und Konsolidierung neuronaler Verbindungen durch einen aktivitätsabhängigen, assoziativen, synaptischen Mechanismus.
Als Ein- und Ausgabemedium dient eine ‚sensible' und intelligent gesteuerte Laserinstallation, die sich mehrerer neuer Technologien bedient: Einer neuen Kristalltechnologie, mit der sich Laserlicht in bis dahin nicht realisierbarer Geschwindigkeit in Helligkeit und Farbe modulieren läßt, sowie eines zum Patent angemeldeten Sensors. Dieser Sensor erkennt Ort, Richtung und Geschwindigkeit, mit der ein Gegenstand in einen Laser-Lichtteppich eintaucht, und macht diese Parameter einer intelligenten Computerauswertung zugänglich.
Über eine Lichtschleuse gelangt der Besucher in einen ca. 10 x 5 Meter großen Raum. Die Decke des Raumes wird von einem bläulichen Lichtteppich gebildet, der in 2,50 Meter Höhe flach aufgespannt ist. Taucht der Besucher seine Hand oder einen Gegenstand in die Lichtfläche, wölbt sie sich im Bereich der Berührung für etwa 2 Sekunden nach oben, um sich dann wieder zu glätten. Entlang des vorherigen Schattenbereichs entsteht eine Farbänderung, die ebenfalls wieder abklingt.
In Abhängigkeit vom Ort der ‚Stimulation' wird ein Ton ausgelöst, dessen Intensität von der Eintauchgeschwindigkeit bestimmt wird und dessen Tonhöhe durch seitliche Bewegung innerhalb der Laserfläche moduliert werden kann. Der Ton klingt parallel zur Farbänderung

Friedrich Förster (D), born 1952, studied natural sciences, graduated as a neurobiologist in 1980. Worked at the Max Planck Institute for Biophysical Chemistry in Göttingen from 1985 to 1989. Independent since 1990, realising inter-medial projects with music, lasers and projections. Artistic collaboration with the Music Ensemble of Benares, Nederlands Dans Theater and the KRONOS Quartet, among others.

■ *«The core of the project 'Das plastische Licht' ('The plastic light') is an educational model on the neuron level: the tracing and consolidation of neural connections through an activity-dependent associative synapsic mechanism.
The input-output medium is provided by a 'sensitive' and intelligence-controlled laser installation which makes use of several new technologies: a new crystal-based technique by which the brightness and colour of a laser light can de modulated at hitherto unattainable speed, as well as a sensor which has been registered for a patent. This sensor perceives the location, direction and speed of an object diving into a laser light carpet and makes these parameters available for an intelligent analysis by computer.
The visitor enters the 10 m x 5 m room through a gate of light. The ceiling of the room consists of a bluish carpet of light suspended at a height of 2.5 meters. When the visitor moves his or her hand or an object into the light surface, it curves upwards at the point of contact for about 2 seconds and then flattens again. Along the previously shaded area, a colour shift takes place which also eventually disappears.
Depending on the point of 'stimulation', a sound is released, of which the intensity is determined by the 'diving speed'. Its pitch can be modulated by lateral movement within the laser surface. Together with the colour change, the sound gradually disappears.
Stimulations of the laser surface within a certain*

INTERAKTIVE KUNST

FRIEDRICH FÖRSTER

allmählich wieder ab. Stimulationen der Laserfläche innerhalb eines gewissen Zeitabschnitts werden als zusammenhängend gelernt. Werden z. B. an verschiedenen Stellen gleichzeitig oder kurz hintereinander die Hände in die Laserfläche getaucht, entsteht ein Streifenmuster. Wird nun von den im Laufe der Zeit verblassenden Streifen nur ein einzelner erneut berührt, wird das komplette Muster wieder abgerufen.

So entstehen im Laufe der Zeit komplexe Muster und Tonfolgen, die nicht nur durch die Aktivität des Publikums, sondern auch durch dessen Reaktionen auf die sichtbar gewordenen Engramme generiert wurden.» (Friedrich Förster)

time interval are 'learned' as being associated in some way. If, for example, hands are plunged in at various places simultaneously or in close succession, a striped pattern emerges. Then, when just one of the gradually fading stripes is touched again, the whole pattern is recalled/recreated.

In time this creates complex patterns and sound sequences, generated not only by the activity of the visitors, but also by their reactions to the engrams which have become visible.» (Friedrich Förster)

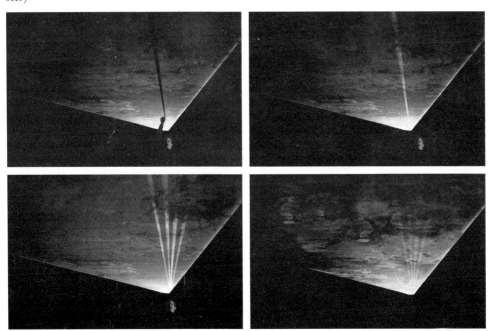

Anerkennung
Das Plastische Licht, 1991–94
HW: Laser, PC
SW: "Digitus", Artist's Proprietary

INTERAKTIVE KUNST

MICHAEL GIRARD/SUSAN AMKRAUT

Michael Girard (USA) studierte Mathematik und Computerwissenschaften an der University of California. Bachelor of Science in beiden Fächern. Weiterführende Studien am Advanced Computer Center for the Arts and Design an der Ohio State University.
Susan Amkraut (USA), Bachelor of Arts und Bachelor of Science in bildender Kunst sowie in Informatik und Computerwissenschaften. Weiterführende Studien im Bereich der Computerkunst am ACCAD.

■ «Mit unserem Entwurf zu ‚Menagerie' wollten wir eine verspielte, dynamisch-lebendige virtuelle Welt erschaffen, die interaktiv-konfrontativ angelegt sein sollte.
Verhaltenssimulationen abstrahierter Tierformen sollten die wesentlichen Begegnungselemente in ‚Menagerie' sein. Durch Türen und Bullaugen, die auf dem unendlichen zu untersuchenden Territorium in unmittelbarer Nähe des Besuchers auftauchen, betreten und verlassen fünf unterschiedliche Tierarten den sichtbaren Raum. Die Tiere scheinen dabei aus einer unsichtbaren Welt hinter den Türen zu kommen, von jenseits der virtuellen Welt, die der Besucher gerade erforscht. Strukturiert ist ‚Menagerie' als eine Folge von Ereignissen mit unterschiedlichen Tierkombinationen, die auftauchen und entsprechend der variierenden Verhaltensszenarien mit dem Besucher interagieren.
Der Charakter der Tiere zeigt sich dabei durch die Interaktion mit dem Besucher. Wenn sich zum Beispiel ein Besucher einem Vogelschwarm nähert, fliegt dieser auf und läßt sich ein Stück weiter wieder nieder. Das fordert den Besucher heraus, sich neuerlich zu nähern, so lange, bis der letzte Vogel durch ein Loch verschwunden ist, das sich sofort hinter ihm schließt.
Die Bewegungen der einzelnen Tiere wurden mittels Algorithmen modelliert, die die physischen Eigenschaften der Bewegung simulieren. Viele der angewendeten Techniken kommen

Michael Girard (USA), studied mathematics and computer science at the University of California. Bachelor of Science degrees in each field. Graduate studies at the Advanced Computer Center for the Arts and Design at the Ohio State University. Susan Amkraut (USA), bachelor's degree in fine arts and in computer and information science from the University of California at Santa Cruz. Graduate studies in the computer art program at ACCAD.

■ *«When we began our design of 'Menagerie', we wanted to create a playful virtual world that was dynamically alive and interactively confrontational.
The central elements of the encounters in 'Menagerie' are behavioral simulations of abstracted animal forms. Five different species of animals enter and exit the visible space through 'portholes' and 'doorways' that materialize near the user as she/he roams the infinite ground plane beneath. The animals appear to come from an invisible world behind the doors, beyond the virtual world explored by the user. 'Menagerie' is structured as a series of events comprised of different combinations of animals that emerge and interact with the user according to varying behavioral scenarios.
Through interaction, the character of the animals is revealed. For example, in one event, as the user moves toward a group of birds gathered on the ground, they take off and land at a slightly further location, baiting the user to advance again, eventually disappearing into a porthole that closes as the last bird flies in.
The motion of the individual animals is modeled with algorithms that simulate the physical qualities of movement. Many of the techniques employed are inspired by the robotics field. Legged animals respond to simulated gravity as they walk and run in various gaits. They are able to spontaneously plan footholds on the ground so that they appear to be dynamically balanced. Gait shifting*

INTERAKTIVE KUNST

MICHAEL GIRARD/SUSAN AMKRAUT

aus der Robotik. Tiere mit Beinen reagieren beim Gehen und Laufen in den verschiedensten Gangarten auf die simulierte Schwerkraft. Sie sind in der Lage, ihre Schritte spontan im voraus zu planen, so daß der Eindruck entsteht, sie befänden sich in einem dynamischen Gleichgewicht. Um die Beeinträchtigung der Dynamik bei Gangartwechseln zu minimieren, wurden Phasenverschiebungsalgorithmen entwickelt. Vögel und andere fliegende Tiere beschleunigen zum Beispiel, indem sie mit den Flügeln schlagen und sich auch realistisch in die Kurve legen.» (Michael Girard/Susan Amkraut)

algorithms were developed that minimize the dynamic perturbation of the body as legs undergo a phase shift during the gait transition period. Birds and other flying creatures accelerate when flapping their wings and bank realistically into turns.» (Michael Girard/Susan Amkraut)

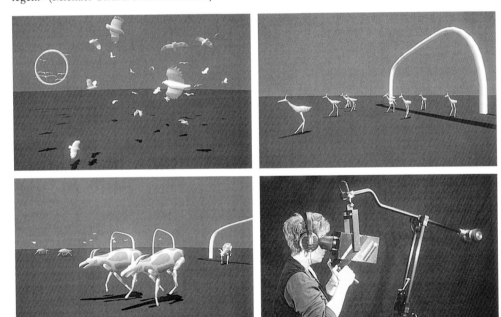

Anerkennung
Menagerie, 1993
HW: SGI Crimson Reality Engine, Fakespace "BOOM 2C", Crystal River "Beachtron" 3-D Sound System
SW: BOOM Software "VLIB-SGI", Beachtron Software, Custom Simulation Software

INTERAKTIVE KUNST

RICHARD KRIESCHE

Richard Kriesche (A), geb. 1940, ist seit 1991 Professor für Theorie und Praxis der elektronischen Bilderzeugung an der Hochschule für Gestaltung in Offenbach/Main (D). Ausbildung als Lehrer für Bildnerische Erziehung. Gründer zahlreicher kultureller Institutionen (u. a. „kulturdata"). Studienaufenthalte am MIT (1985–86), Lehrauftrag an der Technischen Universität Wien (1988–91).

Richard Kriesche (A), born 1940, has been Professor for Theory and Practice in Electronic Image Creation at the Offenbach/Main Hochschule für Gestaltung (Design College). Trained as teacher for Art Education, founder of numerous cultural institutions (including "kulturdata"), study visits at MIT (1985–86), teaching engagements at the Technische Universität in Vienna (1988–91).

■ «‚Telematische Skulptur III' (Produzent: kulturdata) ist ein ‚virtueller Datenraum'. Sie repräsentiert die Informationsmoderne als ‚universellen Warteraum'. Der Raum bzw. die Skulptur definieren sich ausschließlich aus dem digitalen Datenverkehr. Dabei besteht zwischen künstlerischem und alltäglichem Datenverkehr kein Unterschied mehr.
Vielmehr werden die symbolischen Zeichen des Computers im ‚virtuellen Datenraum' nochmals symbolisch aufgeladen: Die materielle Eisenbahnschiene befördert nichts mehr, sondern die immateriellen Symbole sind es, die die Eisenbahnschiene befördern.
Sowohl der Datenverkehr der Kunstwerke als auch der gesamte interne Datenverkehr des Ausstellungsgebäudes selbst, wie Telefon, Fax, Telex etc., steuerten die Bewegung der ‚Telematischen Skulptur III'. Der jeweilige Zustand der Skulptur war in Form der Selbstanzeige am Bildschirm ablesbar. Jeder informationelle Input hatte eine sichtbare Veränderung der immateriellen Symbole und damit eine minimale Bewegungsveränderung der tonnenschweren Skulptur, d. h. eine unsichtbare Verschiebung der Eisenbahnschiene, zur Folge.
Die zeitliche Dauer der Skulptur war, da sie interaktiv bzw. informationsabhängig war, nicht planbar. Das endgültige Ende jedoch war von den physikalischen Grenzen der Kunsthalle selbst bestimmt, an deren Mauern sich die Skulptur durch einen ‚information overload' selbst zerstört hätte, indem die Eisenbahnschiene(!) in den Bildschirm gefahren wäre.»
(Richard Kriesche)

■ «'Telematische Skulptur III' (production: kulturdata) is a 'virtual data space' representing the modern information age as a 'universal waiting room'. The room (or sculpture) defines itself purely on the basis of digital information traffic. It no longer makes any difference whether this is artistic or everyday data traffic. Rather, the symbolic signs of the computer in the 'virtual data room' are once again symbolically loaded: the material rail (as in railway) doesn't carry anything anymore, on the contrary – it's now the non-material symbols which carry the rail.
The movement of the 'Telematische Skulptur III' was controlled not only by the data relating to the art work, but also by the whole internal data traffic of the exhibition building itself, such as telephone, fax, telex, etc. The momentary condition of the sculpture was visible in the form of a status indicator on the screen. Every information input resulted in a visible change in the non-material symbols, which in turn caused a minimal change in the movement of the sculpture (which weighs tons), in other words, an imperceptible shift in the rail.
As the sculpture was interactive (information-dependent), its temporal duration could not be laid down in advance. The final end, however, was determined by the physical limits of the Kunsthalle building itself, at whose walls the sculpture would have destroyed itself – an information overload would have caused the rail itself (!) to crash into the screen.» (Richard Kriesche)

INTERAKTIVE KUNST

RICHARD KRIESCHE

Anerkennung
Telematische Skulptur III, 1993
HW: No Technical Details
SW: Knapp Electronic

INTERAKTIVE KUNST

WOLFGANG KRÜGER

Wolfgang Krüger (D) ist Direktor der Forschungsgruppe „Scientific Visualization" am Höchstleistungsrechenzentrum der Gesellschaft für Mathematik und Datenverarbeitung in Bonn. Studierte Mathematik und Theoretische Physik an der Universität Berlin. Promotion zum Dr. rer. nat. 1972. Mitbegründer von mental images, Berlin, und Art+Com, Berlin. Beteiligung an Management- und Softwareentwicklung für Animationen und Anwendungen von VR-Systemen in Architektur und Design.

Wolfgang Krüger (D), director of the Scientific Visualization Department at the Supercomputer Center of the German National Research Center for Computer Science (GMD) in Bonn. Studied Mathematics and Theoretical Physics at the University of Berlin, Dr. rer. nat. 1972. Cofounder of mental images, Berlin, and Art+Com, Berlin. Involved in management and software development for computer animations and applications of Virtual Reality systems in architecture and design.

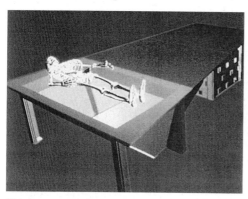

Fig. 1

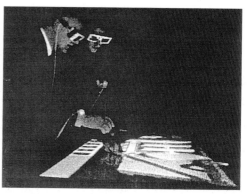

Fig. 2

■ «Virtuelle Objekte und Kontrolleinrichtungen befinden sich auf einer realen ‚Werkbank' (Abb. 1). Die Objekte werden als dreidimensionale computergenerierte Bilder auf die Oberfläche der ‚Werkbank' projiziert. Diese Anordnung entspricht in etwa der Arbeitssituation in einem Architekturbüro, in Operationssälen usw. Ein ‚Guide' kann die virtuelle Arbeitsumgebung benützen, während mehrere Beobachter mittels stereoskopischer Videobrillen den Vorgängen zusehen können (Abb. 2). Die Teilnehmer arbeiten in einem nicht-immersiven virtuellen Umfeld. Abhängig von der Anwendung, können verschiedene Eingangs- und Ausgangsmodule integriert werden, wie etwa Bewegungs-, Gestik- oder Spracherkennungssysteme, die den generellen Trend weg

■ «Virtual objects and control tools are located on a real 'workbench' (fig. 1). The objects, displayed as computer-generated stereo-images are projected onto the surface of the workbench. This setting corresponds to the actual work situation in an architect's office, in surgery environments, etc. A guide uses the virtual working environment while several observers can watch events through stereo shutter glasses (fig. 2). The participants operate within a non-immersive virtual environment. Depending on the application, various input and output modules can be integrated, such as motion, gesture and voice recognitions systems, which characterize the general trend away from the classical human-machine interface. Several guides can work together in similar

INTERAKTIVE KUNST

WOLFGANG KRÜGER

von der klassischen ‚Mensch-Maschine-Schnittstelle' veranschaulichen. Mehrere ‚Guides' können, entweder lokal oder über Breitband-Kommunikationsnetzwerke (Daten-Highways) miteinander verbunden, an vergleichbaren Arbeitsumgebungen zusammenarbeiten. Eine ‚verständnisvolle' Arbeitsumgebung mit ihren leistungsfähigen Graphik-Workstations, Tracking-Systemen (Ortungs-/Steuerungs-Systemen), Kameras und Projektoren ersetzt die traditionelle Multimedia-Workstation auf dem Schreibtisch.
Bisher sind zwei Szenarien realisiert worden: im Design- und Diskussionsprozeß in der Architektur, bei der Landschafts- und (Raum-) Umweltplanung sowie im Bereich chirurgischer Planung und im nicht-sequentiellen medizinischen Trainingsbereich.» (Wolfgang Krüger)

environments either locally or by using broadband communication networks. A responsive environment, consisting of powerful graphic workstations, tracking systems, cameras, projector, and microphones, replaces the traditional multimedia desktop workstation.
Two scenarios have been realized so far: design and discussion process in architecture, landscape and environment planning, and surgery planning and non-sequential medical training.» (Wolfgang Krüger)

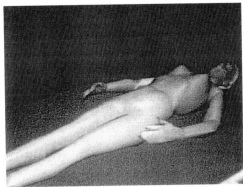

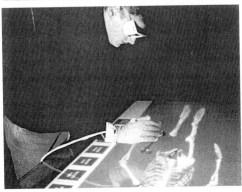

Anerkennung
Responsive Workbench, 1993/94
HW: SGI Onyx Reality Engine 2, Tracking Systems, Beamer, Workbench
SW: SGI GL + Performer, In-House Software

INTERAKTIVE KUNST

BRENDA LAUREL/RACHEL STRICKLAND

Brenda Laurel (USA), Forscherin und Schriftstellerin, die sich in ihrer Arbeit auf die Interaktion zwischen Mensch und Computer sowie auf die kulturellen Aspekte der Technologie konzentriert. Master of Fine Arts und Doktorat in Theaterwissenschaft an der Ohio State University.
Rachel Strickland (USA), Architektin, Video-Filmerin und Interaction-Designerin. Am MIT und am UC in Santa Cruz hat sie Film- und Videoproduktion unterrichtet.

■ «‚PlaceHolder' ist der Name eines Forschungsprojekts, das ein neues Paradigma von Erzählhandlungen in virtuellen Umgebungen untersucht. Die geographische Situation in ‚PlaceHolder' ist inspiriert von drei tatsächlich existierenden Örtlichkeiten im Banff National Park in Alberta/Kanada: Von Middle Spring, einer heißen Schwefelquelle in einer natürlichen Höhle, von einem Wasserfall im Johnston Canyon und einer gespenstischen Formation, die den Bow River überragt.
Dreidimensionale videographische szenische Elemente, räumlich inszenierte Klänge und Stimmen sowie einfache Animationen von Figuren wurden verwendet, um eine zusammenhängende Landschaft zu bilden, die von zwei räumlich getrennten Benützern mit Headphones gleichzeitig besucht werden kann. Eigenheiten und Gegenstände der realen Vorbilder werden hier wieder zusammengefügt und dienen als Treffpunkte zu deren Erforschung oder zum Spielen. Die Personen können darin spazieren gehen, sprechen, mit beiden Händen virtuelle Gegenstände berühren und sie bewegen.
Traditionen und spirituelle Praktiken, aber auch Mythen und Sagen basieren häufig auf jenen Beziehungen, die Menschen zu ihrer Umgebung und den darin vorkommenden Lebewesen haben. Und jene Ikonographie, die sich seit der Steinzeit in die Landschaft eingraviert hat, bestimmt auch die graphischen Elemente in ‚PlaceHolder'. Erzählmotive, die

Brenda Laurel (USA) is a researcher and writer whose work focuses on human-computer interaction and cultural aspects of technology. M.F.A. and Ph.D. in Theater from the Ohio State University. Member of the Research Staff at Interval Research Corporation in Palo Alto, California. Rachel Strickland (USA), architect, videographer, and interaction designer. Her work of the past 20 years has focused on cinematic dimensions of places in people's everyday experience. She has taught film and video production at MIT and UC Santa Cruz.

■ *'PlaceHolder' is the name of a research project which explores a new paradigm for narrative action in virtual environments. The geography of 'PlaceHolder' takes inspiration from three actual locations in the Banff National Park of Alberta, Canada – the Middle Spring (a sulfur hot spring in a natural cave), a waterfall in Johnston Canyon, and a formation of hoodoos overlooking the Bow River.
Three-dimensional videographic scene elements, spatialized sounds and voices, and simple character animation have been employed to construct a composite landscape that may be visited concurrently by two physically remote participants using head-mounted displays. Features and objects found in the actual places are reassembled here to serve as venues for exploration and play. People may walk about, speak, and use both hands to touch and move virtual objects.
People's relationships with places and the creatures who inhabit them have formed the basis of many traditions and spiritual practices, as well as ancient stories and myths. The graphic elements in 'PlaceHolder' are adapted from iconography that has been inscribed upon the landscape since palaeolithic times. Narrative motifs that lend expression to archetypal characters of landscape features and animals have been selected from aboriginal tales.
Four animated spirit critters – Spider, Snake, Fish, and Crow – inhabit this virtual world. A*

INTERAKTIVE KUNST

BRENDA LAUREL/RACHEL STRICKLAND

Landschaften oder Tieren ihren archetypischen Charakter verleihen, wurden Eingeborenenerzählungen entlehnt.

Spinne, Schlange, Fisch und Krähe, vier spirituelle Symboltiere, bewohnen diese virtuelle Welt. Ein Besucher kann in eines dieser Geist-Tiere schlüpfen und erfährt dabei Aspekte der einmaligen Seherfahrung des Tieres, seiner Bewegungsweise und seiner Lautäußerung. In diesem Sinn fungieren diese Wesen als ‚intelligente Kostüme', die den Menschen innerlich mehr verändern als äußerlich.

Die Besucher von „PlaceHolder" verändern die Installation. Spaziergänger beispielsweise hinterlassen in der Natur mitunter Zeichen, Piktogramme, Felsritzungen, Inschriften auf Mauern oder einfach Fußabdrücke. In „PlaceHolder" können sie Stimmspuren hinterlassen – Teile aus Erzählungen –, die von späteren Besuchern abgefragt oder umgruppiert werden können. Durch die Botschaften und Erzählstränge, die die Besucher entlang des Weges hinterlassen, gewinnt die Landschaft an innerer Bedeutung. Wir hoffen, daß „PlaceHolder" das Entstehen neuer, spielerischer Erzählweisen fördern wird.» (Brenda Laurel/Rachel Strickland)

person visiting the world may assume the character of one of these spirit animals and thereby experience aspects of its unique visual perception, its way of moving about, and its voice. Thus the critters function as 'smart costumes' that alter more than the appearance of the person within.

The people who visit 'PlaceHolder' will change it. Travellers sometimes leave marks in natural places – pictograms, petroglyphs, graffiti or trail signs, for example. In 'PlaceHolder', people may create Voicemarks – bits of spoken narrative – that can be listened to and rearranged by subsequent visitors. The virtual landscape accumulates definition through messages and storylines that participants leave along the way. We hope that 'PlaceHolder' will foster the emergence of new forms of narrative play.» (Brenda Laurel/Rachel Strickland)

Anerkennung
PlaceHolder, 1993
HW: SGI Onyx Reality Engine and others
SW: Minimal Reality Toolkit

INTERAKTIVE KUNST

GEORGE LEGRADY

George Legrady (USA), geb. 1950 in Budapest, emigrierte 1956 nach Montreal. Besuchte das Loyola College, Montreal, das Goddard College, Vermont, und promovierte 1976 am San Francisco Art Institute zum Master of Fine Arts. Außerordentlicher Professor an der Kunstabteilung der San Francisco State University für Information Art/Conceptual Design, einem Kunstprogramm, das Kulturtheorie und hochentwickelte Anwendungen digitaler Technologie in den Bereich der Konzeptkunst und zeitgenössischen Kunstpraxis integriert.

■ «‚An Anecdoted Archive from the Cold War' ist eine Installation, bestehend aus einem interaktiven Computerarchiv, das wie ein Ausstellungssystem eines zeitgenössischen Museums konzipiert ist. Die Schnittstelle des Archivs ist angelegt wie der Grundriß des ehemaligen Propagandamuseums der Arbeiterbewegung in Budapest.
Die Inhalte des Archivs sind auf CD-ROM und Bildplatte gespeichert und über Workstations in einem Installations-Umfeld abrufbar, das auch großformatige Texte und Bilder auf den dunklen Wänden der Galerie beinhaltet.
Das Archiv besteht in erster Linie aus öffentlichen und privaten Dokumenten aus Osteuropa, z. B. aus privaten ungarischen Amateurfilmen aus den fünfziger Jahren, aus aktuellem Videomaterial von Orten und Ereignissen in Osteuropa, aus Gegenständen, Büchern, Familiendokumenten, sozialistischer Propaganda, Geld, Tonaufnahmen und Berichten aus meiner Sammlung von Dingen und Geschichten, die mit dem Kalten Krieg zu tun haben. Diese Bestandteile sind in Form von über 80 Geschichten thematisch geordnet und über acht Räume verteilt, die analog dem Orginalgrundriß des Propagandamuseums der Arbeiterbewegung in Budapest angeordnet sind. Dessen ursprüngliche Bestände stehen seit 1990 unter dauerndem Verschluß.
Dieses bis zu einem gewissen Maße autobiogra-

George Legrady (USA), born 1950 in Budapest, immigratd to Montréal in 1956. Attended Loyola College, Montreal, Goddard College, Vermont, and received an MFA from the San Francisco Art Institute in 1976. Associate Professor in Information Arts/Conceptual Design, Art Department at San Francisco State University, an art program that integrates cultural theory and advanced applications in digital technology within the contexts of conceptual art and contemporary art practice.

■ *«'An Anecdoted Archive from the Cold War' is an installation artwork consisting of an interactive computer archive designed in the form of a contemporary museum display. The Archive's interface is based on the floor plan of the former Workers' Movement Propaganda museum in Budapest. The Archive's contents are all contained on CD-ROM and videodisk. These are viewed on workstations in an installation environment that includes large scale text and images on the darkened walls of the gallery. The Archive consists primarily of East European public and personal documents such as 1950's Hungarian home movies, recent video footage of Eastern European places and events, objects, books, family documents, Socialist propaganda, money, sound recordings, and reports in my collection of things and stories related to the Cold War. These items, in the form of over eighty stories, have been arranged thematically in eight rooms superimposed on the original floor plan of the former Workers' Movement Propaganda museum in Budapest – the original contents of which have been in permanent storage since 1990.
Autobiographical to a degree, the artwork adresses the transitional space between two world orders as reflected by my particular hybrid history – I was born in Budapest in 1950 near the end of the Stalin era, and fled with my family to the West during the 1956 Hungarian Revolution.*

INTERAKTIVE KUNST

GEORGE LEGRADY

phische Kunstwerk bezieht sich hauptsächlich auf den Übergangsbereich zwischen zwei Weltordnungen, der sich in meiner eigenen hybriden Geschichte widerspiegelt: Ich wurde 1950 gegen Ende der Stalin-Ära in Budapest geboren und flüchtete während des Aufstandes 1956 mit meiner Familie in den Westen.

Die Zuschauer interagieren nun mit dem Archiv, indem sie mit der Computermaus je nach Interesse Ausstellungsräume auf dem Interface auswählen und Geschichten abrufen. Daraus ergibt sich, daß persönliche Geschichten in unterschiedlichem Ausmaß mit öffentlichen Bildwerken und Dokumenten verwoben werden. Dieser interaktive Ansatz erlaubt es dem Zuschauer, abhängig von seiner Besuchsabfolge und seiner Eindringtiefe in das Museum, mit geringfügig unterschiedlichen Eindrücken bezüglich der Inhalte und Zusammenhänge des Archivs nach Hause zu gehen.» (George Legrady)

Viewers interact with the Archive by using the computer mouse to select and enter rooms and stories according to their own interests. As a result, personal stories are interwoven to varying degrees with public imagery and documents of the era. This interactive approach allows viewers to walk away with slightly different impressions of the Archive's content and context determined according to the sequence of their choices and the depth of their exploration.» (George Legrady)

**Anerkennung
An Anecdoted Archive from the Cold War, 1993
HW: Macintosh Quadra 650
SW: Director**

INTERAKTIVE KUNST

PATTI MAES

Patti Maes (USA), Assistant Professor am MIT-Media-Laboratory seit 1991. Doktorat in Künstlicher Intelligenz der Universität Brüssel 1987. Autorin verschiedener Publikationen, u. a. „Meta-Level Architectures and Reflection" und „Designing Autonomous Agents".

Patti Maes (USA), Assistant Professor at MIT Media-Laboratory since 1991. Ph.D. in Artificial Intelligence from the University of Brussels, Belgium in 1987. Author of several publications, including "Meta-Level Architectures and Reflection" and "Designing Autonomous Agents".

■ «Der Großteil der Virtual-Reality-Systeme stellt für den Teilnehmer keine besonders natürliche oder verbindliche Erfahrung dar. Eines der Probleme besteht darin, daß der Teilnehmer mit Datenhelm und Datenhandschuh komplett verdrahtet werden muß. Zum zweiten gestatten sie dem Teilnehmer üblicherweise nur, sich in eine einfache, eindimensional-lineare Interaktion einzuklinken. Normalerweise kann der Benützer nur durch einen virtuellen Raum navigieren (wobei sich verändert, was er wahrnimmt), und manchmal kann der Teilnehmer auch selber einfache Manipulationen an virtuellen Objekten vornehmen.
Das Ziel des ‚ALIVE'-Systems war es, eine ganz andere Art von Erfahrungen herzustellen. Wir wollten erreichen, daß sich der Teilnehmer in einer sehr viel natürlicheren, unbelasteteren Art und Weise mit vertrauten Bewegungen und ohne störende Ausrüstungsgegenstände mit dem virtuellen Raum auseinandersetzen kann, und haben uns dabei von der Arbeit des Pioniers Myron Krueger inspirieren lassen. Darüber hinaus war es uns wichtig, daß der Benützer mehr tun konnte, als sich nur durch die künstliche Umwelt zu bewegen und ein paar Handgriffe an virtuellen Objekten vorzunehmen. Wir wollten zeigen, daß es weniger darauf ankommt, wie phantasievoll und schnell die Graphiken sind, damit eine virtuelle Umgebung einladend wirkt, sondern vielmehr darauf, wie interessant und vor allem wie sinnvoll die Interaktionen sind.» (Patti Maes)

*■ «The majority of virtual reality systems do not represent a very natural or engaging experience to the participant. The first problem is that they require the participant to be 'wired up' by means of goggles or gloves. The second problem is that they typically only allow the participant to engage in simple, straightforward interactions. Typically, a user can only navigate through the virtual space (thereby changing what he/she perceives), and sometimes the participant can also perform some simple manipulations on virtual objects.
The goal of the 'ALIVE' system was to provide a very different kind of experience. Inspired by the work of pioneer Myron Krueger, we wanted a participant to be able to interact with a virtual environment in a much more natural, unencumbered way, using familiar gestures that do not require any obtrusive equipment. In addition, we wanted the user to be able to do more than just navigate through the environment or manipulate simple objects. We wanted to demonstrate that in order for a virtual environment to be very engaging, it might not be so important how fancy and fast the graphics are, but rather how meaningful and interesting the interactions can be.» (Patti Maes)*

INTERAKTIVE KUNST

PATTI MAES

**Anerkennung
ALIVE: Artificial Life Interactive Video Environment, 1993
HW: SGI Indigo 2
SW: C++, Inventor**

INTERAKTIVE KUNST

CHRISTIAN MÖLLER

Christian Möller (D), geb. 1959, studierte Architektur in Frankfurt und arbeitete als Stipendiat an der Akademie der bildenden Künste in Wien bei Gustav Peichl. Seit 1990 eigenes Architekturbüro mit einem Labor für Elektronische Medien und Softwareentwicklung. Seit 1991 Mitarbeit am Institut für Neue Medien der Städelschule Frankfurt.

■ «Die Installation ‚The Virtual Cage', eine Produktion des Theaters am Turm (Frankfurt), befindet sich in einem Theaterraum mit einer Größe von etwa 10 x 12 Meter. Mittig im Raum steht eine begehbare, bewegliche, hydraulisch gedämpfte gläserne Plattform. Zwei an der Plattform befestigte, 45 Grad geneigte Oberflächenspiegel fächern einen Laserstrahl als Referenzebene in den dunklen Raum. Sensoren übertragen die jeweilige Schrägstellung der Plattform an eine Iris-Indigo-Workstation im Nebenraum. Über ein Netzwerk besteht Verbindung zu einem Indigo-System im Theaterfoyer.
Der Raum wird beschallt durch eine 5-Kanal-Audioanlage, die durch das Indigo-Computersystem individuell gesteuert wird.
In dem Durchgang zwischen den beiden Räumen befindet sich eine Rückprojektionsfläche von 3 x 4 Meter. Im Deckenbereich des Nebenraumes angebracht, projiziert ein Video-Beamer ‚realtime'-Computergraphik von hinten auf die Leinwand.
Auf beiden Computersystemen läuft das gleiche Programm. Die Database enthält ein ‚wire-frame'-Modell des Raumes, in dem sich ein Schwarm von sich verfolgenden Punkten bewegt (die Kreatur). In Relation zur Schräglage der sich unter dem Gewicht des Betrachters neigenden Plattform wird der Schwarm durch den Raum bewegt. Dem Schwarm sind zwei verschiedene Geräusche zugeordnet, die als wahrnehmbare Äußerungen der Kreatur vom Publikum durch den Raum bewegt werden.
Durch die beiden miteinander verbundenen

Christian Möller (D), born 1959, studied architecture in Frankfurt and received a scholarship at the Akademie der bildenden Künste in Vienna where he worked under Gustav Peichl. Has his own architecture firm and laboratory for electronic media and software development since 1990. Associate at the Institute for New Media at the Städelschule in Frankfurt since 1991.

■ «The installation 'The Virtual Cage' is situated in an auditorium (a 'Theater am Turm' production, Frankfurt) approximately 10 m by 20 m. In the middle of the room there is a hydraulically damped glass platform where the viewer can walk around. Two surface mirrors fastened to the platform and tilted at a 45 degree angle reflect a laser beam across the darkened room as a reference plane. Sensors convey the instantaneous inclination of the platform to an Iris-Indigo workstation in the next room. A second Indigo in the theater foyer is connected via a network.
A five channel audio system controlled by the Indigo computer system fills the room with sound. In the connecting space between the two rooms there is a 3 m by 4 m rear-projection screen. A video beamer located close to the ceiling of the next room projects real-time computer graphics onto the screen from behind. The same program runs on both computer systems. The databases contain a 'wire-frame' model of the room, in which a swarm of dots chase each other around (the creature). The swarm is moved around the room in accordance with the angle at which the platform is tilting under the weight of the viewer. The swarm is allocated two different sounds which are moved around the room by the audience as a perceptible utterance.
The connection between the two computer systems allows two simultaneous ways of seeing:
– the viewer finds himself in the 'computer model' of the room and sees the creature as a fleeting shadow on the screen.

INTERAKTIVE KUNST

CHRISTIAN MÖLLER

Computersysteme sind zeitgleich zwei Betrachtungsweisen möglich:
– der Betrachter befindet sich im ‚Computermodell' des Raumes und sieht die Kreatur gelegentlich als Schatten auf der Leinwand;
– der Betrachter sieht im Monitor den gesamten Installationsraum (virtuell) durch eine andere Kameraposition von außen. Das sich darin befindliche schwarmartige Wesen ist aus dieser Sicht permanent zu betrachten, wie es interaktiv von den Betrachtern durch den Raum getrieben wird.» (Christian Möller)

– the viewer sees the whole installation room (virtually) through another camera position (from outside) on the monitor set up in the foyer. The swarm-like creature inside can be seen being chased around the room – interactively – by the viewers.» (Christian Möller)

Anerkennung
The Virtual Cage, 1993
HW: SGI
SW: Custom Software

INTERAKTIVE KUNST

CHRISTIAN MÖLLER/RÜDIGER KRAMM

Christian Möller (D), geb. 1959, studierte Architektur in Frankfurt und arbeitete als Stipendiat an der Akademie der bildenden Künste in Wien bei Gustav Peichl. Seit 1990 eigenes Architekturbüro mit eigenem Labor für Elektronische Medien und Softwareentwicklung. Seit 1991 Mitarbeit am Institut für Neue Medien der Städelschule Frankfurt.
Rüdiger Kramm (D) ist freier Architekt und Professor für Architektur an der Universität Karlsruhe. Er war Teilnehmer an zahlreichen Architekturwettbewerben und internationalen Projekten. Zahlreiche Architekturpreise.

■ «Bei Einbruch der Dämmerung schaltet sich, gemeinsam mit den Frankfurter Straßenlaternen, die ‚Kinetische Lichtplastik' der Frankfurter Zeilgalerie ein. Sie visualisiert die alltäglichen, aber unsichtbaren Phänomene der Straße: das aktuelle Wetter und den aktuellen Geräuschpegel in der Zeil.
Eine Wetterstation auf dem Gebäudedach operiert als Sensor von Wind, Temperatur und Niederschlag. Ein Computersystem steuert und überträgt diese Daten in blau-gelb changierendes Wetterfluten: Die jeweilige Temperatur bestimmt dabei die Menge der Gelbanteile auf der blauen Wand, und von Wind und Regen ist die Verteilung der Gelbanteile auf der Fläche abhängig. Diesen aktuellen Zustandsbericht der Straße ergänzt die Pixelwand im oberen Fassadenbereich.
Sie visualisiert mit einer blitzartig pulsierenden Liniengraphik den jeweiligen Geräuschpegel der nächtlichen Passanten bis zum Morgengrauen. Tagsüber schickt die Pixelwand als großflächige Informationsbörse Schlagzeilen und aktuelle Veranstaltungen über die Fassaden.» (Christian Möller/Rüdiger Kramm)

Christian Möller (D), born 1959, studied architecture in Frankfurt and received a scholarship at the Akademie der bildenden Künste in Vienna where he worked under Gustav Peichl. Has his own architecture firm and laboratory for electronic media and software development since 1990. Associate at the Institute for New Media at the Städelschule in Frankfurt since 1991.
Rüdiger Kramm (D), freelance architect and architecture professor at the University of Karlsruhe. He has taken part in numerous architecture contests and international projects and won many prizes for architecture.

■ «As dusk falls, the street lights of Frankfurt switch on, and so does the 'Kinetic Light Sculpture' in the Frankfurt Zeilgalerie. It visualises the everyday but invisible phenomena of the street, the instantaneous weather and sound level in the Zeil.
A weather station on the roof of the building acts as a wind, temperature and precipitation sensor. A computer system controls and portrays these data in weather currents shimmering in blue and yellow: the momentary temperature determines the amount of yellow areas on the blue background, and the wind and rain readings cause the distribution of the yellow areas across the surface. This momentary situation report on the street completes the pixel wall in the upper area of the facade. With a line image pulsing like lightning, the wall registers and illustrates the individual sound readings from nocturnal pedestrians until the dawn. By day the pixel wall acts as a large-format information exchange, displaying headlines and a calendar of events.» (Christian Möller/Rüdiger Kramm)

INTERAKTIVE KUNST

CHRISTIAN MÖLLER/RÜDIGER KRAMM

Anerkennung
Kinetische Lichtplastik, 1992
HW: SGI
SW: Custom Software

INTERAKTIVE KUNST

CATHERINE RICHARDS

Catherine Richards (CDN), Künstlerin. Universitäre Ausbildung in bildender Kunst und englischer Literatur. Zahlreiche künstlerische Arbeiten und Publikationen im Bereich neuer Technologien. 1993 „Canada Council for the Arts Award" für Medienkunst. 1993–94 Forschungsstipendium für zeitgenössische kanadische Kunst am Centre for the Visual Arts an der National Gallery of Canada.

■ «‚The Virtual Body' ist eine niedrige Säule, die an die Säulenstereoskope aus der Mitte des 19. Jahrhunderts erinnert, als diese neuen optischen Geräte teils wissenschaftliches Instrument, teils ästhetisches Objekt, teils Wahrnehmungsmedium waren. Diese Grauzone zwischen Objekt und Instrument belegt ‚The Virtual Body'.

Die Säule steht auf einer Plattform inmitten eines Raumes. Der Betrachter bemerkt beim Eintreten ein leichtes Glühen in Augenhöhe am oberen Säulenende. Es ist ein winziges, fast vibrierendes, gläsernes Zimmer. Die Wände sind durchsichtig, die bunten Bilder an den Wänden strahlen im Licht, das aus dem Boden kommt. Und wenn der Betrachter näher kommt, nimmt er eine Abbildung eines Rokokoraumes wahr.

Zur Plattform führende Stufen laden zu genauerer Betrachtung ein. Und ganz aus der Nähe bemerkt der Beobachter ein Messingguckloch am oberen Säulenende. Beim Hineinschauen sieht er zuerst ganz kurz die Rokokodecke des Zimmers, die aber anscheinend sofort vom Abbild des Bodens abgelöst wird, und dieses geht wieder über in das Bild der Decke. Das Raumgefüge im Miniaturzimmer wird ‚destabilisiert'.

An der Seite, an der bei einem richtigen Stereoskop ein Knopf angebracht wäre, befindet sich eine Öffnung, durch die man die Hand in den Raum hinein stecken kann ... um damit in den Raum einzudringen. Und mit dieser Interaktion durch den Betrachter beginnt eine dritte

Catherine Richards (CDN) is a visual artist with a university education in the visual arts and English literature. She has produced works and published extensively in the area of new technologies. Canada Council for the Arts' award for Media Arts 1993. Research fellowship in contemporary Canadian art at the Centre for the Visual Arts at the National Gallery of Canada for 1993–94.

■ *« 'The Virtual Body' is a short column, reminiscent of the column stereoscopes of the mid 1800's when the new optical instruments were part scientific instrument, part aesthetic object and part perceptual media. 'Virtual Bodies' occupies this ambiguous ground of instrument and object.*

It stands on a platform in the middle of the room. As spectators enter, they see that the top of the column, at eye level, is glowing. It is an almost vibrating miniature glass room. The walls are transparent. The coloured images on the walls glow with light from the floor within. Approaching, they see that the images are of a Rococo room.

Steps to the platform beckon for a closer look. Standing next to the glass room, spectators notice a brass peekhole in the top/ceiling. Peering inside they see, momentarily, the Rococo ceiling, but just as it appears, it seems to be interrupted by the floor image on the monitor and this floor image, in its turn, is again overtaken by the ceiling. The space in the miniature room destabilizes.

On one side of the room, where a knob on an instrument would be, is a hole to put one's hand inside the room ... to enter. With this intervention by the spectator, the third state begins. To an outsider, the miniature room suddenly becomes opaque and loses all its transparency and detail. Meanwhile, the peering spectator stares down at this hand spread across the room's floor. This floor moves away from him and his hand appears to be infinitely travelling away. It is taking his body

INTERAKTIVE KUNST

CATHERINE RICHARDS

Phase. Von außen betrachtet wird das Zimmer plötzlich lichtundurchlässig, verliert seine Durchsichtigkeit und seinen Detailreichtum. Währenddessen sieht der Beobachter seine auf dem Boden ausgestreckte Hand. Dieser Boden aber entfernt sich von ihm, und die Hand scheint sich unendlich weit wegzubegeben. Sie nimmt den Körper mit – so als ob der kleine Raum in die Unendlichkeit ausgefaltet würde, als würde sich Bewegungslosigkeit in Bewegung entfalten. Der Körper verliert alle Bezugspunkte: innen/außen, riesig/winzig, Betrachter/betrachtetes Objekt, Teil/Ganzes ... Wenn der Betrachter seine Hand wieder zurückzieht, erscheint das durchscheinende kleine Zimmer wieder und glüht noch einmal auf.

‚The Virtual Body' ist ein nostalgisches, materielles Objekt. Auf den ersten Blick sieht es aus wie ein Museumsstück aus verlockenden, warmen Materialien. Es läßt die Idee des Schönen aus dem 19. Jahrhundert aufleben und damit die Bestätigung der klaren Unterscheidung zwischen Betrachter und betrachtetem Gegenstand – ein geläufiger Betrachterstandpunkt –, und sobald der Betrachter mit dem Objekt interagiert, wird dieses vertraute Verhältnis auf den Kopf gestellt.» (Catherine Richards)

with it ... as if miniature space is folded into infinite space, as if stillness is folded into motion. The body loses all references: inside/outside; giant/miniature; spectator/object; part/whole. It becomes an instrumental site and part of the dispersion of events.
As the spectator withdraws, the transparent miniature room reappears, glowing once again.
The 'Virtual Body' is a nostalgic material object. A first sight, the piece seems like a museum object of alluring, warm, fine materials. It re-creates the 19C idea of the beautiful and, with it, the reassurance of the clear distinction between the spectator and the object. This spectator relationship is familiar. It is just this familiar relation that is challenged in new technologies. And once the spectator interacts with the piece, this initial spectator/object relation is turned inside out.» (Catherine Richards)

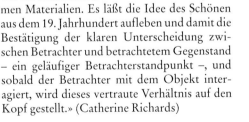

Anerkennung
The Virtual Body, 1993
HW: Amiga 600
SW: AMOS

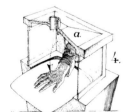

COMPUTERMUSIK

COMPUTERMUSIK

LUDGER BRÜMMER

Ludger Brümmer (D), geb. 1958. Von 1978–83 Studium der Psychologie/Soziologie an der Universität Dortmund. 1980–83 weiterführende Studien in Musik und Kunst. 1983–89 Kompositionsstudium an der Folkwanghochschule in Essen bei Nicolaus A. Huber (instrumentale Komposition) und Dirk Reith (elektronische Komposition). 1990 Musikdirektor am Theater in Bruchsal und Technischer Direktor sowie Workshopleiter beim Kamener Musikforum. 1992 Arbeit mit dem Nederlands Dansteater und dem „Ballett Orchestra", Den Haag, für das Stück „!Tristan und Isolde!", wobei das Orchesterstück „Riti Contour" mehrere Male aufgeführt wurde. 1991–93 Stipendium am Center for Computer Research in Music and Acoustics (CCRMA) an der Stanford University California. 1993 Lehrauftrag am elektronischen Studio der Folkwanghochschule Essen (ICEM).

■ «‚The Gates of H.' verwendet als Ausgangsmaterial Samples eines Volksliedes, das durch einen bulgarischen Frauenchor interpretiert wird. Die Überlegung, ein bereits existierendes Musikstück für eine neue Komposition heranzuziehen, geht davon aus, eine neue Struktur über das Ausgangsmaterial zu legen und damit eine Spannung zwischen der Originalstruktur des Stücks und der vom Algorithmus ausgehenden Struktur herzustellen. Es ist eine Mischung aus unterschiedlichen Zeitkonzepten, wobei der Zuhörer manchmal die Ebene des Algorithmischen, manchmal die Ebene des Ausgangsstücks und manchmal beide gleichzeitig versteht. Der Ausgangsklang hat die Funktion eines bekannten Bezugspunktes, der dann über verschiedene Parameterkonstellationen des Algorithmus neu definiert wird.
Die dynamischen Veränderungen (crescendo/decrescendo), vorwärts oder rückwärts, die neue Positionierung des Klanges im Zeitraster und die Klangdauer, zusammen mit der Umwandlung der Tonhöhen, erzeugen einen Effekt der Maskierung des Ausgangsklanges,

Ludger Brümmer (D), born 1958. 1978–1983 Study of psychology/sociology at the Universität Dortmund. 1980–1983 additional studies in music and art. 1983–1989 studies of composition at the "Folkwanghochschule" in Essen with Nicolaus A. Huber (instrumental composition) und Dirk Reith (electronic composition). 1990 musical director at the theater in Bruchsal. 1990 technical director and workshop trainer at the Kamener Komponistenforum. 1992 Work with the Nederlands Dansteater and the Ballett Orchestra, Den Haag for the piece "!Tristan und Isolde!" where the piece for orchestra "Riti Contour" was played several times. 1991–1993 scholarship at the "Center for Computer Research in Music and Acoustics" (CCRMA) at the Stanford University California. 1993 Teaching position at the electronic Studio of the Folkwanghochschule Essen (ICEM).

■ «'The Gates of H.' uses as the source-sound a sample of a folk piece sung by a Bulgarian female choir. The idea of using an already existing piece of music for a new composition is to put a new structure above the source-piece creating a tension between the original structure of the source-sample and the structure generated by algorithms. It is the mixture between two different time concepts, where the listener understands sometimes the algorithmical, sometimes the source-sound layer, sometimes both layers in its structure. The source-sound has the function of being the known reference which is then restructured by the parameter constellations of the algorithms. The dynamic modifications (crescendo/decrescendo), forward or backward, the new time position of the sound and the durations together with the pitch conversion create this masking effect to the source-sound, so that the image of a voice is sometimes clear and recognizable, but sometimes not. The same masking effect influences the harmonic structure of the piece in that the tonal character

COMPUTERMUSIK

LUDGER BRÜMMER

wodurch das Profil einer Stimme manchmal klar und erkennbar wird, manchmal auch nicht. Derselbe Maskierungseffekt beeinflußt die harmonische Struktur des Stücks insofern, als der Charakter der Klangfarbe des bulgarischen Volksliedes mit der Tonhöhenstruktur des Algorithmus in Konflikt gerät. Diese Methode steuert die Wahrnehmbarkeit entweder des Klangprofils des Ausgangsklanges oder der algorithmischen Komponente.

Der Verwendung des Algorithmus liegt eine zentrale Idee zugrunde: Ein oder mehrere Werte nehmen in unterschiedlicher Geschwindigkeit zwischen zwei beweglichen Grenzbereichen zu oder ab. Diese Werte werden dann auf unterschiedliche Parameter angewendet. Der erste Klang zum Beispiel wurde so erzeugt, daß der Tonhöhenwert zwischen Anfang und Ende des Klangs auf und ab pendelte, der Zeitwert dagegen vorwärts und rückwärts. In diesem Fall schwanken jeweils nacheinander bis zu fünf verschiedene Werte.

Die formale Struktur des Stücks ist sowohl durch klangliche Akzente als auch durch durchgehende dynamische und ansteigende dynamische Niveaus festgelegt. Die eigentliche Komposition beginnt mit zwei dynamischen Extremwerten. Während die ersten 340 Sekunden nur durch Akzente, weiche und laute Niveaus (subito ff oder subito pp) strukturiert werden, entwickelt der anschließende Teil Abschnitte mit ansteigender Dynamik, mit langen crescendi und decrescendi. Diese dynamischen Strukturen sind Verstärkungen der folgenden Wechsel in der Dynamik, wobei ein schnelles Crescendo wie ein Akzent oder ein subito ff wahrgenommen wird. Im Verlauf des Stücks gruppieren sich die Akzente zu immer komplexeren Akzentgruppen, die zwischen der 818. und der 850. Sekunde zu hörbaren Strukturen zusammenwachsen, also an jener Stelle, an der zwei Transpositionen der entstandenen Akzentgruppen zum Klingen kommen.»
(Ludger Brümmer)

of the Bulgarian folk song interferes with the pitch structure of the algorithms. This technique switches the recognizable image between the source-sound and the algorithmic image.

The algorithms use one central idea: one or more values increase or decrease at different speeds between two mobile limits. These values are then applied to different parameters. The first sound, for example, is generated by a pitch bouncing up and down while the time value bounces forward and backward between the beginning and the end of the sound. In this case, several (up to five) different values decrease and increase as the values are used one after the other.

The formal structure of the piece is determined by accents, continuous dynamic levels and ramped dynamic levels. The composition itself starts with two extreme dynamics. While the first 340 seconds have only very soft or very loud levels (subito ff or subito pp) and accents, the following part develops ramped dynamic parts with long crescendi and decrescendi. These dynamics are augmentations of the beginning dynamic switches, where a fast crescendo is perceived like an accent or subito ff.

Throughout the piece the accents combine to form more and more complex accent groups which grow into structures audible in seconds 818–850 of the piece, where two transpositions of the developed accent group are audible.»
(Ludger Brümmer)

Goldene Nica
The Gates of H., 1993, 18.03 min

COMPUTERMUSIK

ÅKE PARMERUD

Åke Parmerud (S), geb. 1953, Komponist und Künstler seit 1978, studierte Musik und ist gelernter Photograph, als solcher arbeitete er von 1972–75. Sein Werk umfaßt Instrumentalmusik, elektroakustische Musik, Multimedia und Video. Seine Werke wurden ausgezeichnet, u.a. beim Bourges Festival für elektroakustische Musik, beim „Prix Noroit" und beim „Stockholm Electronic Arts Award". Mehrere Jahre arbeitete er am EMS (The Electronic Music Studio of Stockholm), wo viele seiner Stücke entstanden. Seit 1987 unterrichtet er Computermusik und Komposition am Konservatorium Göteborg.

■ «In ‚Strings & Shadows' wirken die Saiten einer Harfe so, als wären sie Tore, die sich öffnen und eine Vielfalt instrumentaler, quasi-instrumentaler und manchmal auch vokaler Klänge in einem Strom ständiger Transformationen herausfließen lassen. Diese klangfarblichen ‚Schatten' werden durch Spiegelungen der Harfe mittels einer Vielfalt synthetischer Saitenklänge ergänzt. Allerdings gibt es auch noch eine andere Art musikalischer Schatten. Ein kurzes, melodisches Fragment einer Filmmusik zu einem Greta-Garbo-Film (‚Queen Christina') wird in einer leicht verzerrten Spiegelung der Harfe im Mittelteil des Stückes hörbar. In der Tat wird die melodische Entwicklung der Harfenstimme zu einem großen Teil von dieser Melodie abgeleitet. Die poetische Vision des Stücks ist das Bild einer alten, sterbenden Schauspielerin, die in einem letzten, rauschenden Tanzreigen die Schatten ihrer Vergangenheit revuepassieren läßt, während langsam der Tod als ihr Begleiter zu einem letzten Pas-de-Deux erscheint.
Das Klangmaterial für ‚Strings & Shadows' basiert hauptsächlich auf drei Typen von Klängen:
1. Klänge verschiedener akustischer Instrumente (Holzbläser, Streicher etc.);
2. stimmliche Klänge, die sich in instrumentale und/oder synthetische Klänge umwandeln;

Åke Parmerud (S), born 1953, composer and artist since 1978. Studied music, but also worked as a trained photographer from 1972–75. His list of works contains instrumental music, electroacoustic music, multimedia and video. His works have won awards like Bourges festival for electroacoustic music, "Prix Noroit" and "Stockholm electronic arts award". For many years he worked at EMS (The electronic music studio of Stockholm) where many of his pieces were realized. Teaches computer music and composition at the Music Conservatory of Gothenburg since 1987.

■ «In 'Strings & Shadows', the strings of the harp acts like gates that open up and let out a variety of other instrumental, quasi-instrumental and (sometimes) vocal sounds that flow in a constant stream of transformations. These timbral shadows are complemented with mirroring of the harp using a variety of synthesized string sounds. There is, however, also another kind of musical shadow present. A short melodic fragment from the filmscore of a Greta Garbo film (Queen Christina) can be heard in a slightly distorted mirror image of the harp in the middle section of the piece. In fact, the whole melodic development of the harp part has been to a large extent derived from this melodic theme. The poetic vision of the piece is an image of an old dying actress drawn into a last flowing sequence of dance through the shadows of her past while death slowly appears as her partner in the last Pas-de-deux.
The sound material of 'Strings & Shadows' is based primarily on three types of sounds:
sounds of different acoustic instruments (woodwinds, strings etc);
vocal sounds that transform into instrumental and/or synthetic sounds;
a variety of synthetic string-like sounds.
To obtain the transformations of timbres, I have used all kinds of techniques ranging from simple overlay and mixing to spectral interpolation

COMPUTERMUSIK

ÅKE PARMERUD

3. eine Vielfalt synthetischer Saitenklänge.
Um eine Transformation der Klangfarben zu erzielen, habe ich alle möglichen Methoden von einfacher Überlagerung und Mischung bis zu spektraler Interpolation und Phasenvocoder angewendet.
Die Erzeugung synthetischer Saitenklänge erreichte ich durch Frequenzmodulation, String-Modelling-Algorithmen und abgestimmte Resonanzfilter (mit verschiedenen Klängen als Anschlagimpulse).
Das ursprüngliche Klangmaterial wurde in etlichen Durchgängen durch digitale Signalprozessoren geschickt. Eines der wesentlichen Werkzeuge in der Anfangsphase der Klangbehandlung war das neu herausgekommene GRM-Tool für den Macintosh. Diese Arbeitsoberfläche zum Digital Signal Processing in Echtzeit ist eine spezielle Variante des Sytersystems, das in den achtziger Jahren am GRM in Paris entwickelt wurde. Die so verarbeiteten Klänge wurden dann mit gängigen DSP-Einheiten wie Ensoniq DP-4, RSP-Technologies Intelliverb und Lexicon LXP-300 weiterverarbeitet. Zusätzliches Material wurde später mit dem Eventide UltraHarmonizer erstellt. Für spezielle Arbeitsgänge wie Phasevocoding und komplexe Schleifen wurde nicht-Echtzeittaugliche Software wie TurboSynth und Sounddesigner von Digidesign, SoundHack von Tom Erbe und Infinity von Jupiter eingesetzt.
Mit Max und Vision von IRCAM/Opcode wurden die MIDI-Kontrollabläufe erstellt, und das ganze Material wurde dann im Studio Charybde in Bourges auf Festplatte überspielt. Zusammengefügt und synchronisiert wurde das Stück schließlich unter Verwendung einer 32MB-SampleCell II und einer 8MB-SampleCell I-Karte sowie eines Vierkanal-ProTools-Systems, alle gesteuert von Studio Vision von Opcode.» (Åke Parmerud)

and phasevocoding. The string synthesis was accomplished through frequency modulation, string-modelling algorithms and tuned resonant filters (with various sounds acting as plucking impulses).
The original sound material was put through several chains of digital signal processing. A major tool for the initial phase of treatment was the newly realesed GRM-tools for the Macintosh. This real-time environment for DSP is a special version of the Syter system developed during the 1980's at GRM, Paris. These processed sounds were later further processed using standard hardware DSP-units like the Ensoniq DP-4, RSP-technology's Intelliverb and Lexicons LXP-300. Additional material was later created using the Eventide UltraHarmonizer. Some non-real-time software like Digidesign's TurboSynth and Tom Erbe's SoundHack and Jupiter system's Infinity were used to achieve special processings like phasevocoding, complex loops, etc.
MIDI control processes were created using Opcode/Ircam's Max and Vision. All material was later transferred to harddisk in Studio Charybde at GMEB, Bourges. Assembly and synchronization of the piece was acomplished using 1 SampleCell II card with 32 Mb memory, 1 SampleCell I card with 8 Mb memory and a 4-channel ProTools system, all controlled by Opcode's Studio Vision.» (Åke Parmerud)

Auszeichnung
Strings & Shadows, 1993, 9.45 min

COMPUTERMUSIK

JONATHAN IMPETT

Jonathan Impett (GB), Trompeter, studierte an der Universität London (The City University), in Basel und Den Haag. Auftritte als Solist bei BBC Proms., am IRCAM und bei der Biennale von Venedig. Umfangreiche Arbeit auf dem Gebiet der elektroakustischen Musik als Komponist, Ausführender und Leiter des „Ensemble Metanoia". Arbeit mit Echtzeitkompositionssystemen im Umfeld der „Meta-Trompete" am Centro di Sonologia Computazionale, Padua. Spielt auch Barocktrompete und Kornett und ist Mitglied des Orchestra of the Eighteenth Century und des Amsterdam Baroque Orchestra.

Jonathan Impett (GB), studied at the University of London, The City University, and in Basel and Den Haag. A trumpet player, he has performed as soloist at the BBC Proms, IRCAM and at the Venice Biennale. He has worked extensively with electroacoustic music as a composer, performer, and director of the ensemble Metanoia. Works with real-time composition systems based around a "meta-trumpet", at the Centro di Sonologia Computazionale, Padova. He also plays the baroque trumpet and cornetto, and is a member of The Orchestra of the Eighteenth Century and The Amsterdam Baroque Orchestra.

■ «‚Mirror-Rite' ist eine Echtzeit-Komposition für Meta-Trompete, Computer und elektronische Instrumente. Das Instrument selbst nimmt jene Performanceaspekte, die dem Trompete-Spielen schon innewohnen, und abstrahiert und dehnt sie so aus, daß sie a) Musikmaterial für Kompositionszwecke und b) Werkzeug zur Steuerung anderer Parameter werden. Die erstellten Daten könnten dabei als eine Beschreibung einer umfassenderen Aufführungssituation gesehen werden, wobei der Klang der Trompete nur einen Blickpunkt darstellt.
Ein zentrales Anliegen beim Entwerfen des Instruments war, eine enge und dynamische Verbindung zwischen dem Instrument, seinem Spieler und dem musikalischen Material zu ermöglichen, egal ob es sich dabei um musikalische ‚Vorlagen' aus dem Computerspeicher oder Echtzeit-Aufführungsdaten handelt. Wie bei den meisten erfolgreichen Instrumenten kann man Klangerzeugung und Klangkontrolle vollständig im Instrument integrieren – in diesem Fall durch die tatsächliche Einverleibung des Computers (und damit der Komposition) ins Instrument. Der Ausführende kann damit eine Direktheit und Spontaneität der Kommunikation aufrechterhalten, während er ‚höhere' Ebenen von Abstraktion und Formalisation, sowohl des strukturellen als auch klanglichen

■ «'Mirror-Rite' is a real-time composition for meta-trumpet, computer and electronics.
The instrument itself takes aspects of performance already inherent in playing the trumpet, abstracting and extending them to become: a) musical material for compositional purposes, and b) means of direct control over other parameters. The data generated could be seen as depicting a broader performance situation of which the sound of the trumpet is one view.
A central aim in designing the instrument was to permit a close and dynamic relationship between performer, instrument and musical material, whether computer-stored 'score' or constructed in real time from performance data. As in most successful instruments, the roles of sound source and controller can be fully integrated, in this case by effectively incorporating the computer (and thus the composition) in the instrument. The player can maintain a directness and spontaneity of communication whilst retaining 'higher' levels of abstraction and formalisation of both structural and sound material. This can be seen as part of a move to re-empower not only the performer and performing situation, but thus also the listener.
Several continuous control parameters are implemented without compromising the

COMPUTERMUSIK

JONATHAN IMPETT

Materials, beibehält. Dies kann als ein Vorstoß in Richtung einer ‚Wieder-Aufwertung' nicht nur des Spielers und der Auftrittsituation, sondern auch des Zuhörers gewertet werden.

Mehrere durchgehende Kontrollparameter werden so eingesetzt, daß damit weder die Reichhaltigkeit des Instruments und seiner Spieltechnik beeinträchtigt wird, noch dem Ausführenden fremdartige Techniken aufgesetzt werden; die meisten sind Standard in der üblichen Aufführungspraxis.

Neben der Information in Form der Noten umfassen die Aufführungsparameter Lautstärke (auf zwei Ebenen, um damit sowohl Instrumenten- als auch Atemtöne mit einzubeziehen), Position in einem virtuellen Raum, Richtung und Geschwindigkeit der Bewegung, Neigung, Handdruck, Atemdruck, Ventilpositionen und verschiedene Schalter ...

Das gesamte Material stammt direkt vom Ausführenden an der Meta-Trompete, einem Instrument, das sowohl physikalische als auch musikalische Aufführungsdaten liefert. Diese Informationen werden vom Computer verarbeitet; durch Veränderung und kontextuelle Logik der Komposition entsteht erst die eigentliche Komposition. Es gibt keine Partitur oder sonstige Vorlage. Noten werden Teil des Kompositionsprozesses, wobei die Regeln dafür von den Noten selbst abgeleitet werden. Vorgänge initiieren dynamische Systeme und werden darin aufgenommen. Das Werk an sich wird dadurch zwar erfahrbar, aber nicht steuerbar. ‚Mirror-Rite' könnte man als parallele Sequenzen von Ritualen in unbekannten Sprachen erleben, in denen jede Handlung des Ausführenden ein Teil davon wird. Anders gesagt, eine spiralförmige Abfolge von Spiegelkabinetten unterschiedlichster Formen und Farben, die sich alle mit unterschiedlicher Dynamik bewegen.« (Jonathan Impett)

richness of the instrument and its technique or adding extraneous techniques for the performer – most of the actions already occur in conventional performance.

As well as note information, performance parameters include loudness (on two levels to capture breath and instrument sounds), position in a virtual 'screen', direction and speed of movement, inclination, hand pressure, breath pressure, valve position and various switches. Data is converted to MIDI by a STEIM Sensorlab for transmission to the composers 'Shells' composition and scheduling environment, running on a Macintosh. It is routed to a current 'scene' by input channel, where it can be processed directly or used as material for other processes. Several variable speed schedulers run simultaneously, triggering MIDI events or internal functions. Output controls the various synthesisers, samplers and processors, including mixing. The meta-trumpet is also being used within the integrated environment of the ISPW and could be used with other MIDI processing systems.

All of the material is derived directly from the performer by the meta-trumpet, an instrument which conveys both physical and musical performance data. This information is processed by the computer; by the changing and contextual logic of the composition, it becomes the composition itself. There is no given score or material. Notes become part of compositional processes whose rules derive from the notes themselves. Actions instigate and are taken up into dynamical systems. The work is thus 'knowable' but not 'masterable'.

'Mirror-Rite' could be heard as parallel sequences of rituals in unrecognised languages, of which the performers every action becomes a part. Or a spiral structure of chambers of mirrors, of different shapes and colours, all moving with different dynamics.« (Jonathan Impett)

Auszeichnung
Mirror-Rite, 1993, 24 min

COMPUTERMUSIK

PATRICK ASCIONE

Patrick Ascione (F), geb. 1953, ist seit 1991 Direktor des CAP (Centre d'Art Acousmatique et de Polyphonie Spatiale) in Vierzon. 1991 Mitbegründer der ABSO-Bewegung (Mouvement pour le développement de l'art acousmatique) gemeinsam mit Dhomont, Duchenne, Dufour u.a. Arbeit für die Groupe Experimental de Bourges, mehrere Arbeitsaufenthalte in den wichtigsten Zentren und Studios Frankreich (GMEA, GES, GRM, GMVL, IRCAM, CIRM). Mehrere Auftragskompositionen für GRM.

■ «Aus der gleichzeitigen oder aufeinanderfolgenden Wahrnehmung von in der Luft deutlich getrennten, bildlichen Darstellungen, Bahnen und Sendepolen kann eine besondere Form des Diskurses entstehen. Der Zuhörer, der sich so an die Stelle der traditionellen ‚Tonmischung' setzt, wird der aktive Empfänger der zusammengewürfelten Elemente des Stückes, eine Art von selektivem Katalysator.
‚Espaces Paradoxes' (‚Paradoxe Räume') läßt die Vorstellung einer Kunst ahnen, die es erlaubt, den Raum (eines Ortes) zu konstruieren und zu gestalten, ohne das projizierte Bild eines virtuellen, hinzugefügten Raumes an seine Stelle zu setzen.
Die Verteilung, die Bewegung und die jeweilige Ordnung der Töne im Luftraum wurden im Studio entworfen und verwirklicht – zur selben Zeit, als die Tonelemente und -sätze geschaffen wurden, die ihnen entsprechen. Da die räumliche Bestimmung der Töne (Mischung ‚Töne/Raum') ein wesentlicher Bestandteil des Schöpfungsaktes des Werkes ist, existiert keine ‚Diffusionspartitur', und es bedarf keines Verwaltungssystems – sei es automatisiert oder nicht – für den nachkommenden und mit dem Stück gleichlaufenden Raum. Nur ein Mischpult bleibt notwendig.» (Patrick Ascione)

Patrick Ascione (F), born in 1953, has directed the CAP (Centre d'Art Acousmatique et de Polyphonie Spatiale) in Vierzon since 1991. Co-founder of the ABSO movement (Mouvement pour le développement de l'art acousmatique) in 1991 together with Dhomont, Duchenne, Dufour and others. Work for the Groupe Experimental de Bourges; several working visits to the leading French centers and studios (GMEA, GES, GRM, GMVL, IRCAM, CIRM). Several commissioned works for the GRM.

■ «By means of the simultaneous or successive perception of figured planes, paths and transmission poles in the air, a particular form of discourse can emerge.
The listener, putting himself at the point of the traditional 'sound mixing', becomes the active receiver of the oddly assorted elements of the piece, a kind of selective catalyst.
'Espaces Paradoxes' ('Paradox Spaces') gives an idea of a kind of art which makes it possible to set up and design the space of a location without leaving the projected image of a virtually added space in its place.
The distribution, movement and arrangement of sounds in space are designed and created in the studio – at the same time as the sound elements and phrases were created which refer to them.
In view of the fact that determining the spatial characteristics of the sounds (sound/space mixture) is an essential part of the act of the creative process in this piece, there is correspondingly no diffusion score and no management system – automated or otherwise – requested in advance for the space that follows the piece and that runs concurrently with it. All that is needed is a sound mixer.» (Patrick Ascione)

Anerkennung
Espaces Paradoxes, 1990, 24.20 min

COMPUTERMUSIK

JEAN-FRANÇOIS CAVRO

Jean-François Cavro (F), geb. 1963, Studium der Informatik am Institut Européen Informatique, Lyon. Anschließend Studium elektroakustischer Komposition bei Denis Dufour, Lyon. Weiterführende Studien am IRCAM, Paris, und am Conservatoire National Supérieure de Musique de Lyon, u. a. bei Alain Robbe-Grillet (Bild und Ton).

■ «Schreiben und die Arbeit im Studio bedingen einander wechselweise. Die Ganzheitlichkeit ist dabei nur gewährleistet, wenn beide Elemente zusammenspielen, zum Beispiel beim Hören einer Aufnahme oder einer Aufführung. So vermittelt das Lesen der Partitur oder das Abhören der Aufnahmekomponenten (Sampler, Festplatte, DAT-Band …) höchstens einen unvollständigen Eindruck des Werks. Unter Rücksichtnahme auf die Einheitlichkeit wurden der elektronische Teil und instrumentale Materialien direkt verknüpft. Im Gegensatz zu den konkreten Klängen kommen alle Transformationen und voraufgezeichneten Klänge aus der Partitur und stehen damit in einer direkten Beziehung zu den Klangelementen des Werks. Die Idee ähnelt einer Spirale. Der elektronische Teil nährt sich aus dem Instrumentalen, was manchmal im elektronischen Chaos hörbar wird. Dieser Grundsatz wird zur ‚Conditio sine qua non' beim Gebrauch elektronischer Medien im Einklang mit dem Instrumentalen. Die Klänge, die ich aus voraufgezeichneten Fragmenten entnommen habe, werden – manchmal bis zur Unkenntlichkeit manipuliert – anschließend dem musikalischen Diskurs wieder zugeführt. Dann versuche ich, ihnen spezifische Rollen zuzuweisen: entweder kontrapunktische, rhythmische, auch morphologische oder als Begleitung und zur Hervorhebung der Instrumente.» (Jean-François Cavro)

Jean-François Cavro (F), born 1963, studied Computer Science at the Institut Européen Informatique, Lyon. Subsequently studied electroacoustic composition under Denis Dufour, Lyon. Continuing studies at IRCAM, Paris, and at the Conservatoire National Supérieure de Musique de Lyon, under Alain Robbe-Grillet (pictures and sound) and others.

■ «Writing and work in the studio are co-dependent on each other. The integrity of the work can only exist when these two elements are combined. For example, during the performance or when listening to the recording. Thus, reading the score or listening to the recorded elements (sampler, hard drive, DAT tape,…) will only give an incomplete idea of the work.
With a view to coherence, the electronic part is directly connected to the instrumental materials. Except for the concrete sounds, all the transformations and all the pre-recorded sounds come from the score and are therefore in direct relationship with the sound elements of the work. This idea is akin to a 'spiral'. The electronic part nourishes itself from the instrumental with the instrumental sometimes becoming audible in the electronic chaos. This axiom has been the condition 'sine qua non' for the use of the electronic medium in keeping with the instrumental.
These sounds are extracted from pre-recorded fragments, then manipulated, sometimes rendered unrecognizable, and then returned to the musical discourse. I then try to assign them a specific role: contrapuntal, rhythmic, also morphologic; as a single accompaniment to highlight the instruments.» (Jean-François Cavro)

Anerkennung
L'aube sublime de la tyrannie, 1992, 18 min

COMPUTERMUSIK

AKEMI ISHIJIMA

Akemi Ishijima (J), studierte angewandte Chemie an der Waseda Universität und elektroakustische Musik am EMS und am Royal College of Music in Stockholm. Erhielt ein Stipendium der Schwedischen Musikakademie, Master of Music in elektroakustischer Komposition der University of East Anglia. Dort derzeit Doktoratsstudium.

Akemi Ishijima (J), studied Applied Chemistry at Waseda University and Electroacoustic Music at EMS and The Royal College of Music in Stockholm. Recipient of the Swedish Music Academy Scholarship; Master of Music in electroacoustic composition from the University of East Anglia. Currently studying for the degree of Ph.D.

■ «Eine der einmaligsten Eigenschaften der elektroakustischen Musik ist ihre Fähigkeit, einen virtuellen Raum, der physikalisch gesehen nicht existiert, zu projizieren und ihn damit erscheinen zu lassen.
Die räumliche Wahrnehmung akusmatischer, elektroakustischer Musik resultiert aus der Interaktion zwischen den auf Band gestalteten akustischen und psycho-akustischen Bedingungen und der Hörsituation. Dadurch, daß so viele unvorhersehbare Faktoren beteiligt sind, ist die Raumwahrnehmung instabil und individuell verschieden. Trotzdem glaube ich, daß das Erstellen von Grundsätzen für räumliche Kompositionen eine Geschlossenheit schaffen sollte, und zwar nicht nur die Raumwahrnehmung betreffend, sondern auch in Hinblick auf eine generelle ästhetische Wertschätzung.
Ausgangspunkt bei der Komposition ‚Ab ovo' war die Bewegung eines Pendels. Ich mußte mir eine Art Klang vorstellen, vielleicht ein leichtes Vibrieren der Luft, wenn das Pendel vorbeischwingt, und ihn in einem elektroakustischen Klangraum musikalisch darstellen. ‚Ab ovo' ist die endgültige Abstraktion eines solchen Kompositionsprozesses. Obwohl der Klang des Pendels in seiner Urform nicht mehr vorhanden ist, werden zwei Aspekte der Bewegung auf verschiedenste Weise das ganze Stück hindurch reflektiert: die Periodizität und das Anhalten der Bewegung durch irgendeine Störung.» (Akemi Ishijima)

■ *«One of the most unique features of electroacoustic music is its capacity to project a virtual space which does not physically exist as such, but which is made to appear to do so.*
The spatial perception of acousmatic electroacoustic music is a result of the interaction between the acoustic and psycho-acoustic conditions composed on the tape and the listening situation. Since there are so many unpredictable factors involved, this perception of space is unstable and individual. Nevertheless, I believe that creating principles for spatial composition should give some sort of coherence not only to spatial perception, but also to the overall aesthetic value of the musical work.
The starting point for composing 'Ab ovo' was the motion of a pendulum. This means that I have to imagine a sort of sound, perhaps a tiny air vibration caused by the passage of a pendulum, and represent it musically in an electroacoustic sound space. 'Ab ovo' is the final abstraction of such a compositional process. Although the primal pendulum sound I made is no longer left in its original form, two aspects of the motion of the pendulum – periodicity and the stopping of motion caused by some interference – are reflected in various ways throughout the piece.» (Akemi Ishijima)

Anerkennung
Ab Ovo, 1993, 13.50 min

COMPUTERMUSIK

PAUL KOONCE

Paul Koonce (GB), geb. 1956, studierte Komposition bei Herbert Brün und Salvatore Martirano an der University of Illinois und bei Roger Reynolds an der University of California, San Diego. Dort Ph.D. in Musik. Produzierte Kompositionen für Computer, elektronische und instrumentale Medien. Auszeichnungen und Kompositionsaufträge, u. a. von der Luigi Russolo International Competition for Composers of Electronic Music und von der National Flute Organisation. Fellowship bei der McKnight Foundation.

■ «‚Hothouse‘ (1992) entstand auf einer NeXT Workstation unter Verwendung einer Vielfalt von Klangbibliotheken mit Instrumental- oder Umweltgeräuschen, die mit CMUSIC verarbeitet wurden.
Bei der Komposition von ‚Hothouse‘ war mir wichtig, die sich eröffnende Erfahrung eines Spaziergangs durch die exotischen Gemärke eines Tropenhauses hervorzurufen, eines Tropenhauses mit seiner reichhaltigen Sammlung von Pflanzen, die ganz offenbar ihrer angestammten Umgebung, den Gesetzen der Wildnis entrissen, im dunstigen Tropenhaus mit seinem unwirklichen Lebensraum in die unwirkliche Nachbarschaft anderer Pflanzen wiederangesiedelt wurden.
Jetzt, aus der Distanz zur feuchten Erfahrung bei der Komposition des Werks mit seinen dichtbewachsenen Blumeninseln und auskragenden Markisen, bin ich überwältigt von seiner hervorragenden Qualität der Übergänge von einer Welt zur anderen, auf die das Ohr entlang eines hauchdünnen Fadens von Entdeckungen mitgenommen wird. ‚Hothouse‘ wurde durch ein Fellowship für Komposition der McKnight Foundation unterstützt.» (Paul Koonce)

Paul Koonce (GB), born 1956, studied composition with Herbert Brün and Salvatore Martirano at the University of Illinois, and with Roger Reynolds at the University of California, San Diego where he received a Ph.D. in Music. He has produced compositions in the electronic, computer and acoustic media. Awards and commissions from the Luigi Russolo International Competition for Composers of Electronic Music and the National Flute Association; Recipient of a McKnight Foundation fellowship.

■ «'Hothouse' (1992) was created on the NeXT workstation using a variety of instrumental and environmental sound libraries processed with the sound-synthesis language CMUSIC.
In composing 'Hothouse', I was interested in evoking the unfolding experience of walking through the exotic confines of a hothouse with its rich collection of flora conspicuously removed from the environs and orders of the wild to the unlikely habitats and neighbors of the steamy hothouse interior.
Now distanced from the humid experience of composing the work, with its crowded enclaves and spreading canopies, I am struck by its overriding quality of transition which leads the ear past different worlds of sound on little else than a thread of discovery. 'Hothouse' was supported by a composer fellowship from the McKnight Foundation.» (Paul Koonce)

Anerkennung
Hothouse, 1992, 9 min

COMPUTERMUSIK

MESIAS MAIGUASHCA

Mesias Maiguashca (EC), geb. 1938, erhielt seine musikalische Ausbildung am Conservatorio de Quito, der Eastman School of Music, Rochester, NY, dem Instituto di Tella, Buenos Aires, und an der Kölner Musikhochschule. Produktionen im Studio für elektronische Musik des WDR, im Centre Européen pour la Recherche Musicale, Metz, und im IRCAM, Paris.

■ «Ausgangspunkt von ‚The Spirit Catcher' sind fünf Spektren unterschiedlicher Ausdehnung und Tonlage, aber mit vielen allgemeinen Teilbereichen, die eine harmonische Geschlossenheit gewährleisten. Der Klangobjekt-Generator hat die Klangereignisse gemäß vorher festgelegter Parameter erstellt. Der ‚Führungsparameter' heißt ‚Klangfarbe'. Die allgemeine Richtung ist von ‚lärmend' nach ‚klangvoll'.
Das Instrument löst die Computerklänge aus, durch MIDI-Pedale oder andere passende Mittel. Die ausgelösten Klänge sind räumliche Erweiterungen der instrumentalen Klänge. Sie entwickeln aber oft ein Eigenleben und rufen damit weitere Aktionen des Solisten hervor. Das Stück ist als ‚open-form-environment' angelegt, bei dem der Solist Klangereignisse nach seinem Belieben auslösen kann. Trotzdem ist diese Version als eine eigenständige Komposition ausgearbeitet worden. Melodie und Harmonie werden zur Gänze von den Spektren vorgegeben. Der Instrumentalklang wird während der Aufführung mittels eines MAX-Patch in der NeXT-ISPW-Oberfläche verarbeitet. Die Schnittstelle ist eine ‚Mathews-Drum'... Der hauptsächliche Zweck des Patch ist es, Instabilität in den Instrumentalteil zu bringen, gewissermaßen eine Un-Wirklichkeit. Erreicht wird das vom ‚Mathews-Drum'-Spieler, der improvisatorisch nach seinem Geschmack, den akustischen Verhältnissen usw. vorgeht.» (Mesias Maiguashca)

Mesias Maiguashca (EC), born in 1938 in Quito, Ecuador. Musical training at the Conservatorio de Quito, the Eastman School of Music in Rochester, New York, the Instituto di Tella, Buenos Aires, and at the Cologne Musikhochschule. Productions in the WDR Studio for Electronic Music, the Centre Européen pour la Recherche Musicale in Metz and in the IRCAM in Paris.

■ «The point of departure of the composition 'The Spirit Catcher' is 5 spectra with different ambitus and registers, but with many 'common partials' to assure harmonic cohesion. The 'sound object generator' created the events according to predefined parameters. The 'leading-parameter' is 'Klangfarbe'. The general direction is: noisy – with tone. The instrument triggers the computer sounds, either with MIDI-pedals or any other suitable means. The triggered sounds are spatial extensions of the instrumental sounds, however, they often develop their individuality and provoke new actions from the soloist. The piece is conceived as an 'open-form' environment where the soloist can trigger the events she/he wishes. However, the present version has been worked out as an independent composition. Melody and harmony are given entirely by the spectra. The instrument is processed during the performance by means of a MAX-Patch in the Next-ISPW environment. The interface is a 'Mathews-Drum'. The patch is a mixture of harmonizer, ring modulator and amplitude modulator, which produces spacialization by means of a circuit that generates Lissajou-curves. The main intention of the patch is to create instability in the instrumental part, a certain irreality. The performer on the 'Mathews-Drum' is to accomplish this improvisingly, according to taste, acoustics, etc.» (Mesias Maiguashca)

Anerkennung
The Spirit Catcher, 1992/93, 10.20 min

COMPUTERMUSIK

JULIET KIRI PALMER

Juliet Kiri Palmer (NZ), geb. 1967, studierte Klarinette, Komposition, elektronische Musik und intermediale Performance an der University of Auckland, Neuseeland. Seit 1990 in New York. In der Folge Zusammenarbeit mit Meredith Monk und Michael Gordon. Auftritte u. a. in John Zorns „Cobra" in der Knitting Factory, New York.

Juliet Kiri Palmer (NZ), born 1967, completed graduate studies in clarinet, composition, electronic music and intermedia performance at the University of Auckland, New Zealand. Subsequently worked with performance artist Meredith Monk, and Michael Gordon. She has among others performed at the Knitting Factory in John Zorn's Cobra.

■ «Ausgehend von einem mir sehr lieben Foto, auf dem meine Großeltern stolz ganze Büschel Grapefruits herzeigen, die in ihrem Garten gewachsen sind, habe ich begonnen, dieses persönliche Sinnbild in meiner besessenen Ausdrucksform widerhallen zu lassen. Ich wollte die Grapefruit zu Klang machen. Grapefruit. Ich suchte Texte, in denen die Worte ‚Fruchtfleisch', ‚Saft', ‚saftig', ‚Grapefruit', ‚ausquetschen', ‚abschälen' … vorkamen. Dann fand ich Leute, die mir für jene Szenarios und Eindrücke, die die Texte hervorriefen, ‚geeignet' erschienen, und nahm sie auf. Ich nahm die Geräusche der Früchte auf, wie sie in Stücke geschnitten, gelutscht, entsaftet und getrunken werden. Als ich die Aufnahmen anhörte, stellten sich für mich jene Momente als die interessantesten heraus, in denen die Leute versuchten, die Identitäten anzunehmen, die die Texte vorschrieben, und in denen sie sich dabei unbelauscht wähnten … Ich wollte eine intensive körperliche Aktion mit der Frucht selbst auf die Bühne bringen. So entstand eine Kadenz für Mixer und 75 Grapefruits, die nun der Angelpunkt der gesamten Aufführung ist. Innerhalb der ersten zehn Minuten schneide ich fieberhaft so viele Früchte wie nur möglich in Stücke, die das Publikum verzehrt, bevor ich den übriggebliebenen Grapefruits den endgültigen Schlag zukommen lasse. Was bleibt dann noch anderes übrig, als tief in sich hineinzutrinken und dann zu singen?» (Juliet Kiri Palmer)

■ *«Beginning with a photograph I hold dear of my grandparents proudly displaying bunches of home-grown grapefruit, I set out to make this image resonate through my obsessive expression of this personal icon. I wanted to turn the grapefruit into sound.*
Grapefruit.
I searched for texts using the words pulp, juice, juicy, grapefruit, squeeze, peel … Then I found and recorded people who seemed 'right' for the scenarios and characters these texts evoked.
I recorded the fruit themselves: cut into pieces, sucked, juiced and drunk. I listened to the recordings and found that the most interesting moments were when the tape recorder caught people off-guard in their attempts to assume the new identities the written texts suggested. Not only did these 'found' words take me to a place apparently far from my family and the fruit, but my friends' voices and personalities tapped into stories and emotions I had not expected. I wanted to stage an intense physical interaction with the fruit itself. A cadenza for blender and 75 grapefruit was born and is now the fulcrum of the entire performance piece. During the first 10 minutes I chop feverishly as many fruit as possible into segments which the audience devour before I deal the final electric blow to the remaining fruit. In the end, all that remains is to drink deeply and to sing.» (Juliet Kiri Palmer)

Anerkennung
Citrus, 1994, 20.30 min

COMPUTERMUSIK

MICHEL REDOLFI

Michel Redolfi (F), geb. 1951, seit 1986 Leiter des Centre International de Recherche Musicale (CIRM) in Nizza. 1969 Mitbegründer der Groupe de Musique Expérimentale de Marseille (GMEM). Zwischen 1974 und 1984 Zusammenarbeit mit Bregman Electronic Music Studio am Dartmouth College, Center for Music Experiment an der University of California in San Diego und dem elektroakustischen Studio des California Institute of the Arts.

■ «Anmerkungen des Komponisten aus der Sicht des Malers
1989: Stürmisches Treffen mit dem Opfer in einer Hotelhalle in São Paulo in Brasilien.
1991: Portrait Celeas in Nizza in den CIRM-Studios. Vor dem Mikrophon spielt er frei den Kontrabaß. Drei Aufnahmetage in Form von Klangskizzen.
1991: Ein paar Monate später Komposition der elektroakustischen Sequenzen im Studio; Versuch, Klang und Persönlichkeit Celeas einzufangen (Integration seiner Stimme).
Das Portraitprojekt wurde durch Zufall eine Galerie verschiedener Portraitstile, die Facetten des Solisten, vom wilden Experimentalisten bis zum lyrischen Jazzer, darstellen. Die Uraufführung für Kontrabaß und Tonband war als Duo/Duell zwischen Celea und seinen Klangportraits aus den Lautsprechern angelegt.
Der Solist Jean-Paul Celea
Französischer Bassist, geboren 1951. Mitglied des L'Ensemble Intercontemporain am IRCAM (mit Pierre Boulez, Luciano Berio und Karlheinz Stockhausen), entschied sich aber dann, sich dem Jazz und der improvisierten Musik zu widmen. Welttourneen u. a. mit Gitarrist John MacLaughlin, dem Vienna Art Orchestra. Derzeit Leiter von Meisterklassen am Konservatorium in Lyon, weiterhin Solokarriere.» (Michel Redolfi)

Michel Redolfi (F), born 1951. Director of the Centre International de Recherche Musicale (CIRM) in Nice since 1986, co-founder of the Groupe de Musique Expérimentale de Marseille (GMEM) in 1969. From 1974 to 1984, collaboration with Bregman Electronic Music Studio at Dartmouth College, Center for Music Experiment at the University of California in San Diego, and in the electroacoustic Music Studio of California Institute of the Arts.

■ *«Notes by the composer in the role of the painter*
1989: Stormy meeting with the subject in Brazil in a crowded São Paulo hotel lobby.
1991: Portrait of Celea in Nice at the CIRM studios. He plays the double bass freely. Three days of recording in the form of sound sketches.
1991: A few months later, composition of electroacoustic sequences in the studio to try to capture the sound and personality of Jean Paul Celea (integrating his voice).
This portrait project eventually became a gallery of various styles of portraits depicting facets of the soloist, from the experimentalist ferocious to the lyrical jazzman. The premiered version for double bass and tape was a duel/duo between Celea and his sound portraits playing from the loudspeakers.
The soloist Jean-Paul Celea
French bass player, born 1951. Member of L'Ensemble Intercontemporain at IRCAM (with Pierre Boulez, Luciano Berio and Karlheinz Stockhausen), he then decided to devote himself to jazz and improvised music. World tours, e. g. with guitarist John MacLaughlin and the Vienna Art Orchestra. Currently in charge of master classes in Lyon, he continues to pursue a carreer as soloist.» (Michel Redolfi)

**Anerkennung
Portrait of Celea with Double Bass, 1991–93, 18 min**

COMPUTERMUSIK

MICHAEL VAUGHAN

Michael Vaughan (GB), geb. 1954, studierte Musik am Dartington College of Arts und an der Nottingham University, wo er den Doktorgrad in Komposition erwarb. Sein Werk umfaßt instrumentale und elektroakustische Stücke. Lebt als Komponist in Cheshire und ist Lehrbeauftragter an der Universität Keele.

■ «‚Crosscurrents' verwendet den Aufbau eines Konzerts als Modell, indem das Tonband unter Verwendung verschiedener Kombinationen synthetischer und aufgenommener Klänge das Cembalomaterial erweitert und ausdehnt. Die Klänge wurden unter Einsatz verschiedenster elektroakustischer Methoden der Klangerzeugung und -Manipulation mit Computer, MIDI und traditionellen Techniken der ‚Musique Concrète' erzeugt. Im Stück selbst geht es um die verschiedenen Extreme einer Wechselbeziehung zwischen Cembalo und Tonband, die von unterschiedlichen Charakteristiken der Klangwelt des Instruments ausgehen. Im weiteren Verlauf dieses Teils tendiert das Tonband dazu, immer unabhängiger vom Cembalo zu werden, was schließlich in einem Tonbandsolo kulminiert. Dann folgt eine Cembalo-‚Kadenz' mit dem Rest des Werks, das sich zunehmend um eine Wiedervereinigung der beiden Teile bemüht, um so zu einer zyklischen Form zu finden. Der Großteil des Tonbandteils wurde aus sequenzierten Varianten von Abschnitten des Cembaloparts zusammengestellt, um damit verschicdene synthetische und gesamplete Klänge abzuleiten, so daß ähnliche gestische Profile während des Stücks erhalten blieben. Zur graduellen Entwicklung von Textur und Klangfülle im Cembalopart wurden algorithmische Kompositionstechniken angewendet.» (Michael Vaughan)

Michael Vaughan (GB), born 1954, studied music at Dartington College of Arts and at Nottingham University where he holds a Ph. D. in composition. His work consists of both instrumental and electroacoustic pieces. He lives in Cheshire working as a composer and lecturer at the University of Keele.

■ «'Crosscurrents' for harpsichord and tape uses the idea of concerto as a model, with the tape providing expansions and extensions of the harpsichord material using different combinations of synthesized and recorded sounds. These were created using various electroacoustic techniques of sound generation and manipulation including computer synthesis, MIDI and the traditional techniques of musique concrète.
The piece deals with various extremes of interaction between the harpsichord and tape arising from different characteristics of the sound world produced by the instrument. In the first large section of the piece, the tape and harpsichord combine to produce a form of 'meta-instrument'. As this section progresses, the general tendency is for the tape to become progressively more independent of the harpsichord culminating in a tape 'solo'. A harpsichord 'cadenza' follows this section with the remainder of the work working towards a further fusion of the two parts, thereby creating a cyclic form.
Most of the tape part was created by using a sequenced version of sections of the harpsichord part to drive various synthesized and sampled sounds in order to retain similar gestural profiles throughout the work. The gradual evolution of texture and register in the harpsichord part is composed using algorithmic techniques.» (Michael Vaughan)

Anerkennung
Crosscurrents, 1990, 14.50 min

COMPUTERMUSIK

ALEJANDRO VIÑAO

Alejandro Viñao (RA), geb. 1951, studierte Gitarre und Komposition in Buenos Aires. Studien am Royal College of Music und an der City University London. Ph.D. in Komposition an der City University. Kompositionsaufträge u. a. von IRCAM, MIT, Ensemble Intercontemporain, KRONOS-Quartett. Goldene Nica (1. Preis) beim Prix Ars Electronica 92.

■ «‚Borges y el Espejo' (‚Borges und der Spiegel') basiert im weitesten auf einem halbklassischen türkischen Lied. Ich war vorwiegend an der rhythmischen Komplexität und am Melisma der ottomanischen und prä-ottomanischen Musiktradition der Türkei interessiert. In dieser Art des Gesangs scheint das Melisma der zentrale Punkt zu sein, von dem aus repetitive Rhythmen ausgelöst und vervielfacht werden und komplexe und unterschiedliche Phrasen entstehen lassen, wobei sie aber einen starken Ausdruck von Einheit behalten. In ‚Borges y el Espejo' habe ich durch einfache Wiederholungen melismatischen Gesangs komplexe Rhythmen und eine sich dauernd verändernde Wahrnehmung einer Schwebung geschaffen. Die melismatischen Phrasen werden kopiert, wiederholt und transformiert, indem Spiegel sie in die Perfektion der Symmetrie oder in die Tiefe besessener Wiederholungen hineinvervielfachen. Spiegel und der Islam, das waren zwei Lieblingsthemen von Borges und, wenn man es im übertragenen Sinn sieht, sind sie auch das Thema dieses Werks.
Der Text in ‚Borges y el Espejo' hat nur wenig oder gar keinen Sinn. Größtenteils sind die verwendeten Wörter türkisch, sie wurden aber nach kompositorischem und musikalischem Bedarf umgruppiert, so daß sie den Regeln der türkischen Sprache nicht unbedingt folgen. Der Text ist fiktiv und wurde von mir erfunden.» (Alejandro Viñao)

Alejandro Viñao (RA), born 1951, studied composition, guitar and conducting in Buenos Aires. Studies at the Royal College of Music and the City University in London. PH. D. in composition at the City University. Commissions from various performing groups and institutions such as IRCAM, commission for KRONOS quartet for the 1994/95 season, MIT, the Ensemble Intercontemporain. "Chant d'ailleurs" won the 1st Prize "Golden Nica" at Prix Ars Electronica 92.

■ «'Borges y el Espejo' (Borges and the Mirror) is loosely based on a Turkish semi-classical song. I was primarily interested in the rhythmic complexity of melismatic singing in the Ottoman and pre-Ottoman musical traditions of Turkey. In this type of singing, the melisma seems to be the centre point from which repetitive rhythms are triggered and multiplied, creating complex and diverse phrases and yet, retaining a great sense of unity.
In 'Borges y el Espejo', I used the simple repetition of melismatic singing to generate complex rhythms and to create an ever changing perception of pulse.
The Turkish melismatic phrases are copied, repeated and transformed by mirrors which multiply them into the perfection of symmetry or the abysm of obsessive repetition. Mirrors and Islam, two of Borges' favourite subjects and, in a metaphorical sense, the subject matter of this work too.
The text in 'Borges y el Espejo' has little or no semantic meaning. Most of the words are in Turkish and have been re-arranged according to the musical needs of the composition and do not necessarily follow the syntactical rules of the Turkish language. The text is a fiction which I have invented.» (Alejandro Viñao)

**Anerkennung
Borges y el Espejo, 1992, 12 min**

COMPUTERMUSIK

FRANCES WHITE

Frances White (USA), (Computer-)Komponistin, studierte bei Lawrence Moss, Charles Dodge und Paul Lansky. Mehrere Preise und Ehrenmitgliedschaften, darunter zwei Spitzenpreise beim Festival in Bourges 1990. 1985 Assistentin von John Cage für sein Werk „Essay". Auf CD sind ihre Werke in der Serie „Computer Music Currents" bei Wergo, in der Serie „CDCM" bei Centaur und auf „Cultures Electroniques #5" bei „Le chant du monde" erschienen. Frances White lebt in Princeton, New Jersey.

Frances White (USA), composer, primarily of computer music. Studied with Lawrence Moss, Charles Dodge, and Paul Lansky. Various awards and fellowships, including two top prizes in the 1990 Bourges International Electroacoustic Music Competition. 1985 assistant to John Cage for the creation of his "Essay" compositions. Her music appears on compact disc in the Wergo Computer Music Currents series, on Centaur's CDCM series, and on Le chant du monde's Cultures Electroniques #5. Frances White lives in Princeton, New Jersey.

■ «‚Winter aconite' ist eine blühende Knollenpflanze. Ihre kleinen, gelben, butterschüsselförmigen Blüten gehören zu den ersten, die jedes Jahr erscheinen; im Nordosten sogar schon im Februar, wenn noch Schnee liegt. Wie viele der frühblühenden Pflanzen verbreiten sie sich gerne, wuchern und bilden große Polster. ‚Winter Aconites' (für Klarinette, Vibraphon, Elektrogitarre, Klavier, Cello, Kontrabaß und Tonband) war ein Auftragswerk für die ASCAP Foundation und das ‚Bang On A Can'-Festival in memoriam John Cage.
Kurz nachdem ich begonnen hatte (und noch bevor ich einen Titel dafür hatte), träumte ich, ich brächte John Cage eine Schale voll mit ‚Winter aconites'. Er war hocherfreut darüber – er liebte ja Pflanzen und Blumen –, und später, während meines Traumbesuchs bei John Cage, machten wir uns Sandwiches mit einigen Blüten drinnen (dabei weiß ich gar nicht, ob man sie überhaupt essen kann). Wie diese Blumen, so ist auch dieses Stück ein Geschenk an John Cage.
Der Tonbandteil von ‚Winter aconites' entstand am Winham Laboratory an der Princeton University auf einer NeXT Workstation unter Verwendung der Programme Cmix und Csound software.» (Frances White)

■ «The winter aconite is a species of flowering bulb (Eranthis hyemalis). Its small, yellow, buttercup-like flowers are among the very first to appear each year; in the northeast, it can bloom as early as February, while there is still snow on the ground. Like so many of the little early bulbs, winter aconites will naturalize – they will propagate themselves and form large colonies.
The piece 'Winter Aconites' (for clarinet, vibraphone, electric guitar, piano, cello, double bass, and tape; duration: 15 minutes) was commissioned by The ASCAP Foundation and the Bang On A Can Festival in memory of John Cage.
Shortly after I began work on it (and before it had a title), I had a dream in which I brought a pot of winter aconites to Cage. He was delighted – he loved flowers and plants – and later during my visit, we made sandwiches with some of the blooms (I have no idea whether winter aconites are actually edible or not). Like the flowers in my dream, this piece is a gift for John Cage.
The tape part of 'Winter Aconites' was created at the Winham Laboratory at Princeton University on a NeXT workstation, using Cmix and Csound software.» (Frances White)

Anerkennung
Winter Aconites, 1993, 15 min

PRIX ARS ELECTRONICA

JURY

PRIX ARS ELECTRONICA

VORSITZENDER DER GESAMTJURY
HANNES LEOPOLDSEDER

Hannes Leopoldseder (A), geb. 1940, Dr. phil. Seit 1967 als Journalist beim Österreichischen Rundfunk, Fernsehen, tätig, seit 1974 Landesintendant des ORF, Landesstudio Oberösterreich. 1979 Mitbegründer von Ars Electronica und der Linzer Klangwolke, 1987 Initiator des Prix Ars Electronica, 1993 Initiator des Ars Electronica Center, Präsident des Oö. Presseclubs, Vorsitzender des Landeskulturbeirates, Mitglied des PEN-Clubs, Mitglied des European Board des Circom Regionale.

Hannes Leopoldseder (A), born 1940, Ph.D., has been working for the Austrian Broadcasting Corporation since 1967. Since 1974 he has been General Manager of the Upper Austrian Regional Studios. In 1979 he co-founded Ars Electronica and the Linz Sound Cloud, in 1987 he initiated the Prix Ars Electronica, and in 1993 the Ars Electronica Center. He is President of the Upper Austrian Press Association, a member of the State Culture Advisory Board, a member of the PEN Club and of the European Board of Circom Regionale.

GESAMTJURY

PRIX ARS ELECTRONICA

JURY
GRAPHIK & ANIMATION

Michael Tolson (USA), geboren 1947, ist Mitbegründer und Präsident der Animationsfirma XAOS Inc., San Francisco, sowie federführender Wissenschafter bei XAOS Tools Inc. Studierte Mathematik und Physik an der University of Chicago, anschließend Studium der Malerei an der Cooper Union in New York City. Goldene Nica bei Prix Ars Electronica 93 in der Sparte Computergraphik für seine „Founders Series".

Michael Tolson (USA), born 1947, is co-founder and President of the animation production company XAOS Inc. in San Francisco, and principal scientist at XAOS Tools, Inc. He studied mathematics and physics at the University of Chicago, then transferred to the Cooper Union in New York City where he studied painting. Golden Nica at the Prix Ars Electronica 93 in the Computer Graphics category for his "Founders Series".

Michael Bielicky (D) studierte bei Nam June Paik an der Kunstakademie Düsseldorf und war Stipendiat der Cité Internationale des Arts in Paris, wo er an der École Nationale Supérieure des Arts décoratifs studierte. Zuvor Photograph und Pferdekutscher in den USA. 1991 Berufung an die Kunstakademie Prag als Gründungsdozent (Abteilung Neue Medien). Lebt in Prag und Düsseldorf.

Michael Bielicky (D) studied under Nam June Paik at the Kunstakademie Düsseldorf, received a scholarship at the Cité Internationale des Arts in Paris, and studied at the École Nationale Superieure des Arts Décoratifs. Previously, photographer and coachman in the USA. Appointed as lecturer at the newly estabished Department for New Media at the Prague Art Academy. Lives in Prague and Düsseldorf.

Rolf Herken (D), geb. 1954, studierte Theoretische Physik und Mathematik an der Freien Universität Berlin. 1986 gründete er in Berlin die Firma „mental images", die auf die Entwicklung von Hochleistungs-Visualisierungssoftware spezialisiert ist. Sein Hauptinteresse gilt der Computergraphik, v. a. der Bildsynthese, und der künstlichen Intelligenz, v. a. der Rolle von Vorstellungsbildern.

Rolf Herken (D), born 1954, studied Theoretical Physics and Mathematics at the Freie Universität Berlin. In 1986 he founded the company 'mental images' in Berlin, which specializes in the development of high image quality visualization software. His main professional interests are in computer graphics with special emphasis on image synthesis, and in artificial intelligence, specifically mental imagery and vision.

PRIX ARS ELECTRONICA

JURY
GRAPHIK & ANIMATION

Matt Mullican (USA), geb. 1951, Künstler. Lebt in New York. Bachelor of Fine Arts am California Institute of the Arts (1974). Seit 1973 zahlreiche Ausstellungen in den USA, Europa und Japan.

Matt Mullican (USA), born 1951, artist. Lives in New York. B.F.A. from the California Institute of the Arts (1974). Since 1973 several solo and group exhibitions in the USA, Europe and Japan.

Lucy Petrovich (USA) studierte Computerkunst (Electronic Visualization Department) an der University of Illinois, Chicago. Ausstellungen ihrer Arbeiten in den USA, Europa und Japan. 1988 Teilnahme an der ACM SIGGRAPH als Ausstellungsleiterin, 1989 in der Theaterjury und Course Speaker. Produzierte die 20-Jahr-Retrospektive für die SIGGRAPH 93 und ist Vizeintendantin des Electronic Theatre 1994. Mitglied des Computergraphik-Teams der Fernsehserie „Max Headroom". Lehrte Computerkunst an der University of Wisconsin. Derzeit Professorin für Computerkunst am Savannah College of Art and Design, wo sie Programmieren und Geschichte der Computerkunst unterrichtet.

Lucy Petrovich (USA), studied computer art at the University of Illinois, Chicago in the Electronic Visualization Department. Her personal work has been exhibited in the U.S., Europe and Japan. She has participated in the ACM SIGGRAPH conference as Art Show Chair in 88, Electronic Theater jury in 89, Course speaker in 89. She produced the 20 year retrospective for SIGGRAPH 93 and is the Electronic Theater Co-Chair for 94. She was a member of the computer graphics team for "Max Headroom" (the television series), taught computer art at the University of Wisconsin, and is currently Professor of Computer Art at the Savannah College of Art and Design where she teaches programming and History of Computer Art.

PRIX ARS ELECTRONICA

JURY
INTERAKTIVE KUNST

Roger Frank Malina (USA), geb. 1950, Bachelor in Physik am Massachusetts Institute of Technology (MIT). Dr.Phil. der Astronomie an der University of California, Berkeley. Executive Director am Center for EUV Astrophysics in Berkeley, Kalifornien. Principal Investigator für Raummissionen des Extreme Ultraviolet Explorer Observatory der NASA. Herausgeber des Kunstjournals „Leonardo" und Redakteur der Zeitschrift für Elektronik „Leonardo Electronic Almanac".

Roger Frank Malina (USA), born 1950, Bachelor's Degree in physics at MIT, Ph.D. in astronomy at the University of California, Berkeley. Presently Executive Director at the Center for EUV Astrophysics in Berkeley, California. He is the NASA Principal Investigator for Mission Operations of the Extreme Ultraviolet Explorer Observatory. Exective Editor of the art journal "Leonardo" and an editor of the electronic journal "Leonardo Electronic Almanac".

Roy Ascott (GB), geb. 1934, Künstler, ist Leiter des Centre of Advanced Inquiry in the Interactive Arts am Gwent College, Wales. Pionier der telematischen Kunst: „Terminal Art" (1980), „La Plissure du Texte" (Electra 1983), Biennale Venedig 1986, Ars Electronica 89. Zahlreiche internationale Veröffentlichungen. 1975–78 Dekan am San Francisco Art Institute, 1985–92 Professor für Kommunikationstheorie an der Hochschule für angewandte Kunst, Wien.

Roy Ascott (GB), born 1934, artist, Director of the Centre for Advanced Inquiry in the Interactive Arts, Gwent College, Wales. Pioneer of telematic art: "Terminal Art" (1980), "La Plissure du Texte" (Electra 1983), Venice Biennale 1986, Ars Electronica 89. Noumerous articles published internationally. Dean, San Francisco Art Institute, California 1975–78; Professor for Communication Theory, Academy of Applied Art, Vienna 1985–92.

Johnie Hugh Horn (USA), geb. 1951, Elektronik-Künstler. Ausstellungen in den USA, Europa und Japan. Produzierte und leitete in den letzten 12 Jahren Elektronik- und Computerkunstfestivals sowie einschlägige Großereignisse. Seine Zusammenarbeit mit SIGGRAPH begann 1983, Leitung des Electronic Theatre 1989, 1991, 1993 und 1994. 1988 Regie beim ersten Video-Katalog für interaktive Kunst der SIGGRAPH. Mitbegründer von „big Research". Derzeit technischer und künstlerischer Leiter von HUXLEY 101.

Johnie Hugh Horn (USA), born 1951; electronic artist whose work has been shown extensively in the U.S., Europe, and Japan. Produced and directed computer/electronic art festivals and large-scale events for the past 12 years. Associated with SIGGRAPH since 1983, directed the Electronic Theater in 89, 91, 93, and 94. Directed the first video catalogue of Interactive Art for SIGGRAPH in 1988. Co-founder of "big Research". Currently he is art/technical director for HUXLEY 101.

PRIX ARS ELECTRONICA

JURY
INTERAKTIVE KUNST

Michael Naimark (USA) war 12 Jahre lang unabhängiger Medienkünstler, bevor er 1992 zu Interval Research Corporation stieß. Lehraufträge am San Francisco Art Institute, an der San Francisco State University, am California Institute of the Arts, am MIT und an der University of Michigan. Mitherausgeber von „Presence" und „Leonardo Electronic Almanac". Bachelor of Science für Kybernetische Systeme der University of Michigan (1974) und Master of Science für visuelle Studien und Raumplanung am MIT (1979). Seine künstlerischen Arbeiten wurden international ausgestellt.

Michael Naimark (USA) independent media artist for twelve years before joining Interval Research Corporation in 1992. Faculty appointments at the San Francisco Art Institute, San Francisco State University, California Institute of the Arts, MIT and the University of Michigan. Member of the Editorial Boards of "Presence" and "Leonardo Electronic Almanac". Bachelor of Science in Cybernetic Systems from the University of Michigan (1974), Master of Science in Visual Studies and Environmental Art from MIT (1979). His artwork has been exhibited internationally.

Florian Rötzer, geb. 1953, lebt als freier Journalist und Autor (u. a. bei „Kunstforum International") in München. Er arbeitet überwiegend über Kunsttheorie sowie Medientheorie und Ästhetik. Publikationen: Florian Rötzer (Hg): Digitaler Schein, Ästhetik der elektronischen Medien, Frankfurt 1991; Peter Weibel und Florian Rötzer (Hg): Strategien des Scheins. Im Irrgarten der Begriffe der Medien, Frankfurt 1991; Künstliche Spiele (Mitherausgeber), München 1993; Das neue Bild der Welt (Hg.), Kunstforum International, Köln 1993; Cyberspace (Hg. mit Peter Weibel), München 1993.

Florian Rötzer (D), born 1953, lives in Munich as a free-lance journalist and author (e.g. for "Kunstforum International"). He writes mostly about art and media theory, as well as aesthetics. Publications: Florian Rötzer (ed.): "Digitaler Schein, Ästhetik der elektronischen Medien", Frankfurt 1991; Peter Weibel und Florian Rötzer (ed.): "Strategien des Scheins. Im Irrgarten der Begriffe der Medien", Frankfurt 1991; "Künstliche Spiele" (co-editor), München 1993; "Das neue Bild der Welt" (ed.), "Kunstforum International", Köln 1993; "Cyberspace" (co-edited with Peter Weibel), Munich 1993.

PRIX ARS ELECTRONICA

JURY
COMPUTERMUSIK

Charles Amirkhanian (USA), geb. 1945; Komponist, Perkussionist, Klangpoet und Radioproduzent. Er ist einer der führenden Vertreter der elektroakustischen Musik und Text-Klang-Kompositionen. Werkaufnahmen bei Empreintes Digitales (CDN), Starkland (USA) und Centaur (USA). Derzeit leitender Direktor des Djerassi Resident Artists Program in Woodside, Kalifornien, wo jährlich 60 Künstlern Studiokapazität und Unterkunft zur Verfügung gestellt wird, damit sie in der Einsamkeit konzentriert an ihren Projekten arbeiten können. Außerdem leitet er das jährliche „Other Minds Music Festival" in San Francisco.

Charles Amirkhanian (USA), born 1945; composer, percussionist, sound poet and radio producer. He is a leading practitioner of electroacoustic music and text-sound composition. Works recorded on Empreintes Digitales (CDN), Starkland (USA) and Centaur (USA). Currently managing director of the Djerassi Artists Program in Woodside, California, where every year studio time and accomodation is made available to 60 artists to facilitate concentrated work on their projects. Also heads the annual "Other Minds Music Festival" in San Francisco.

Lars-Gunnar Bodin (S), geb. 1935 in Stockholm; freier Komponist und Vorsitzender des Komitees für künstlerische Entwicklung an der Königlich-schwedischen Musikakademie. Studierte Komposition bei Lennart Wenström. Als Komponist elektroakustischer Musik Autodidakt. Lehrte elektroakustische Musik am staatlichen Musik-College in Stockholm und am Dartmouth College in den USA. Lars-Gunnar Bodin ist einer der Pioniere der elektroakustischen Musik in Schweden, darüber hinaus auch engagiert in den Bereichen Kammermusik, intermediale und visuelle Kunst, instrumentelles Theater und Happening. Von 1978 bis 1989 Direktor des Instituts für elektroakustische Musik in Stockholm. Mitbegründer der International Confederation for Electroacoustic Music (ICEM).

Lars-Gunnar Bodin (S), born 1935 in Stockholm; independent composer/artist and chairman of the Committee for Artistic Development at the Royal Academy of Music in Sweden. Studied traditional composition under Lennart Wenström. Self-taught composer of electronic music. Taught electroacoustic music at the State College of Music in Stockholm and Dartmouth College, USA. Lars-Gunnar Bodin is one of the pioneers of electroacoustic music in Sweden, and is also involved in chamber music, inter-media, happenings, instrumental theater and visual arts. From 1978 to 1989 he was Director of the Institute for Electroacoustic Music in Stockholm. Co-founder of the International Confederation for Electroacoustic Music (ICEM).

PRIX ARS ELECTRONICA

JURY
COMPUTERMUSIK

Werner Jauk (A), geb. 1953 in Kapfenberg, ist Universitätsassistent und Lehrbeauftragter für Systematische Musikwissenschaft an der Universität Graz. 1980 Promotion zum Dr. phil. mit einer Dissertation über Musikpsychologie und Kybernetik an der Musikhochschule Graz. Gründer und Leiter des Studios „Grelle Musik" für experimentelle Formen der akustischen und visuellen Künste. Aufführungen eigener elektroakustischer und intermedialer Arbeiten auf Festivals im In- und Ausland. Permanente Klanginstallationen für öffentliche Einrichtungen. Arbeitsaufenthalte am IRCAM in Paris. Früher Lehrbeauftragter für experimentelle Ästhetik an der Musikhochschule Graz. Verfasser von wissenschaftlichen Publikationen in den Bereichen Musikpsychologie, Musiksoziologie, Computermusik und Rock-Avantgarde, wobei ihn die Übertragung technologieimmanenter Prinzipien auf die Ästhetik von Musik interessiert.

Werner Jauk (A), born 1953 in Kapfenberg; assistant professor and lecturer in systematic musicology at the University of Graz. Doctorate in 1980 with a dissertation on psychology of music and cybernetics at the Graz College of Music. Founder and director of the "Grelle Musik" studio for experimental acoustic and visual art forms. Performances of his own electroacoustic and intermedial works at festivals at home and abroad. Permanent sound installations for public institutions, working visits to IRCAM in Paris. Previously lectured experimental aesthetics at the Graz College of Music. Author of scientific works in the areas of psychology of music, sociology of music, computer music and avantgarde rock, with the emphasis on the carrying over of principles inherent in technology into the aesthetics of music.

Ivanka Stoianova (BG), geb. 1945 in Sliven, ist künstlerische Leiterin des Ricordi-Verlags in Paris sowie Professorin an der Abteilung Musik an der Universität Paris VIII. Studien in Sofia, Moskau, Basel, Berlin und Paris (Geige und Musikwissenschaft). Doktorat und Professur in Paris. Daneben Tätigkeit im IRCAM und CNAC „Georges Pompidou". Preis der Académie Charles Cros für das beste französische Musikbuch des Jahres 1985 (Luciano Berio/Chemins en musique). Zahlreiche weitere musikwissenschaftliche Veröffentlichungen weltweit.

Ivanka Stoianova (BG), born 1945 in Sliven, is Artistic Director of the Ricordi Publishing House in Paris and a professor in the music department at the University of Paris VIII. Studied in Sofia, Moscow, Basle, Berlin and Paris (violin and musicology). Doctorate and professorship in Paris and activity at IRCAM and CNAC "Georges Pompidou". Académie Charles Cros prize for best music book of the year (Luciano Berio/Chemins en Musique). Many musicological writings published worldwide.

PRIX ARS ELECTRONICA

JURY
COMPUTERMUSIK

Trevor Wishart (GB), geb. 1946, Komponist. Werke: u. a. „Red Bird", elektroakustisch; „Tuba Mirum" (Musiktheater für präparierte Tuba); „Anticredos" (unter Anwendung erweiterter Vokaltechniken). Entwicklung von Software für Komposition, u. a. Spektral-Transformations-Programm für „VOX 5". Verfasser von „On Sonic Art". Gründungsmitglied von „Composer's Desktop Project", das leistungsfähige Musik-Computer-Werkzeuge für Komponisten zugänglich macht. Vorstandsmitglied von „Sonic Arts Network" für elektroakustische Musik.

Trevor Wishart (GB), born 1946, composer. His musical works include "Red Bird" (electroacoustic), "Tuba Mirum" (music-theatre for prepared tuba), "Anticredos" (exploring extended vocal techniques) and the "VOX" cycle of vocal works. He has developed much software for musical composition, including the spectral transformation programs used to make "VOX-5". Founder member of the "Composer's Desktop Project", an open-access group attempting to make powerful music-computing tools available to composers. In 1985 he published "On Sonic Art". Committee member of "Sonic Arts Network".

PRIX ARS ELECTRONICA

TEILNEHMER 94

TEILNEHMER 94

COMPUTERGRAPHIK

Abe Yoshiyuki
3-20-27 Meguro
Meguro-Ku, Tokyo 153
J

Abratowicz Gabriel
Helene-Mayer-
Ring 12/8
80809 München
D

Acevedo Victor
9561/2 N. Vista St.
Los Angeles, CA 90046
USA

Adler Barbara
Gernersgade 65
1319 Copenhagen
DK

Adt Reinhold
Hofgut Geroldseck
72172 Sulz/Neckar
D

Aitchison Martha
12 River Grove Park
Beckenham
Kent BR3 IHU
GB

Alexander Pat
19 E 83rd Street #4b
New York,
NY 10028
USA

Astrahan Ilene
Tru-Image
P.O. Box 660/Cooper
Station
New York, NY 10276
USA

Bac Bongsung
ACCAD
1224 Kinnear Road
Colombus,
OH 43212-1154
USA

Bachschneider Wolfgang
Unertlstr. 11
80803 München
D

Bailly – Basin Hervé
„Le Bosquet" Les Plans
74230 Thones
F

Ballhausen Achim
Mauerstraße 19
52064 Aachen
D

Barclay Daria
Abaci Gallery of
Computer Art
312 NW Tenth Ave.
Portland, OR 97209
USA

Barlow Jason
Texas A&M University
216 Langford Center
College Station,
TX 77843-3137
USA

Bauer Harald
Büro für graphische
Gestaltung
Thoracker 16
96052 Bamberg
D

Bean Celeste
2 1/2 Clark Place
Columbus, OH 43201
USA

Becker Scott
1528 N. Elk Grove
Street
Chicago, IL 60622
USA

Bellamy John Ashley
Art Images
2200 N. Haskell
Dallas, TX 75204
USA

Bellows Fenner Ruth
MiraCosta College
One Barnard Drive
Oceanside, CA 92056
USA

Benda Lubor
Total Vision
Bulharska 960
530 02 Pardubice-4
CZ

Berdel Thomas
Reichstr. 21 a
6800 Feldkirch
A

Böhme Steffen
Ahornweg 1
31275 Lehrte
D

Bonde Niels
Vendersgade 29, 4th
1363 Copenhagen K
DK

Bossi Lodovico/
Quinn Andrew
Visuals-Images &
Image Proc.
Via Watt 5
20143 Milan
I

Boztepe Tuncay/
Iranzo Jose
Sebastianplatz 5/2/20
1030 Wien
A

Briggs Jeffrey
1820 Lehner Road
Columbus, OH 43224
USA

Brock Owen A.
Zender + Associates
2311 Park Ave.
Cincinatti, OH 45206
USA

Brown Paul
PO Box 1292
Miss. State, MS 39762
USA

Büchler Uwe
Aspergstraße 58
70186 Stuttgart
D

Buchwald Michael
Heisesgade 19
2100 Kopenhagen Ö
DK

Burden Jeff
Columbus College
4225 University
Columbus, GA 31907
USA

Burris Jon
125 Concord Street
Brooklyn, NY 11201
USA

Cambilhou J.-M.
Dahinden
2 et 10, rue Française
75062 Paris Cedex 02
F

Canali Mario
Correnti Magnetiche
Viale Bligny 29
20136 Mailand
I

Caneparo Luca
Archimedia
Via Pigafetta 37
10129 Torino
I

Cassin Craig
P.O. Box 217
Talmage,
CA 95481-0217
USA

Catania Nicolò
Dunckerstr. 5
10437 Berlin
D

Chafchaouni
Mohammed Aziz
Hochschule für Medien
Peter-Walter-Platz 2
50676 Köln
D

Chang Rodney
2119 North King
Street #206
Honolulu, HI 96819
USA

Chauvet Hélene
Dahinden
10 rue Française
75002 Paris
F

Chmelewski Kathleen
University of Illinois
408 E. Peabody Drive
Champaign, IL 61820
USA

Clifford Paul
West Sussex Institute
1 College Lane
Chichester PO19 5PE
GB

Cole Michael
4948 Burnside Road
Sebastopol,
CA 95412
USA

Conrad Ralf
Karikaturen Konrad
Heresbachstraße 12
46459 Rees
D

Cooper Gene
Arizona State University
Box 872102
Tempe, AZ 85287-2102
USA

Cottingham Keith
1235 Bay St. #9
San Francisco, CA 94123
USA

Csuri Charles
Ohio State University
1224 Kinnear Road
Columbus, OH 43212
USA

Cummings Peter
L.I.H.E./Benedict Art
Centre
Woolton Road
Liverpool LI6 8ND
GB

Czerwinska-
Romanowska Ewa
Postfach 710748
81457 München
D

Dade Roger
Bournemouth and Poole
College
Shelley Park,
Beechwood Ave.
Bournemouth BH5 1NE
GB

Daggett Wright
Texas A&M University
College Station,
TX 77843-3137
USA

Daigneault Ginette
8427 Oscar Roland
Montreal, H2M 2T1
CDN

Davies Molly
684 BWay 10E
New York, NY 10012
USA

De Bardonneche-
Berglund Dominique
Rue Louis de Savole, 49
1110 Morges
CH

De Siqueira Nino/
Maria Do Carmo
07 Rue du General
Leclerc
94220 Charenton Le
Pont
F

Degtyarev Vladimir
P.O. BOX 1298
330114 Zaporozhye
UKR

Delappe Joseph
University of Nevada
Art Dept. 224
Reno, NV 89557
USA

Dement Linda
15/21 St. Neot Av.
Potts Point
Sydney, N.S.W. 2011
AUS

Diaz-Infante Juan
Cveston 192
Mexico D.F. 01900
MEX

Dimitrov Dimiter
Mega Art
78 Samokov Blvd.,
Bl.305, AP 61
1113 Sofia
BG

Dimon Roz
2 Charlton Street
New York,
NY 10014-4916
USA

Doksansky Simone
Pilgersheimer Str. 50
81543 München
D

Dombis Pascal
61, Rue Boursault
75017 Paris
F

Draves Scott
Carnegie Mellon
University
Box 159
Pittsburgh, PA 15213
USA

Drewinski Jadwiga
Flotowstraße 1
10555 Berlin
D

Drewinski Lex
Flotowstraße 1
10555 Berlin
D

Drott Hajo
Platanenstraße 3
82024 Taufkirchen bei
München
D

Düker Bodo
Karlstr. 15
67473 Lindenberg
D

Dulosy Maria
Am Westrand
2301 Schönau a.d.
Donau
A

Dunn Richard
9 Commercial Str.
Gl50 2AU Cheltenham
GB

Eames Angela
Univ. of Wolverhampton
Molineux St.
Wolverhampton
GB

Eberlein Gerhard
Postfach 1622
91006 Erlangen
D

Effertz Karin
Kleistraße 21
69514 Laudenbach
D

Egas Eric
Advanced Graphics
Box 600
Greenville,
NY 12083-0600
USA

Eike
Kl. Campestr. 8
38102 Braunschweig
D

Elsässer Jürgen
Heusteigstr. 59
70180 Stuttgart
D

Endl Kurt
Universität Giessen
Iheringstr. 6
35392 Giessen
D

Endo Susumu
3-13-3 Jingumae,
Shibuyaku
Tokyo 150
J

Engeli-Klemetti Riitta
Lettenstraße 8
9507 Stettfurt
CH

Esser Thomas
Washburn Univ. of Topeka
Topeka, KS 66611
USA

Evans Brian
Vanderbilt University
105 Computer Center
Nashville, TN 37240
USA

Fadon Vicente Carlos
Rua Livreiro Saraiva 236
01237-020 São Paulo
BR

Faiguenboim Irene
I & F Co.
R. Quimico Antonio
Victor, 211 Jaboatao
PE 54450-010
BR

Farrell Anne
VideoGraficArts
131 Huddleson Street
Santa Fé, NM 87501
USA

Fenster Diane
San Francisco State Univ.
1600 Holloway
San Francisco, CA 94132
USA

Fischnaller Franz
F.A.B.R.I.CATORS
Via Fratelli Bronzetti 6
20129 Milano
I

Flassig Willy
TWS GMBH
Inselstr. 3
63741 Aschaffenburg
D

Foltyn Andreas
Große Neugasse 1/10
1040 Wien
A

Fordyce Jon
301 W. Jefferson St.
New Carlisle, OH 45344
USA

Freeman Nancy J.
3550 Wilson Blvd.
Arlington, VA 22201
USA

Funk Gerhard
Robert-Stolz-Str. 5
4020 Linz
A

Furio Jean Marc
49, rue Montmartre
75002 Paris
F

Furio Morgane
Ensad A.I.I.
31, rue d'Ulm
75005 Paris
F

Gai Marilena
Archimedia
Via Pigafetta 37
10129 Torino
I

Galvao Erika
ACCAD
1224 Kinnear Road
Columbus, OH 43212
USA

Garvey Gregory
Concordia University
1455 de Maisonneuve Blvd. West
Montreal, QC H3G 1M8
CDN

Geiger Kevin
ACCAD
1224 Kinnear Road
Columbus, OH 43212
USA

Gellman Rachel
192 Bleecker Street #21
New York, NY 10012
USA

George Phillip
Zographics
11 Miller St., Bondi
Sydney, N.S.W. 2026
AUS

Germann Bea
Nordstraße 185
8037 Zürich
CH

Giedzinski Alison
11752 Miranda St.
Garden Grove,
CA 92645
USA

Giloth Copper
Univ. of Massachusetts
364 Fine Arts Center
Amherst,
MA 01003-4640
USA

Giménez-Noguera Josep
CREA
Bonaire 8
08720 Vilafranca
(Barcelona)
E

Giordani Massimo
Via Lorenzo Delleani, 8
10141 Torino
I

Giraud Jean-Luc
88 Quai de la Fosse
44100 Nantes
F

Gleeson Madge
Western Washington University
Bellingham, WA 98225
USA

Gloggengiesser Christine
Lerchenfelderstr. 50/2/18
1080 Wien
A

Glynn David
619 1/2 South Detroit Street
Los Angeles, CA 90036
USA

Goidaci Geo
Zum Künstlerhof 3
80634 München
D

Goldberg Marina
Weidenweg 43
10249 Berlin
D

Goldmann Harvey
41 Fisher Road
Westport, MA 02790
USA

Gönner Gottfried
Barbarossaring 8
55118 Mainz
D

Grancher Valéry
20, rue de la Charité
69002 Lyon
F

Gränicher Thomas
Hammerstraße 44
8008 Zürich
CH

Grey Michael-Joaquin
425 W. 13th St.
New York, NY 10014
USA

Gröller Eduard
TU Wien
Karlsplatz 13/186/2
1040 Wien
A

Gutzer Silke
Burg Giebichenstein,
Neuwerk 7
06108 Halle/Saale
D

Guzak Karen
707 So. Snoqualmie #5A
Seattle, WA 98108
USA

Haiden Claus
EDV-Ges.m.b.H.
Hofmühlgasse 3–5
1060 Wien
A

Hallier Valerie
445 W. 19th Street, #46
New York, NY 10011
USA

Harwood Graham
49 Sherwin Hse,
Kennington Road
London, SE11 5SB
GB

Haxton David
139 Spring Street
New York, NY 10012
USA

Heindl Joseph
Münchnerstraße 35
82069 Hohenschäftlarn
D

Hennig Carl
University of Waterloo
University Ave. W.
N2L 3G1 Waterloo, ON
CDN

Hermentin Ingrid
Salzköppel 9
35041 Marburg 21
D

Hermsdorf Thomas
Brüsseler Straße 25
13353 Berlin
D

Hervol Uta
Gabrielenstr. 2/II
80636 München
D

Hinker Gottfried
Streitmanngasse 53
1130 Wien
A

Hinreiner Christian
Bergkieferweg 6
80939 München
D

Hinteregger Herbert
Aschauerstr. 44
6365 Kirchberg/Tirol
A

Hmeljak Matjaz
University of Trieste
Via Valerio 10
34127 Trieste
I

Hoffman Paul
Unit 6/50 Ormond Road
Melbourne,
Victoria, 3184
AUS

Holt Charlie
7 Westhead Rd. Croston
Preston, Lancs,
PR5 7RQ
GB

Hörtner Horst
x-space
Kernstockgasse 22–24/II
8020 Graz
A

Howe A. Scott
Kajima Corporation
6-5-30 KI Building,
Akasaka
Minato-ku, Tokyo 107
J

Huff Randolph
344 West 14th St. #D4
New York, NY 10014
USA

Ibach Dick
523 w 17
Spokane WA 99203
USA

Iida Yoshihiro
Gifu Prefectural Ind.
Arts
1554 Yamada-cho
Takayama, Gifu 506
J

Ikam Catherine/
Fleri Louis
Territoires Virtuels
8, Rue des Haies Fleuris
93100 Montreuil
F

Irbe Igors
University of Illinois
106 Jefferson Hall
Chicago, IL 60680-4348
USA

Jacobsen Mogens
Rysensteengade 16-2T.V.
1564 Copenhagen V.
DK

Jahrmann Margarete
Stammgasse 5/3
1030 Wien
A

James Faure Walker
88 Greenwood Road
E8 1NE London
GB

Jamison Alexander
872 North
Longfellow St.
Arlington, VA 22205
USA

Jindrich Cieslicki
Rumunska 28
12000 Praha 2
CZ

Johnson Craig
Salonelectron
63 Providence Ave.
Doylestown, PA 18901
USA

Johnson James
University of Colorado
Boulder, CO 80309-0318
USA

Johnson Robert
16407 Woodlawn East
South Holland, IL 60413
USA

Jonczyk Leon
Franz-Joseph-
Straße 30/5
80801 München
D

Julia Tucholke
Atelier Art-Design
Pistoriusstraße 9
13086 Berlin
D

Kac Eduardo
725 W Melrose 2F
60657 Chicago, IL 60657
USA

Kahrs John
Blue Sky Prod.
100 Executive Blvd.
Ossining, NY 10562
USA

Kajdanski Carmen
Dietramszeller Str. 10
81371 München
D

Katterbauer Gerhard
Etrichstr. 32/2/13
1110 Wien
A

Kaufer Raoul
Richard-Wagner-Str. 6
93055 Regensburg
D

Keim Barbara
161 Llewllyn Drive
Westfield, MA 01085
USA

Kessels Sander
N.Z. Voorburgwal 130A
1012 SH Amsterdam
NL

Kiel Ronaldo
Hard Drive Studios
661 Metropolitan Ave.
3L
Brooklyn, NY 1121
USA

Kiera Werner
Maya Environments
Bennauerstr. 53
53115 Bonn
D

Kindlinger Gerhard
Stanglmühlstraße 9/2/13
8041 Graz
A

Kirgis Werner D.
Photo Graphics
1-11 Monmouth Terrace
Hong Kong
HK

Kirk Roberta
Kirkworks
1621 Hwy. 101
Yachats, OR 97498
USA

Kofler Michael
Schönaugasse 17
8010 Graz
A

Kofler Wilfried
Baptist-Türk-Str. 11
9500 Villach
A

Kopare Jerry
Kamomillgatan 10
75447 Uppsala
S

Kopp Manfred
TU Wien
Karlsplatz 13-186/2
1040 Wien
A

Korkor Josef
bildo akademie
Drontheimerstr. 21
13359 Berlin
D

Koyama Akira
8-1-1 Grakuen-
nishimachi
Nishi-ku, Kobe
J

Krause Dorothy S.
Massachusetts College
of Art
621 Huntington Ave.
Boston, MA 02115
USA

Kreeb Marion
Kriegsstraße 5
76137 Karlsruhe
D

Krenzien Sirius
DTP Werbetuning
Mittenwalderst. 61
10961 Berlin-Kreuzberg
D

Krzysztof Kiwerski
Krowoderska 53/7
31141 Kraków
PL

Kubelka Werner
Rua C, 396 Aldeia Itaipu
24355-260 Niteroi
BR

Kurz Harry
Weidesgrün 18
95152 Selbitz
D

Kwakman Jawek
KREM Medialab
Muntstraat 4f
1621 GB Hoorn
NL

Laing Rosemary
3A Gladstone Str.,
Lilyfield
2040 Sydney
AUS

Lantz Frank
1302 Park Ave #3N
Hoboken, NJ 07030
USA

Lapadula Karin
13810 SE Eastgate Way,
#500
Bellevue, WA 98005
USA

Latham William
IBM
NR. Winchester
S023 Hants
GB

Laurence M. Gartel
270-16b Grand Central
Parkway
Floral Park, NY 11005
USA

Le g.r.eggco
Görres Straße 30
c/o Cooper
80798 München
D

Legrady George
602 20th Street
San Francisco, CA 94107
USA

Lenk Helmut
Breslauer Straße 8
36151 Burghaun
D

Letertre Didier
Accaan Amh
40 Rue Pasteur
76300 Sotteville les
Rouen
F

Lintermann Bernd
Univ. Karlsruhe
Kaiserstr.12
76131 Karlsruhe
D

Löschner Andreas
Am Kirchtor 14
06108 Halle/S.
D

Lugert Jerry
2504 Ellentown Rd.
La Jolla, CA 92037
USA

MacClean Mark
EBU-Optik
42 Witcombe Point
SE15-5EH Yarnfield
GB

MacKay Don
University of Waterloo
200, University Ave.
Waterloo, Ontario
N2L 3G1
CDN

Macko Nancy
Scripps College
1030 Columbia
Claremont, CA 91711
USA

Macot Maurice
487 Pierre Boileau
Ile Bizard, Quebec
H9C 1T8
CDN

Makowska Jolanta
213 Rue de Versailles
92410 Ville d'Avray
F

Maltz Peter
Op de Elg 14
22393 Hamburg
D

Marc Jourdain
Hoscheidterhof
9458 Hoscheidterhof
L

Maros Vera
Szinyei Merse utc 16.
1063 Budapest
H

Martinez Ana
Plaza del Pais
Valenciano 2, 4
Xativa 46800 Valencia
E

Maxedon Terry
718 Broadway 9d
New York, NY 10003
USA

McSherry Stewart
6115 Carlisle ct.
New Orleans,
LA 70131
USA

Meads Mickey
University of Western
Ontario
N6A 5B7 London
(Ontario)
CDN

Metz Valerie
775 Greenwood Road
West Vancouver,
V7S 1X8
CDN

Michel M.
Franz-von-Waldeck-
Straße 3
48167 Münster
D

Miller Gavin/
Greene Ned
Apple Computer, Inc.
1 Infinity Loop
Cupertino, CA 95014
USA

Minogue Gerard
1 Albert Street
3181 Windsor, Victoria
AUS

Monaci Steven
SM Video
1118 Abbot Ave.
San Gabriel, CA 91776
USA

Morita Sui
3-15-2 Sengen-cho
Higashikurume-shi,
Tokyo 203
J

Moschik Ingrid
Wurmbrandgasse 2
8010 Graz
A

Mühleck Georg
data village art
Im Schellenkönig 56a
70184 Stuttgart
D

Munzner Tamara/
Levy Stuart/
Maxwell Delle
University of Minnesota
1300 South Second
Street # 500
Minneapolis, MN 55454
USA

Navarrete Carlos
Casilla 3395
Santiago
RCH

Neumann Ilka
Treskow Str. 23
13156 Berlin
D

Nikolic Svetislav
TRG Republike 1a
11000 Beograd
YU

Nixon Sean
Access Images
467 Central Park West
12-F New York City,
NY 10025
USA

North Mike
Loughborough College
of Art
Radmoor
LE11 3BT Loughborogh
GB

Notzelman Greg
37 Hall Ave.
W. Somerville,
MA 02144
USA

Okano Hideki
Polygon Pictures
Bond Street T 11 2-2-43
Higashi Shinagawa,
Tokyo 140
J

Opalach Agata
University of Sheffield
Regent Court 211
Portobello st
SIO 3ES Sheffield
SI 40 P
GB

Orest Dubay
Mudronova 49
81103 Bratislava
SK

Ortlepp Bernhard
Königsbergerstr. 6a
64579 Gernsheim
D

Paashuis Nelis
Kakeberg 22
6211 KN Maastricht
NL

Paloma Pippi
Wilhelm-Busch-Str. 63
09127 Chemnitz
D

Panev Dimitre
Delitzscher Str. 105a
04129 Leipzig
D

Parrish David
Texas A&M University
College Station,
TX 77840-3437
USA

Patchen Peter
University of Toledo
620 Grove Pl.
Toledo, OH 43620
USA

Paul Edie
Video Cats
4724 Lincoln Blvd. #270
Marina Del Rey,
CA 90292
USA

Perlman David
59 Stoneham Dr.
Rochester, NY 14625
USA

Pfeiffer Michael
Stresemannstr. 6
81547 München
D

Phillips Francesca
46 Hornton Street
London W8 4NT
GB

Pinter Gyula
Bajza utca 70 fsz. 2/A
1062 Budapest
H

Pirofsky Daniel
2173 N.E. Multnomah
Portland, OR 97232
USA

Porte Blaise
P.O. Box 20175
New York, NY 10009
USA

Priore Maria Luigia
Archimedia
Via Pigafetta 37
10129 Torino
I

Radke Marek
Dr.-Wurm-Str. 15
33104 Paderborn
D

Rand Harry/
Stanczak Julian
The Cleveland Inst. of
Art
11141 East Blvd.
Cleveland, OH 44106
USA

Ratner Peter
6391 W. Donnagail Dr.
Penn Laird, VA 22846
USA

Reichelt Ottomar
Clemens-Cassel-Str. 23
29223 Celle
D

Reiff Sabine
Correnti Magnetiche
Viale Bligny 29
20136 Milano
I

Revesz Laszlo L.
Eszter u. II
1022 Budapest
H

Robiner Steven
21 Topsail 4P
Marina Del Rey,
CA 90292
USA

Rogers Christopher
University of Georgia
Athens, GA 30606
USA

Rolf Simonetta
Willikonerstraße 52
8618 Oetwil am See
CH

Rollins Kent
5920 Hillsboro Rd.
Nashville, TN 27315
USA

Rosen Avi
Technion I.I.T.
Technion City
32000 Haifa
IL

Rosenberger Isa
Stuwerstr. 16/9
1020 Wien
A

Rubin Cynthia Beth
8 Sunset View RP.
South Hero, VT 05486
USA

Ruff Marianne
Schweighofstraße 91
8045 Zürich
CH

Ryszard Horowitz
R/GA Print
350 West 39th Street
New York, NY 10018
USA

Sakakibara Motonori
#6D, 10 River Road
Roosevelt Island,
NY 10044
USA

Salomo Eberhard
Friebelstraße 26
01219 Dresden
D

Sandor Ellen
(Art)n Laboratory
3255 S. Dearborn Ave.
Chicago, IL 60616
USA

Schatzl Leo/
Von Suess Petra Rosa
Art+Space Solution
Lorenz-Mandl-Gasse 33
1160 Wien
A

Schultheiss Ralf
Theodor-Heuß-Ring 1
50668 Köln
D

Schulz Günter
comPUTERARTstudio
Georgstr. 5
32756 Detmold
D

Sedlak Michael
Ringmauergasse 8/6/22
9500 Villach
A

Sen Quido
Arbachstr. 65a
6340 Baar
CH

Seun Wen Hwa
ACCAD
1224 Kinnear Road
Columbus,
OH 43212-1154
USA

Sherman John F.
University of Notre
Dame
Notre Dame,
IN 46556-5639
USA

Sherwin David
Rockette Works
P.O. BOX 3426
Berkeley, CA 94703
USA

Sidjanin Predrag
TU Delft
Berlageweg 1
2628 CR Delft
NL

Siegel Leah
95 Christopher Str. 4H
New York, NY 10014
USA

Slutzky Ernst
Nesselbuschstr. 1
60439 Frankfurt/Main
D

Smith Alexa
1860 West Shryer Ave.
Roseville, MN 55113
USA

Smith C. J.
881 Church Street
Woodburn, OR 97071
USA

Smith Gregg
Pratt Institute
106 W. 13th St.
New York, NY 10011
USA

Sorensen Soren L.
Herremagasinet Film &
TV Aps.
Nyvej 17
1851 Frederiksberg C.
DK

Soshea Steven
2054 Golden Gate
Avenue
San Francisco, CA 94115
USA

Sperling Bodo
P.O.Box 4711
64669 Zwingenberg
D

Spoke Lena
1862 Bathurst St. #601
Toronto (Ontario),
M5P 3K8
CDN

Steiner Michael
Lucestraße 6
33397 Rietberg
D

Steinkamp Jennifer
Art Center College of
Design
1700 Lida Street
Pasadena, CA 91109
USA

Stern Roland
Spectrospin AG
Industriestraße 26
8117 Fällanden
CH

Stösser Achim
Universität Karlsruhe
76128 Karlsruhe
D

Struwe Gerd
Heinrichstr. 45
50676 Köln
D

Suchodrew Edith
Oppenhoffallee 63
52066 Aachen
D

Suffern Kevin
University of Sydney
PO BOX 123 Broadway
NSW 2007
AUS

Tanneberger Sylvia-Kathrin
Bonndata GmbH
Poppelsdorfer Allee 27–33
53115 Bonn
D

Thiemann Karl-Hermann
Wuhrstr. 36
79664 Wehr
D

Thomas Michael
School of Art
University of Michigan
2000 Bonisteel
Ann Arbor, MI 48109
USA

Thomas Plazibat
23254 Sagebrush
Novi, MI 48375
USA

Tisma Alexandra
TU Delft
Berlageweg 1
2628 CR Delft
NL

Torinus Sigi
185 Collingwood St.
San Francisco, CA 94114
USA

Torsten Elger
Choriner Straße 37
10435 Berlin
D

Treinish Lloyd
IBM Research
P.O.Box 704
Yorktown Heights, NY 10548
USA

Tremblay Pierre
38 rue Hérault
92190 Meudon
F

Truckenbrod Joan
14 Cari Ct.
DeKalb, IL 60115
USA

Turre Michele
P.O. Box 338
Conway, MA 01341
USA

Ursula Reiprich
Weissenseestraße 4
81539 München
D

Ursyn Anna
Univ. of Northern Colorado
Greeley, CO 80639
USA

Vaden Jean
26, rue des renards,
1000 Bruxelles
B

Valesco Frances
135 Jersey St.
San Francisco, CA 94114
USA

Van Kerkhoff Sonja
Andre Severinweg 47
6214 PL Maastricht
NL

Van Zwaaij Walter
Virtual Design
Reijmerweg 39
6871 HA Renkum
NL

Verostko Roman
5535 Clinton Ave 5
Minneapolis, MN 55419
USA

Voci Peter
NYIT
Old Westbury Campus
Old Westbury, NY 11568
USA

Vogel Bernhard
Zillertalstr. 41
5020 Salzburg
A

Wackernagel Wolfgang
14 ch. de la Cocuaz
1253 Vandoeuvres
CH

Wagner Anna/ Roidinger Adelhard
188 First Ave. #4
New York City, NY 10009
USA

Waite Clea
Kunsthochschule für Medien
Peter-Welter-Platz 2
50676 Köln
D

Watz Marius
Artware
Sagveien 11A
0458 Oslo
N

Weber Ralf
Markgrafenstr. 10
76131 Karlsruhe
D

Weintraub Anette
City College of New York
138th Street/Convent Avenue
New York City, NY 10031
USA

Wennberg Teresa
40, Rue Benoit Malon
13005 Marseille
F

Werler Hannelore
Karl-Liebknecht-Siedlung E4
39118 Magdeburg
D

Werler Karl-Heinz
Karl-Liebknecht-Siedlung E4
39118 Magdeburg
D

Wesely Raimund
Keplerstr. 4
4400 Steyr
A

Westerdorf Helmut
Görresstr. 27
12161 Berlin
D

Whitaker Corinne
1530 Hillcrest Avenue
Pasadena, CA 91106
USA

Whitehill-Ward John
University of Washington
Seattle, WA 98195
USA

Wild Dennis
Lasting Impressions
RSD 173A Samuel Street
Elizabeth Town
Tasmania 7304
AUS

Wilgus Jack
6216 Tramore Road
Baltimore, MD 21214
USA

Wilson Mark
18 River Road
West Cornwall, CO 06796-0023
USA

Windlin Cornel
Quellenstraße 27
8005 Zürich
CH

Wittmer Thomas
Predigerstraße 3
79098 Freiburg
D

Woelpl Guimaraes Julian
Fractals-FTI
R. Carlos de
Carvalho 28–54
04531-080 São Paulo
BR

Wolfe Charles N.
1705 Siva Avenue
Anaheim, CA 92804
USA

Wolfram Schmidt
Im Gewerbepark D36
93059 Regensburg
D

Wood McCrystle
University of Cincinatti
Cincinatti, OH 45221
USA

Woytas-Voy Iwona
Altestadt 6/8
40213 Düsseldorf
D

Wysotski Andrew
1224 Cedar St.
Oshawa LIJ 3S2
CDN

Ying Hui-Chu
University of Akron
Akron, OH 44325-7801
USA

Young Emily
Portland State
University
P.O. Box 751
Portland,
OR 97207-0751
USA

Yourman Judith
1900 Princeton Ave.
St. Paul, MN 55105
USA

Zapf Reinhard
Lehenstr. 34
70180 Stuttgart
D

Zelic Zeljko
Osterwaldstr. 90
80805 München
D

COMPUTERANIMATION

Agnelli Jarbas
TV Cultura-Fundacao
Padre A.
R. Cenno Sbrighi, 378
Cep 05090-010
BR

Alaux Robert
Pandore
9 rue de Mulhouse
75002 Paris
F

Arcadias Laurence
Apple Computer Inc.
301-35-1 Infinity Loop
Cupertino, CA 94709
USA

Azarbayejani Ali
MIT-Media Lab.
20 Ames St.
Cambridge, MA 02139
USA

Bastier Eric
TEVA
24 Cours Michelet
92069 Paris la Défense
F

Batsry Irit
18 rue de l'Hôtel de Ville
75004 Paris
F

Batten Trevor
Kanaalstraat 15
1054 WX Amsterdam
NL

Bauer Michaela
LUX
Deutsches Museum
80306 München
D

Bayrle Thomas
Städelschule
Daimler Straße
60433 Frankfurt/M.
D

Benayoun Maurice
Z.A Production
64, rue de la Folie
Méricourt
75011 Paris
F

Bériou
AGAVE SA.
Cap. 108
67 Rue Robespierre
93558 Montreuil
F

Bishko Leslie
Simon Fraser University
Burnaby, BC V5A I56
CDN

Buscarini Juan Bablo
Univ. de les Illes Balears
Can. Valldemossa
07071 Palma, Balears
E

Cadoz Claude
ACROE
INPG-46 av. Félix
Viallet
38031 Grenoble Cedex
F

Callas Peter
7/8 Munro Street
North Sydney,
N.S.W. 2060
AUS

Caro Marc
Midi minuit
17 rue de la Croix Nivert
75015 Paris
F

Carpot Alain
A.I.I. ENSAD
31, rue d'Ulm
75005 Paris
F

Casadesus Xavier
Univ. de les Illes Balears
Can. Valldemossa
07071 Palma (Balears)
E

Cecchini Piero
Global Design
Corso di Porta Romana
20122 Milano
I

Chamney Martin
School of TV and
Imaging
Perth Road
DD1 4HT Dundee
GB

Chang Yina
ACCAD
1224 Kinnear Rd.
Columbus, OH 43212
USA

Coignoux Eric
Mikros Image
7 rue du Transvaal
75020 Paris
F

Conn Peter
Homer & Associates
1420 N. Beachwood Dr.
Hollywood, CA 90028
USA

Curran Michael
School of TV and
Imaging
Perth Road
DD1 4HT Dundee
GB

Currin Bena
CALTECH
391 S. Holliston
Pasadena, CA 91125
USA

Daggett Wright
Texas A&M University
College Station,
TX 77843-3137
USA

Darnell Eric/
Collery Michael
Pacific Data Images
1111 Karlstad Drive
Sunnyvale, CA 94089
USA

De Juan Jose Luis
Texas A&M University
College Station,
TX 77843-3137
USA

De Korczak-
Leszczynski Maciej
TVP SA BWZ
ul. Woronicza 17
00-950 Warschau
PL

Delabie Caroline
A.I.I. ENSAD
31, rue d'Ulm
75005 Paris
F

Dissaux Annie
12 rue Ganneron
75018 Paris
F

Draves Scott
Carnegie Mellon
University
Box 159
Pittsburgh, PA 15213
USA

Ellis Janiee
Texas A&M University
College Station,
TX 77840
USA

Fantôme
51 Rue Pierre
92110 Clichy
F

Faubert Jean-Luc/
B de F Rashel
„En Faruselle"
31290 Mauremont
F

Ferko Mariah
Dostojevskeho Rad 3
81109 Bratislava
SK

Fiersbach Andreas
Inst. f. Mediengestaltung
Weißliliengasse 2
55116 Mainz
D

Fildes Simon
School of TV and
Imaging
Perth Road
DD1 4HT Dundee
GB

Fitzgerald Sean
Easter Kilmany
Farmhouse
FIFE KYIS 4PT
Kilmany Nr. Cupar
GB

Fletcher Paul
P.O. Box 126
3126 Canterbury
AUS

Fleurova Marina
Av. Pushkin 38-91
Minsk, Byelorussia
BLR

Fuchs Michael
C A M F
Aignerstraße 78
5026 Salzburg
A

Garves Olaf
IMF
Wolfenbüttelstr. 9
38106 Braunschweig
D

Gibson Jim
Northern State
University
1200 South Jay Street
Aberdeen, SD 57401
USA

Giloth Copper
364 Fine Arts Center
Amherst,
MA 01003-4640
USA

Giraud Jean-Luc
88 Quai de la Fosse
44100 Nantes
F

Goldman Jeremy
Texas A+M University
College Station,
TX 77843
USA

Govil Shalini
201 Washington St.
Princeton, NJ 08540
USA

Grauel Günther
Grabenweg 6
34281 Gudensberg
D

Green Brian
Texas A&M University
College Station,
TX 77843-3137
USA

Greg Schmidt
Texas A&M University
College Station,
TX 77840
USA

Guilminot Virginie
DEUS
100 Rue du FBG
75012 St. Antonie
F

Haarhaus D.
Inst. f. d. Wissenschaftl.
Film
Nonnenstieg 72
37075 Göttingen
D

Haggerty Mary Beth
Texas A&M University
College Station,
TX 77843-3137
USA

Hallier Valerie
445 W. 19th Street, #46
New York, NY 10011
USA

Harris Irene
School of TV and
Imaging
Perth Road
DD1 4HT Dundee
GB

Harrison Gaye
450 Forrest Ave. R-200
Norristown, PA 19401
USA

Hazenfield Carol
Apple Computer, Inc.
1 Infinity Loop
Cupertino, CA 95014
USA

Hempel Irmo
Spandlg. 32
1220 Wien
A

Herbst Claudia
4822 Fernley Sq.
Baltimore, MD 21227
USA

Hershman Lynn
1935 Filbert Street
San Francisco, CA 94123
USA

Herzog Alexander
Dunckerstr. 5
10437 Berlin
D

Hong Won-Hwa
23 Country Club Way
Demarest, NJ 07627
USA

Huitric Hervé/
Nahas Monique
Université Paris 7
LUAP 33-43
2, Place Jussieu
75251 Paris-Cédex 05
F

Hurmusiadis Vassili
Bournemouth
University
Fern Barrow, Dorset
BH12 5BB
GB

Ikam Catherine/
Fleri Louis
Territoires Virtuels
8, Rue des Haies Fleuries
93100 Montreuil
F

Imura Takahiko
4-50-4 Yamato Cho,
Nakano-KU
Tokyo 165
J

Inakage Masa
The Media Studio Inc.
2-24-7 Shichrigahama-
higashi
Kamakura
J

Japon Beatriz
Univ. de les Illes Balears
Can. Valldemossa
07071 Palma
E

Jean-François Colonna
LACTAMME
Ecole Polytechnique
91128 Palaiseau Cédex
F

Jeong Eugene
Art Center College of
Design
1700 Lida St.
Los Angeles, CA 90041
USA

Jiempreecha Wichar
26-30, Amphawa
75110 Amphawa
T

Kachaer Valery
„PILOT" Moscow
Animation Stud.
Maly Vuzovsky per. 4/6
109028 Moskau
R

Kaltenbacher Brigitte
Siemensstraße 6
94327 Bogen
D

Karczewski Piotr/
Vaerman Bruno
A.I.I. ENSAD
31, rue d'Ulm
75005 Paris
F

Kaul Dave
ACCAD
1224 Kinnear Rd.
Columbus,
OH 43212-1154
USA

Kawaguchi Yoichiro
University of Tsukuba
1-1-1 Tennodai
Tsukuba-Science
City 305
J

Kim Man-Kyu/
Jin Su-Ha
KBS ArtsVision
18 Yoido-dong,
Youngdungpo-gu
Seoul, 150-790
ROK

Kisseleva Olga
4, allée de la Genetzière
78620 Etang-la-ville
F

Kobrin Vladimir
ul. Amundsena 10, apt. 3
129343 Moskau
R

Kogler Peter
Bechardg. 16
1030 Wien
A

Köhler Axel
media design
Augsburger Straße 57
01309 Dresden
D

Kroyer Bill
12517 Chandler Bl.
Suite 203
North Hollywood,
CA 91607
USA

Krupka Uwe
Dahlweg 76
48153 Münster
D

Lagarce Jean-Luc
3 Cité Falguière
75015 Paris
F

Lakicevic Johanan
IBA-Israel Television
Torah M210N St.,
Po.Box 7139
Jerusalem
IL

Landis Hayden/
Preston Henry
XAOS Inc.
600 Townsend,
Suite 271E
San Francisco, CA 94103
USA

Landreth Christopher
NCSC
3021 Cornwallis Rd.
Research Triangle P.
NC 27709-2889
USA

Lannaud Olivier
A.I.I. ENSAD
31, rue d'Ulm
75005 Paris
F

Larsen Teresa
The Scripps Research
10666 N. Torrey
Pines Rd.
La Jolla, CA 92037
USA

Latham William
Artworks/IBM
NR. Winchester
S023 Hants
GB

Lecutiez Sandrine
A.I.I. ENSAD
31, rue d'Ulm
75005 Paris
F

Lee Maylin
BBC Graphic Design
Wood Lane
W128QT London
GB

Legenstein Walter
Putstone Ideafactory
Barth.-Arnoldi-
Straße 72
61250 Usingen
D

Léger Roberte/
Bourigault Christian
Art Video Danse
89 route de Colmar
67100 Strasbourg
F

Levin Benny
Isreali Television
1 Sary Isreal
96757 Jerusalem
IL

Limber Michael
Angel Studios
5962 La Place Court,
Suite 100
Carlsbad, CA 92008
USA

MacDonald Iain
BBC Television
Wood Lane
W12 7R5 London
GB

Magyar Adam
VTV PECS, Hungary
Lanc u.6
7626 Pecs
H

Mai Sabine/
Pröscholdt Frank
Friedrichstr. 17
90762 Fürth
D

Mapes Kate
School of TV and
Imaging
Perth Road
DD1 4HT Dundee
GB

Marsan Dino
Pubbliteam Photo
Caldirolo, 84
44100 Ferrara
I

Maxwell Faye
16/145 Fitzroy St.
St Kilda
3182 Melbourne
AUS

McCormack Jon
43 Birkenhead Street
3068 North Fitzroy
(Victoria)
AUS

McFadden Robert
8185 rue Berri
H2P 2G1 Montreal
(Quebec)
CDN

Meierhofer Christine
Praterstr. 76/9a
1020 Wien
A

Mermoud Philippa
Ecole cantonale d'art
46, rue de l'Industrie
1030 Bussigny
CH

Miller Gavin/
Greene Ned
Apple Computer, Inc.
1 Infinity Loop
Cupertino, CA 95014
USA

Minako Sugiura
HD/CG
34–12 36th Str.
Astoria, NY 11231
USA

Moilanen Milla
Kroma Productions
Magnusborg
06100 Porvoo
SF

Moragues Jordi
Univ. de les Illes Balears
Can. Valdemossa
07071 Palma
E

Munzner Tamara
University of Minnesota
1300 South Second
Street # 500
Minneapolis, MN 55454
USA

Muren Dennis/
Dippé Mark
Industrial Light & Magic
P.O.Box 2459
San Rafael, CA 94912
USA

Myers Dale
Microtech Graphics
9602 Hartel
Livonia, MI 48150
USA

Nakamae Eihachiro/
Yamashita Hideo
Hiroshima University
1-4-1 Kagamiyama
Higashi-hiroshima 724
J

Netzstadt Projektgruppe
Glauburgstr. 74
60318 Frankfurt/M.
D

Nieto Natalia
Univ. de les Illes Balears
Can. Valldemossa
07071 Palma
E

Pacal
A.I.I. ENSAD
31, rue d'Ulm
75005 Paris
F

Pakesch Muki
Mühlgasse 22/13
1040 Wien
A

Pardo Ignacio
Hortaleza 54 – 4B
28004 Madrid
E

Paternoster Nance
Panting SNO Prod.
546 Wisconsin Street
San Francisco, CA 94107
USA

Pearce Celia/Codd Matt
IWerks Entertainment,
Inc.
4540 W. Valerio St.
Burbank, CA 91505
USA

Petiot Francoise
Actis
52 cours Aristide Briand
69300 Caluire
F

Pier Paolo De Fina
Alphaville Studio Srl.
Via Lovanio 4
20121 Milano
I

Pio Patrizia
S.B.P.
Via E. Jenner 147
00183 Rom
I

Platt Tim/Wyatt Jane/
Chaudoir Mark
Presentation Graphic
Design
Wood Lane, Room 201
W12 London
GB

Provenzano Paul
Acclaim
71 Audrey Ave.
Oyster Bay, NY 11771
USA

Pukema Bruce
230 10th Ave. So.
Suite 301
Minneapolis, MN 55415
USA

Radchenko
Vyacheslav V.
Albatros Studio
Universitetski pr., 1
630090 Novosibirsk
R

Rezeau Caroline
A.I.I. ENSAD
31, rue d'Ulm
75005 Paris
F

Riphead Buggy G.
EBU-Optik
42 Witcombe Point
SE15-5EH Yarnfield
GB

Robiner Steven
21 Topsail 4P
Marina Del Rey,
CA 90292
USA

Robinson Michelle
6200 Franklin Ave., #800
Hollywood, CA 90028
USA

Roosens Michel
Imagique RTBF
52 Boulevard a. Reyers
1044 Brüssel
B

Ross Aaron
643 Divisadero St. 202
San Francisco, CA 94117
USA

Ross Bert
School of TV and
Imaging
Perth Road
DD1 4HT Dundee
GB

Roulin Pascal
ExMachina
22, rue Hégésippe
Moreau
75018 Paris
F

Roveda Stefano
Correnti Magnetiche
Viale Bligny 29
20136 Milano
I

Rüdiger Hirt
Gärtnerstraße 86
20253 Hamburg
D

Sandin Daniel
Univ. of Illinois
851 South Morgan,
Room 1120
Chicago, IL 60607
USA

Santifaller Louis
Eurodata
Kennedystraße 33
39055 Leifers-Bozen
I

Santos Ernesto
Hard Drive Studios
661 Metropolitan
Ave. 3L
Brooklyn, NY 1121
USA

Santos Manuel
Inesc-Centro
Multimedia
Av.Duque D'Auila,
23-4 Esq
1017 Lisboa Codex
P

Schatz Gebhard
Pfarrgasse VIII
6460 Imst
A

Schatzl Leo/
Von Suess Petra Rosa
Art+Space Solution
Lorenz-Mandl-Gasse 33
1160 Wien
A

Schmidt Jochen
Lightmare
Bonner Straße 10
50677 Köln
D

Scott Jill
Hochschule der Bild. Künste
Keplerstraße 3–5
66117 Saarbrücken
D

Seblatnig Heidemarie
Krallgasse 6
1220 Wien
A

Smythe Douglas/
Ralston Ken
Industrial Light & Magic
P.O.Box 2459
San Rafael, CA 94912
USA

Struwe Gerd
Heinrichstr. 45
50676 Köln
D

Sutherland Robert
37 Chrystobel cres.
Hawthorn
3122 Hawthorn
AUS

Szleszynsri Jacek
UL. Zielniskiego 28/44
53-534 Wroczaw
PL

Terzopoulos Demetri
University of Toronto
10 King's College Rd.
Toronto, Ontario
M5S 1A4
CDN

Testa Armanda
ExMachina
22, rue Hégésippe Moreau
75018 Paris
F

Tonkin John
P.O.Box 3126,
Grenfell St.
5000 Adelaide
AUS

Toth Michael
University of Cincinnati
Cincinnati,
OH 45221-0016
USA

Treinish Lloyd
IBM Research
P.O.Box 704
Yorktown Heights,
NY 10548
USA

Vaccarino Giorgio
Imagescript
Strada Maddalena 44/6
10020 Reviglasco (TO)
I

Verpillat Frank
Seize Neuvièmes Productions
27 rue Lusien Voilin
92800 Puteaux
F

Von Ruggins Otto
Virtual Reality
6618 Ovington Court
New York, NY 11204
USA

Vuong Pascal
Cougar Films
40 Boulevard Gouvion
St. Cyr
75017 Paris
F

Walczek Diana/
Kleiser Jeff
6105 Mulholland Hwy
Hollywood, CA 90068
USA

Walden Anne Marie
A.I.I. ENSAD
31, rue d'Ulm
75005 Paris
F

Waliczky Tamás
ZKM
Gartenstr. 71
76049 Karlsruhe
D

Walker John
Texas A&M University
College Station,
TX 77843
USA

Wasner Gerhard
Straßgangerstr. 51
8020 Graz
A

Watanabe Jun
Links Corporation
2-14-1 Higashi-Gotanda
Tokio, Shingawa-ku
J

Wedge Chris
Blue Sky Prod., Inc.
100 Executive Blvd.
Ossining, NY 10562
USA

Whitney John
17298 Herradura
Pacific Palisades,
CA 90272
USA

Wieser Horst
Fachhochschule f. Druck
Nobelstraße 10
70563 Stuttgart
D

Wooten Wayne
Georgia Institute of Technolgy
Atlanta, GA 30332-0280
USA

Zajec Edward
Syracuse University
Art Media Studies Dept.
Syracuse, NY 13244
USA

Zancker Thomas
mental images Ges.
Rankestr. 9
10789 Berlin
D

Zeiler Michael/
Schuch Josef
TU Wien
Karlsplatz 13/186/2
1040 Wien
A

INTERAKTIVE KUNST

A.J. Weigoni
Birkenstr. 117
40233 Düsseldorf
D

Amkraut Susan/
Girard Michael
Unreal Pictures
951 Moreno Avenue
Palo Alto, CA 94303
USA

Auber Olivier
Poiesis
4 Passage Saint Avoye
75003 Paris
F

Balzer Thomas
Pl. d. Vereinten
Nationen 27
10249 Berlin
D

Berry Benott
19 rue Clavel
75019 Paris
F

Bertrand Ennio
Via Giulia di Barolo 48
10124 Torino
I

Binkley Timothy
School of Visual Arts
209 E. 23rd St.
New York, NY 10010
USA

Blinov Alexei/
Grafov Vladimir
1e Oosterparkstraat, 26e
1091 HC Amsterdam
NL

Boissonnet Philippe
De l'esplanada 5294
Montreal H2T 25
CDN

Brandmayr Tanja
Aumühlstr. 17
4050 Traun
A

Brown Paul
P.O.Box 1292
Miss. State, MS 39762
USA

Brown Sheldon
University of California
9500 Gilman
Drive #0327
La Jolla, CA 92093
USA

Campbell Jim
1161 De Haro Street
San Francisco, CA 94107
USA

Campione Marcello/
Canali Mario
Correnti Magnetiche
Viale Bligny 29
20136 Milano
I

Cannon Bruce
2200 Adeline 240
Oakland, CA 94607
USA

Carpenter Loren
Cinematrix
82 Queva Vista
Novato, CA 94947
USA

Coniglio Mark
6143 Alcott Str. Apt. #1
Los Angeles, CA 90035
USA

Corominas Alejandro
Hortaleza 54 4
Madrid
E

Courchesne Luc
School of Industrial
Design
P.O.Box 6128
Montreal, Quebec
H3C 3J7
CDN

Davenport Glorianna
MIT Media Lab
20 Ames Street,
E15-435
Cambridge MA 02139
Massachusetts
USA

David Vera
Hermina u. 3
1146 Budapest
H

De Groot Han H.
Music Design
Burgemeester
Weertstr. 25
6814 HL Arnhem
NL

Dement Linda
15/21 St. Neot Av./
Potts Point
Sydney, N.S.W. 2011
AUS

Demers Loius-Philippe/
Vorn Bill
534 Cherrier #3
H2L 1H3 Montreal,
(Quebec)
CDN

Desparois Louis
Laboratoire Inc.
5042 Clark
Montreal,
Quebec H2T 2T8
CDN

Detev Jordan Petrov
State Academy of Music
Evlogi Georgievbul. 94
1505 Sofia
BG

Diemer Bernd
HdBK SAAR
Keplerstr. 3–5
66117 Saarbrücken
D

Dimke H-P. Karl
Weidenstieg 4
20259 Hamburg
D

Don Ritter
130 rue McGill, Studio 3
Montréal (Quebec),
H2Y 2E5
CDN

Dutton Brett/Cooper
Gene/Malloy Judy
Submissive Talent
824 S. Mill Ave.
Tempe, AZ 85281
USA

Eike
Kl. Campestr. 8
38102 Braunschweig
D

Elliott Edward
MIT Media Lab
20 Ames St., Bulding
E15-435
Cambridge, MA 02139
USA

Elsenaar Arthur
Schuitendiep 1020
9711 RJ Groningen
NL

Fairclough John
Elan School of Fine Arts
Private Bag 92019
Auckland
NZ

Ferigo Paolo
Via oscolo 60
39012 Meran
I

Fietzek Frank
Tönsfeldtstr. 9
22763 Hamburg
D

Fleischer Joachim
Schlosserstr. 5
70180 Stuttgart
D

Fleischmann Monika/
Strauß Wolfgang/
Bohn Christian-A.
GMD
Schloß Birlinghoven
53757 Sankt Augustin
D

Fleri Louis
Territoires Virtuels
8, Rue des Haies Fleuries
93100 Montreuil
F

Förster Friedrich
Hechingerstr. 203
72072 Tübingen
D

Frankel Ari
231 West 16th Street, 1ER
New York, NY 10011
USA

Fuchs Mathias
Sebastianplatz 2/11
1030 Wien
A

Garvey Gregory
Concordia University
1455 de Maisonneuve Blvd. West
Montreal, QC H3G 1M8
CDN

George K. Shortess
Lehigh University
17 Memorial Drive East
Bethlehem, PA 18015
USA

George Phillip/
Wayment Ralph
Zographics
11 Miller St., Bondi
Sydney, N.S.W., 2026
AUS

Giddy Allan
Blumenstraße 23
66111 Saarbrücken
D

Giers Walter
Badmauer 14
73525 Schwäbisch-Gmünd
D

Gillerman JoAnn
Viper Optics
950 61st ST.
Oakland, CA 94608
USA

Goldberg Ken
Univ. of Southern California
3737 Watt Wat
Los Angeles, CA 90089-0273
USA

Gönner Gottfried
Barbarossaring 8
55118 Mainz
D

Gortais Bernard
Galerie Natkin-Berth
124 Vieille-Dutemple
75004 Paris
F

Grace Sharon
Send/Receive
258 Clara Street
San Francisco, CA 94107
USA

Graf Ralf
R.A.L.F.
Clara-Feystr. 1A
6369 Simplveld
NL

Gruchy Tim
Gruchy Productions
P.O.Box 286
2010 Darlinghurst
AUS

Hadlich Brigitte
Sonnige Lehne 3
95466 Weidenberg
D

Hegedüs Agnes
Martin-Luther-Str. 1
76307 Langensteinbach
D

Heindl Joseph
Münchnerstraße 35
82069 Hohenschäftlarn
D

Hershmann Lynn
1935 Filbert Street
San Francisco, CA 94123
USA

Hirano Saburo
Yamaha Corporation
Nakazawa-cho 10-1
Hamamatsu-city 430
J

Hiroyuki Moriwaki
A/02, 7-8-22 Nakagawa-Kouhoku
223 Yokohama
J

Hmeljak Matjaz
University of Trieste – DEEI
Via Valerio 10
34127 Trieste
I

Hu Klaus
Weisestr. 18
12049 Berlin
D

Hübner Guido
Das Synthetische Mischgewebe
13, rue Tiffonet
33800 Bordeaux
F

Ishii Haruo
Trident School of Design
1-15-3 Noritake
Nakamura-ku
453 Nakamura-shi
J

Janney Christopher
PhenomenArts, Inc.
75 Kendall Rd.
Lexington, MA 02173
USA

Jauk Werner
Grelle Musik
Ludwig-Benedek-G. 19
8054 Graz
A

Jimenez Alejandra
7A Milton Rd.
SE24 ONL London
GB

John KP Ludwig
Scharnhorststr. 42
04275 Leipzig
D

Kapan Hillary
Univ. of Maryland
4505 Wilkens Ave.
Baltimore, MD 21229
USA

Kärkkäinen Aarre
OY Ueikkaus AB
Karhunkirros 4
02320 Espoo
SF

Kaufer Raoul
Richard-Wagner-Str. 6
93055 Regensburg
D

Kelly Daniel
Artist House Inc.
4077 Crystal Drive
Beulah, MI 49617
USA

Kerekes Laszlo
Stuttgarterstr. 49
12059 Berlin
D

Kolbe Krystian/
Lüsebrink Dirk
designer arena
Schönhauserallee 8
10119 Berlin
D

Kriesche Richard/
Hoffmann Peter
Kulturdata
Sackstraße 22
8010 Graz
A

Krüger Wolfgang
GMD – HLRZ.VIS
Pf 1316
53731 Sankt Augustin
D

Lakner Yehoshua
Ahornstraße 1
5442 Fislisbach
CH

Laurel Brendal/
Strickland Rachel
Interval Research
1801 Page Mill Road
Build. C
Palo Alto, CA 94304
USA

Lechner Wolfgang J.
Gottschalkstraße 27
13359 Berlin
D

Legrady George
602 20th Street
San Francisco, CA 94107
USA

Lensing Jörg U.
Theater der Klänge
Winkelsfelderstr. 21
40477 Düsseldorf
D

Lindquist Jonas
Klippgatan 16 II
11635 Stockholm
S

Lozano-Hemmer Rafael
Modesto Lafuente 28,
3A
28003 Madrid
E

Lyall Marta
1521 NW 60th #104
Seattle, WA 98107
USA

MacMurtrie Chico
Amorphics Robotics
1777 Yosemite
San Francisco, CA 94124
USA

Madel Mark
De Ruyterkade 149
1011 AC Amsterdam
NL

Maes Pattie
M.I.T. Media Lab
20 Ames Street
Cambridge, MA 02139
USA

Mahin Bruce P.
University/CMT
Box 6968
Bedford, VA 24142
USA

Mauermann Karl
Kupferdreher Str. 174
45257 Essen
D

McNabb Michael
120 Virginia Avenue
San Francisco,
CA 94110-5137
USA

Messner Sabine
Pflügerstr. 79 I
12047 Berlin
D

Miller George Bures
1217 6A, Avenue South
T1J 1G9 Lethbridge
(Alberta)
CDN

Miller Tracy
359 Ludlow #8
Cincinnati, OH 45220
USA

Mine Mark
University of North
Carolina
CB#3175
Chapel Hill, NC 27516
USA

Miwa Masahiro
Kunsthochschule für
Medien
Peter-Welter-Platz 2
50676 Köln
D

Mizerovsky Harald
Wagner Martin
Hirschstettnerstr. 22
1220 Wien
A

Möckel Axel/
Gebe Uwe-Malte
Prinzenallee 25/26
13359 Berlin
D

Möller Christian
Meisengasse 28
60313 Frankfurt/Main
D

Morgenstern Susanna
Währingerstraße 24/31
1090 Wien
A

Mott Iain
1076 Lygon Street
Nth. Carlton
Melbourne,
Victoria 3054
AUS

Mühleck Georg
data village art
Im Schellenkönig 56a
70184 Stuttgart
D

Musil Wolfgang/
Rodler Andreas
Grundsteingasse 44
1160 Wien
A

Myers Rita
131 Spring Street 4EF
NY 10012
USA

Nagashima Yoichi
10-12-301, Sumiyoshi-5
Hamamatsu,
Shizuoka 430
J

Netzstadt Projektgruppe
Glauburgerstr. 74
60138 Frankfurt/M.
D

Noffz Micheal
Woogstr. 42
67117 Limburgerhof
D

Novakovic Gordana
Neznanog Junaka 21a
11000 Belgrad
YU

Oki Keisuke
Artlab
40-17-301, Oyamacho,
Shibuyaku
151 Tokio
J

Pachero Candice
D'CUCKOO
6114 LaSalle Rue
STE 414
Oakland, CA 94611
USA

Paterson Nancy
475 The West Mall #1513
Etobicoke, Ontario
M9C 4Z3
CDN

Ponton European Media
Art Lab
Koppel 66
20099 Hamburg
D

Prehn Horst
Inst. f. Biomedizin.
Technik
Glockenstraße 4
35305 Grünberg
D

Ranft-Schinke Dagmar
Ges. für Mathematik u.
Datenv. Darmstadt
Adelsbergstraße 318
09127 Chemnitz
D

Rapoport Sonya
6 Hillcrest Court
Berkeley, CA 94705
USA

Rath Alan
830 E. 15th Str.
Oakland, CA 94612
USA

Ratner Peter
6391 W. Donnagail Dr.
Penn Laird, VA 22846
USA

Reed Hazen
65 South Sixth St.
Brooklyn, NY 11211
USA

Rees Jörg
Bismarkstr. 108
63065 Offenbach
D

Reiff Sabine/
Alman Flavia/
Roueda Stefano
Correnti Magnetiche
Viale Bligny 29
20136 Milano
I

Richards Catherine
41, Delaware Ave.
Ottawa (Ontario),
K2P OZ2
CDN

Rodemer Michael
Dept. of Art
112 South Michigan Ave
Chicago, IL 60603
USA

Rogala Miroslaw
ZKM
Gartenstr. 71
76135 Karlsruhe
D

Sanders Philip
Intern. Painting
P.O.Box 10176
Beverly Hills, CA 90213
USA

Sarkis Mona
Flemingstraße 42
81925 München
D

Schäfer Sabine
Liegnitzer Str. 4A
76139 Karlsruhe
D

Schedel Gerhard
Elisabethstraße 39
80796 München
D

Schmidt Arthur
Gerichtstr. 23
13347 Berlin
D

See Henry
4371 Christophe
Colomb
H2J 3G4 Montreal
(QC)
CDN

Seifert Manfred
Schleiersbacher Str. 5
64407 Fränk.-Crumbach
D

Selichar Günther
Seidengasse 26/2
1070 Wien
A

Sermon Paul
Eisenbahnstraße 89
04315 Leipzig
D

Sharp Lloyd
28 Bellevue Street Glebe
2037 Sydney, N.S.W.
AUS

Smolan Rick
Aao Productions
P.O.Box 1189
Sausalito, CA 94966
USA

Sommerer Christa/
Mignonneau Laurent/
Ray Tom
NCSA/Beckman
Institute
405 N. Mathews Ave.
Urbana, IL 61801
USA

Steindl Helmut
Währingerstr. 131/11
1180 Wien
A

Steinfl Andrea
Schälss A./Reich C.
Szadecky + Steinfl
Zinckg. 20–22
1180 Wien
A

Steinkamp Jennifer
Art Center College of
Design
1700 Lida Street
Pasadena, CA 91109
USA

Stocker Gerfried/
Hörtner Horst
x-space
Kernstockgasse 22–24/II
8020 Graz
A

Struwe Gerd
Heinrichstr. 45
50676 Köln
D

Svarovsky Petr
Academy of Fine Arts
U Akademie 4
170 00 Praha 7
CZ

Tamblyn Christine
SF State University
Inter-Arts Cen.
CA354,
1600 Holloway Ave
San Francisco, CA 94132
USA

Timcke Henning
Kunstdesign Werft 22
Stadtturmstr. 54
5400 Baden
CH

Tolonen Pekka
Koskelantie 25 B13
00610 Helsinki
SF

Tosa Naoko
2-33-9-3A Ogikubo,
Sugiami-ku
Tokyo 167
J

TRANSIT
Wilhelm-Greil-Str. 1
6020 Innsbruck
A

Trimpin
4136 Meridian Ave.N.
Seattle, WA 98103
USA

Uehara Kazuo
The Osaka University of
Arts
469 Higashiyama,
Minamika.-gun
Osaka
J

Ungvary Tamas
Royal Inst. of
Technology
Box 70014
10044 Stockholm
S

Vaccarino Giorgio
Imagescript
Strada Maddalena 44/6
10020 Reviglasco (TO)
I

Vargas Xabela
Atelier Markgraph
Schloss-Str. 92
60486 Frankfurt
D

Vasulka Steina
RR 6. P.O.Box 100
Santa Fé, NM 87501
USA

Verde Giacomo
Via Lanzaghe 116
31057 Silea (TV)
I

Vesna Victoria
University of California
Santa Barbara, CA 93106
USA

Viuff Harald
Frydenborgvej 20
6092 Stenderup
DK

Waite Clea
Kunsthochschule für Medien
Peter-Welter-Platz 2
50676 Köln
D

Wallmann Johannes
Im Siepen 14
42555 Velbert-Langenberg
D

Welzel Burkhard
Mariannenplatz 6
10997 Berlin
D

Whitehill-Ward John
University of Washington
Seattle, WA 98195
USA

Wilfried Maret
Marken & Produktentwicklung
Bleichimattweg 5
6300 Zug
CH

Wilson Stephen
San Francisco State University
1600 Holloway Avenue
San Francisco, CA 94132
USA

Winne Wolfgang
Computer Aided Art
Postfach 448136
28281 Bremen
D

Woolford Kirk
Zülpicher Str. 17
50674 Köln
D

Yarbrow Teri
3454 Standish Dr.
Encino, CA 91436
USA

TEILNEHMER 94

COMPUTERMUSIK

Adkins Mathew
Cocksparrow Street 7
Warwick CV34 4ED
GB

Adolfo Núnez
LIEM-CDMC
Santa Isabel 52
28012 Madrid
E

Ainger Marc
334 E. Beechwold Blvd.
Columbus, OH 43214
USA

Albright William
2555 Roseland Drive
Ann Arbor, MI 48103
USA

Alexander Blechinger
Neue-Welt-Gasse 318
1130 Wien
A

Alford Ronald
1075 Space Park
Way #322
Mountain View,
CA 94043
USA

Allik Kristi
788 Cedarwood Drive
Kingston ONT K7P
1M7
CDN

Alvarez Javier
23, Barrington Rd
N8 8QT London
GB

Appleton Jon
Dartmouth College
6187 Hopkins Center
Hanover, NH 03755
USA

Ascione Patrick
Les Augerats
18510 Menetou-Salon
F

Austin Larry
University of North
Texas
Denton, TX 76203
USA

Averill Ron
University of
Washington
Seattle, WA 98195
USA

Bahn Curtis
Princetown
University, D.o.M.
Princeton, NY 08540
USA

Barrett Natasha
Birmingham University
Birmingham B15 5TT
GB

Bebris Egils
223 Wright Ave.
Toronto, CDN M6R
1L4
CDN

Becher Johannes
Wimmergasse 6/18
1050 Wien
A

Belda Juan
c/ Las Fueutes N.5 1D
Madrid
E

Bennett Justin
Leeghwaterstr. 125
2521 CN Den Haag
NL

Berger Roman
Exper. Studio Radio
Bratislava
Mytna 1
81290 Bratislava
SK

Berkus Günther
Gallery 5
5 Bridge Str.
Cork City
IRL

Bermann Georges
Midi minuit
17 rue de la Croix Nivert
75015 Paris
F

Bertin Yves
S.C.R.E. DAPHNIS
19 Ter Bd Devaux
78300 Poissy
F

Bestor Charles
University of
Massachusetts
Amherst, MA 01003
USA

Bimstein Phillip Kent
P.O.Box 301
Springdale, UT 84767
USA

Bless Markus
Lederergasse 9
4861 Schörfling
A

Briggs Jeffrey
1820 Lehner Road
Columbus, OH 43224
USA

Brümmer Ludger
Hohenzollernstr. 66
45128 Essen
D

Brunson William
Tourbergsgatan 27B, 6tr.
11856 Stockholm
S

Burt Warren
Flat 18, 102 Park St.
St. Kilda West,
Victoria 3182
AUS

Burt Warren/
Mann Chris
Flat 18, 102 Park St.
St. Kilda West,
Victoria 3182
AUS

Butt Katrin
Freistädter Straße 17
4040 Linz
A

Cadoz Claude
ACROE INPG
46 av. Félix Viallet
38031 Grenoble Cédex
F

Calon Christian
GMEM Marseille
4 rue Bernard de Bois
13001 Marseille
F

Camilleri Lelio
Conservatory of
Music"Martini"
Piazza Rossini 2
40126 Bologna
I

Castellano Pierluigi
Via Calcinaia 63
00139 Rom
I

Castle Harry/
Short Damon
620 Prospect
DeKalb, FL 60115
USA

Cavro Jean François
25 rue Imbert Colomes
69001 Lyon
F

Cee Werner
Waldschmidtstr. 8
35576 Wetzlar
D

Cerullo Stefano
Idra Strumenti Musicali
Via Diaz 20
21047 Saronno
I

Chagas Paulo
WDR Köln Studio f.
elektr. M.
Annastr. 86
50678 Köln
D

Charvet Pierre
IRCAM
1 place Stravinsky
75004 Paris
F

Choi Insook
Nat. Center for
Supercomputing
605 E. Springfield Ave.
Champaign, IL 61820
USA

Cifariello Ciardi Fabio
Via Pietro Giannone, 28
00195 Rom
I

Cizek Martina
Rotenlöwengasse 9/22
1090 Wien
A

Cohen Patric
41 Loomis Drive,
Apt. B1
West Hartford,
CT 06107
USA

Cort Lippe
IRCAM
1, Place Stravinsky
75004 Paris
F

Cospito Giovanni
AGON
Piazzale Egeo 7
20126 Milano
I

Dallosto Diego
Corso Palladio, 114
36100 Vicenza
I

David Chesworth
11 Teak Street
Caulfield South
VIC 3162
AUS

De Man Roderik
1e Tuindwarsstraat 3
1015 RT Amsterdam
NL

De Smet Francis
Generaal Lemanlaan 151
8310 Brügge
B

Dennis Elwyn
„Clouds"
Stawell West, VIC 3380
AUS

Dhomont Francis
3355, Chemin Queen
Mary; App. 31
H3V 1A5 Montreal
(Québec)
CDN

Dimchev Valeri
T. Komitov Str. 65
2700 Blagoevgrad
BG

Dinicola Donald
360 Cabrini Blvd.,
Apt. 5G
NY 10040
USA

Dolden Paul
2161 Bonaccord Dr.
Vancouver V5P 2N8
CDN

Duesenberry John
514 Harvard St. #3B
Brookline, MA 02146
USA

Dunn David
1274 Calle de
Commercio #5
Santa Fé, NM 87505
USA

Eduardo R. Miranda
University of Edinburgh
12, Nicolson Square
EH8 9DF Edinburgh
GB

Evelyn Ficarra
100 Highbury Hill
N5 1AT London
GB

F. Randomiz/Jan Werner
Zülpicherstr. 35
50674 Köln
D

Francesco Galante
Via Taranto 178/9b
00182 Roma
I

Frankel Ari
231 West 16th Street,
1ER
New York, NY 10011
USA

Frei Andreas M.
Nußdorferstraße 40/9
1090 Wien
A

Fried Joshua
277 N. 7th Str., 4R
Brooklyn, NY 11211
USA

Fritz Fro/Gue Schmidt
RBW 21
Rüdigergasse 10/5
1050 Wien
A

Gerber Jerry
9 Sutro Heights
San Francisco, CA 94121
USA

Gold Roderich
Haeberlinstr. 3
60431 Frankfurt/M.
D

Goldman Harvey
41 Fisher Rd.
Westport, MA 02790
USA

Gressel Joel
cfx Inc.
584 Broadway, Suite 201
New York, NY 10012
USA

Greuel Christian
FAKESPACE Inc.
4085 Campbell Ave.
Menlo Park, CA 94025
USA

Grippe Ragnar
Strindbergsgatan 43
115 31 Stockholm
S

Guglielmino Roberto
Hans-Resel-Gasse 19
8020 Graz
A

Habla Frank-Michael
CRAZED LAB
Otto-Weininger-G. 5/2
1130 Wien
A

Hackl Franz
303 E. 94th Str. Apt.
New York, NY 10128
USA

Halac Jose
544 Court St. #3
Brooklyn, NY 11231
USA

Harel Ilan
IBA-Israel TV
Tora M`Zion
St./P.O.Box 7139
91071 Jerusalem
IL

Harris Craig
686 47th Ave.
San Francsico, CA 94121
USA

Hass Jeffrey E.
Indiana University
Bloomington, IN 47405
USA

Hauksson Thorsteinn
P.O.Box 1196
121 Reykjavik
IS

Heifetz Robin-Julian
14543 Burbank Blvd.
#201
Van Nuys,
CA 91411-4314
USA

Helmuth Mara
Texas A+M University
404 Academic Bldg.
College Station,
TX 77843
USA

Hingel Wolfgang/
Koschmieder Bernd
Tulbeckstr. 39
80339 München
D

Hoffmann Norbert
Föhrenwald 464
6100 Seefeld
A

Hollinetz Klaus
Steinhumergutstr. 1
4050 Traun
A

Howard Earl
24 - 46 29th st 3a
Astoria, NY 11102
USA

Humpert Hans
Hochschule f. Musik
Köln
Dagobertstr. 38
50668 Köln
D

Hyde Joseph
University of
Birmingham
Edgbaston Birmingham
B15 2TS
GB

Impett Jonathan
50 Haliburton Road
TWI IPF Twickenham
GB

Indomiti
Soundvideo
International
Uferweg 7
6060 Hall in Tirol
A

Ingrid Häussler
Paracelsusgasse 6
1140 Wien
A

Ishijima Akemi
39 Wymer Street
Norwich NR2 4BJ
GB

Jack Tamul
JIM STUDIOS Inc.
1541 Boulevard
Jacksonville, FL 32206
USA

Jaffe David
295 Purdue Ave.
Kensington
CA 94708
USA

Jolly Kent
10101 Ditch Rd.
Carmel, IN 46032
USA

José Manuel Berenguer
COCHLEA
Sardenya 516-6-2
08024 Barcelona
E

Karlsson Erik Mikael
Tranebergs Strand 53
161 32 Bromma
S

Katmeridu Aphrodite
Komplex Ljulin,
Bl.006, VH.A/8
1343 Sofia
BG

Kato Hideki
205 2nd Ave. #6C
New York, NY 10003
USA

Kato Hitoshi
Büro M4 –
Rainer Kürvers
Messeplatz 4
80339 München
D

Kaufmann Dieter
Inst. f. Elektroakustik
Rienösslgasse 12
1040 Wien
A

Kazuo Uehara
The Osaka University of
Arts
469 Higashiyama,
Minamika.-gun
Osaka
J

Klammer Josef
Grieskai 40/2/8
8020 Graz
A

Knittel Krzysztof
Society For
Contemporary Music
Mazowiecka 11
00-052 Warsaw
PL

Koller Gerald
Froschaugasse 7/59
8010 Graz
A

Koonce Paul
1005 13th Street South
Moorhead, MN 56560
USA

Kosk Patrick
Stengardsgatan 1C/8
00260 Helsinki
SF

Kossenko Sergei
Dartmouth College
HB 6187 Dartmouth
College
Hanover, NH 03755
USA

Kostelanetz Richard
Archae Editions
P.O. Box 444, Prince St.
New York,
NY 10012-0008
USA

Koustrup Frank
4882, Av. de l'Esplanade
Montreal, Quebec
H2T 2Y7
CDN

Krbavac Karl
Brunnweg 4/8/3
1100 Wien
A

Kretz Johannes
Giesshübler Str. 95
2371 Hinterbrühl
A

Kreuzer Michael
Gesellenhausstraße 23
4020 Linz
A

Kruppa Birgitta
Peter-Strasser-Weg 17
12101 Berlin
D

Kucharz Lawrence
Int. Audio Chrome
P.O.Box 1068
Rye, NY 10580
USA

Kupper Leo
Studio de Recherches
23, Avenue Albert-
Elisabeth
1200 Bruxelles
B

Laffage Annie
VINYL VIDEO
Mont-Roland
39100 Dôle
F

Lanza Alcides
shelan publications
6351 Trans Island Ave.
H3W 3B7 Montreal
CDN

Lazarov Simo
12 Postojanstro
1111 Sofia
BG

Lazarov Valentin
12 „Postojanstvo" str.
bl. 253
1111 Sofia
BG

Leduc Daniel/
Müller Wilhelm
15 rue Waterman
app. 606
Saint-Lambert
Quebec J4P 1R7
CDN

Lejeune Jacques
8 Rue Truffaut
75017 Paris
F

Lenk Helmut
Breslauer Straße 8
36151 Burghaun
D

Lesso Drew
201 S. Santa Fe Ave. #207
Los Angeles,
CA 90012-4339
USA

Link Stan
Princeton University
Princeton, NJ 08544
USA

Lo Yee On
BOX 75/2
Stanford
CA 94309
USA

Lopez Tom
28 Rue Cassini
06000 Nice
F

MacDonald Alistair
127 Highbury Rd.
B14 7QW Birmingham
GB

Mader Heinrich
Georgestr. 6
3100 St. Pölten
A

Maiguashca Mesias
Gaisbühlstr. 1
76532 Baden-Baden
D

Maldonado Gabriel
Via Donna Olimpia 166
00152 Roma
I

Mangele Andy
Engerthstr. 51/11/14
1200 Wien
A

Manion Michael
21 Orlando Street
Milford
Milford, CT 06460
USA

Manrique José
Travesia del norte 2,1
28293 Madrid-Zarzalejo
E

Mason Charles
Birmingham Southern
College
900 Arkadelphia Rd.
Birmingham, AL 35254
USA

Mathias Wolfgang
Belfortstr. 5
81667 München
D

Maurina Franco
Via Gorani 5
20123 Milano
I

McMenamin Patrick
168 Glacier Drive
Livermore, CA 94550
USA

Melcher Leslie
321 East 43rd Street
AP#209
NY 10017
USA

Mikolasek Bohdan
Milchbuckstr. 57
8057 Zürich
CH

Mittendorf Hans
Les Ateliers Uipc
Audionaut Enterprises
35 A Bisson Rd.
E15 2RD London
GB

Monro Gordon
University of Sydney
Sydney, NSW 2006
AUS

Moore Adrian J.
University of
Birmingham
B15 2TT Birmingham,
Edgbaston
GB

Morleo Luigi
Via Cesare Battisti, 22
72020 Erchie
I

Mott Iain
1076 Lygon Street
Nth. Carlton
Melbourne,
Victoria 3054
AUS

Mowitz Ira
1111 Falmouth Ave.
Teaneck, NJ 07666
USA

Nakamura Shigenobu
Kyoto College of Art
2-116 Uryuyama
Kitashirakawa
Kyoto 606
J

Neitchev Vladimir D.
Republika Street 53D
App.103
1220 Sofia
BG

Neuwirther Erich
Allerheiligen 51
8412 Herberstorf
A

Newcomb Robert S.
Alfred & Rose Music
POB 743
Hanover,
NH 03755-0743
USA

Nitsche Uwe
Tönsfeldtstr. 9
22763 Hamburg
D

Norman Katharine
18 Northcote Road
London E17 7DU
GB

Normandeau Robert
2994, Avenue de
Soissons
H3S 1W2 Montréal
(Québec)
CDN

O'Rourke Jim
4721 N. Odell
Harwood HTS 60656
USA

Olsanik Otakar
Digital Audio Studio
32-DAS32
Kosmakova 30
61500 Brno
CZ

Orschakowski Wolfgang
Musikversuch-Station
Rehhoffstr. 16
20459 Hamburg 11
D

Osborn Ed
Box 9121
Oakland, CA 94613
USA

Ostertag Robert
824 Shotwell Str.
San Francisco, CA 94110
USA

Pachero Candice
D'CUCKOO 6114
LaSalle Rue STE 414
Oakland, CA 94611
USA

Palmer Glenn
7728 Loma Vista Dr.
Kansas City, MO 64138
USA

Palmer Juliet
Princeton University
Princeton,
NJ 08544-1007
USA

Parmerud Åke
Backeskärsgatan 27
42159 Västra Frölunda
S

Penrose Christopher
Princeton University
Princeton, NJ 08544
USA

Perez Ileana
Dartmouth College
6187 Hopkins Center
Hanover, NH 03755
USA

Petkov Grisha
OTKROVENIE
18, Bitolia Str. Block 63
1680 Sofia
BG

Pinter Gyula
Bajza utca 70 fsz. 2/A
1062 Budapest
H

Polonio Eduardo
Josep Pla. 39; 7o 1a
08019 Barcelona
E

Proy Gabriela
Lacknergasse 100/24
1180 Wien
A

Qin Daping
Sibelius Academy
P.Rautatiekatu 9
00100 Helsinki
SF

Rabl Günther
3532 Rastenberg 10
A

Redolfi Michel
CIRM
33 Av. Jean-Medecin
06000 Nice
F

Reitz Lothar/
Witschke Dirk
Auto composer tools
Lange Str. 55
60311 Frankfurt
D

Resch Gernot
Fabidab Productions
Naglerg. 56
8010 Graz
A

Rocha Manuel
108 rue des Pyrénées
75020 Paris
F

Roedelius Hans
Antonsgasse 19/9/3
2602 Blumau
A

Roland Harry-Ed
Kurfürstenstr. 126
10785 Berlin
D

Rosas Cobian Michael
72 Redcliffe GDNS.
London SW10 9HE
GB

Rothstein Jordon
72 Nassau Drv.
Great Neck, NY 11021
USA

Rowe Robert
New York University
35 W. 4th St. Room 777
New York, NY 10003
USA

Ruschkowski André
Hochschule
„Mozarteum"
Mirabellplatz 1
5020 Salzburg
D

Ruzicka Rudolf
Serikova 32
63700 Brno
CZ

Rychkov Sergei
Komlev Str. 8–22
420012 Kazan
R

Sani Nicola
Via Orti della
Farnesina 141
00194 Roma
I

Savic Miroslav
Students Cultural
Center
Srpskih Vladara 48
11000 Belgrad
YU

Schäfer Sabine
Liegnitzer Str. 4A
76139 Karlsruhe
D

Scheiflinger Eberhard
Tonstudio Angermann
Bahnhofstraße 17
9800 Spittal/Drau
A

Schneider Patrick
Neugasse 84
8005 Zürich
CH

Schobert Rolf
Rotebühlstr. 154
70197 Stuttgart
D

Schulze Gerald
Raumerstraße 34
10437 Berlin
D

Schwarz Jean
13, Rue Duchâtel
78220 Viroflay
F

Schweizer Frank
Hohlohstraße 7
76189 Karlsruhe
D

Shaun Rigney
3/236 Canterbury Rd.
St. Kilda
3182 Melbourne
AUS

Sims Ezra
1168 Mass. ave.
Cambridge MA 02138
USA

Siwinski Jaroslaw
ul. Lubomelska 9 m. 2
01-805 Warschau
PL

Skrleta Erich
Octopus
Fleischmarkt 16
1010 Wien
A

Spitzer-Marlyn Eric
The Hit Box
Altenburg 116
3591 Altenburg
A

Stammet Arthur
29, rue Léon-Metz
4238 Esch-Sur-Alzette
L

Stange-Elbe Joachim
Hämmerlegäßle 4a
78112 Freiburg i.Br.
D

Stengel Wolfgang
Anton-Anderer-Pl. 7
1210 Wien
A

Stroppa Marco
11 rue des Rosiers
93220 Cagny
F

Strubinsky Ursula
Laxenburgerstraße 97/5
1100 Wien
A

Szigeti Istvan
Ungar. Rundfunk
Brody S. u. 5-7
1800 Budapest
H

Tagliente Domenico
Mexikoplatz 12
1020 Wien
A

Taninaka Suguru
M Sound Design Institute
255-6 Hachigasaki,
Matsudo-shi
Chiba
J

Teruggi Daniel
INA-GRM
116 Av. du Président Kennedy
75786 Paris Cédex 16
F

Thoma Ernst
Flurweg 377
8260 Stein a. Rhein
CH

Thompson Robert Scott
Ancourant Records
P.O. Box 672902
Marietta,
GA 30061-0049
USA

Tiensuu Jukka
Nervanderinkatu 7 B 21
00100 Helsinki
SF

Todoroff Todor
Faculté Polytechnique de Mons
9, rue de Houdain
7000 Mons
B

Tremblay Marc
ACREQ
4001 Berri
Montréal H2L 4H2
F

Ungvary Tamás
Royal Inst. of Technology
Box 70014
10044 Stockholm
S

Vaggione Horacio
Université de Paris – VIII
2, Rue de la Liberté
93526 Saint Denis – Cédex 02
F

Vaughan Michael
University of Keele
Keele Staffs ST5 5BG
GB

Veeneman Curt
University o. t. Pacific Conser.
3601 Pacific Ave.
Stockton, CA 95211
USA

Veith Ralf
Motionmania Music
Rolandstr. 11
46539 Dinslaken
D

Verin Nicolas
41 bd. de Revilly
75012 Paris
F

Viñao Alejandro
27 Coolhurst Rd.
London N8 8ET
GB

Vinao Ezequiel
108 Wooster St. Ph 6A
New York, NY 10012
USA

Von Ruggins Otto
Virtual Reality
6618 Ovington Court
New York, NY 11204
USA

Weinger Lauren
School of the Art Institute
112 S. Michigan Ave.
Chicago, IL
USA

Weixler Andreas
Schaftalbergweg 33
8044 Graz
A

White Frances
9 Patton Ave.
Princeton, NJ 08540
USA

Wiggins John
HBO
120 A. East 23rd St.
NYC, NY 10010
USA

Wolman Amnon
University-School of Music
711 Elgin Rd
Evanston,
IL 60208-1200
USA

Wraggett R.D.
R.D. Music
679 Greycedar Cresc.
Mississauga
ONT L4W 3J4
CDN

Zanesi Christian
G.R.M.
116, Av du Président Kennedy
75016 Paris
F

Zimbaldo Daniel
L.I.E.M./C.D.M.C.
Santa Isabel 52
28012 Madrid
E

BILDNACHWEIS

Portraits:
S. 60: Gert Heide, Graz
S. 100: Alexandra Eizinger, Wien
S. 121: Gert Heide, Graz

Der Bildnachweis gibt die uns bekannten Rechtsinhaber an. In einigen Fällen konnten die Rechtsinhaber leider nicht oder nur ungenau ermittelt werden. Sollten dadurch Urheberrechte verletzt worden sein, wird der Verlag nach Anmeldung berechtigter Ansprüche diese entgelten.